The Worst Loss

BARBARA D. ROSOF

The Worst Loss

How Families Heal
from the Death of a Child

HENRY HOLT AND COMPANY · NEW YORK

Henry Holt and Company, Inc.
Publishers since 1866
115 West 18th Street
New York, New York 10011

Henry Holt® is a registered
trademark of Henry Holt and Company, Inc.

Published in Canada by Fitzhenry & Whiteside Ltd.,
195 Allstate Parkway, Markham, Ontario L3R 4T8.

Library of Congress Cataloging-in-Publication Data
Rosof, Barbara D.
The worst loss: how families heal from the death of a child /
Barbara D. Rosof—1st ed.
p.   cm.
Includes bibliographical references and index.
1. Bereavement—Psychological aspects.   2. Children—Death—
Psychological aspects.   3. Family.   4. Parent and child.
5. Brothers and sisters—Death—Psychological aspects.   I. Title.
BF575.G7R68   1994   94-9255
155.9'37'085—dc20   CIP

ISBN 0-8050-3240-1

Henry Holt books are available for special promotions and
premiums. For details contact: Director, Special Markets.

First Edition—1994

Designed by Victoria Hartman

Printed in the United States of America
All first editions are printed on acid-free paper. ∞

1   3   5   7   9   10   8   6   4   2

Contents

Part Three

Families Speak 153

Part Four

The Rest of Your Life 237

Acknowledgments

No book ever gets written without the help of the unseen people who point the author in the right direction, advise, educate, and encourage her, indulge her, reorient her when she loses her way, and generally cheer her on. In the course of my inquiries, the people I have spoken with have been unfailingly generous with their knowledge and their time. They include Leslie Swager, M.S.W.; Nancy Anderson, M.F.C.C.; Nina Gorbach, M.F.C.C.; Al Vigil; Susan Blanchard, L.C.S.W.; Michelle Dietz, R.N.; Lisa Beck, M.S.N.; Liz Sumner, R.N.; Molly Drummond, L.C.S.W.; Judith Feigon Schiffman, Ph.D.; Toby Eisenberg; Anne Groves, L.C.S.W.; Murray Dubin; Libby Rosof-Dubin; Joan Hoff, M.A.; Donna Schuurman, Ed.D.; Jeremy Forbes; Anne Armstrong Dailey; Elliot Rosen, Ed.D.; Connie Black; Peg Macy, L.C.S.W.; Judy Davis, L.C.S.W.; Paul Oas, Ph.D.; Sidney Zisook, M.D.; Diane Roberts; and Steve Alper, L.C.S.W. My thanks also to the staffs of Children's Hospice International, National Hospice Organization, the University of California at San Diego Library, and local chapters and national office staffs of MADD, Compassionate Friends, Parents of Murdered Children, and Sharing and Healing.

The staff of Community Hospice Care of San Diego, where I worked part-time while I was writing much of the book, provided a congenial milieu and many helpful perspectives. Cynthia Vartan, my editor, provided encouragement, praise, and latitude in just the right proportions, at just the right times.

The parents who gave me their time and trusted me with their stories are the major contributors, without whose generosity this book could not have happened. I thank you all for your help and your willingness to help other parents.

My colleague Gay Hybertsen, L.C.S.W., encouraged me in the most difficult times. From the outset, she has been a stalwart supporter, a discerning reader, and a good friend.

Thank you, all.

Preface

I have practiced psychotherapy for more than a quarter of a century, and in that time I've learned more about loss and about helplessness than I had ever intended. Loss and helplessness are the two most painful experiences that human beings have to bear, and most people who seek psychological help have had too much in their lives of one or both. Early on I learned that my commitment to listen respectfully to my patients and my willingness to hear their pain and their helplessness were the most powerful therapeutic tools I possessed.

Sitting with other people's pain is an arduous discipline. It exposes me to my patients' experiences of loss and helplessness. Their sadness sets off resonances of my own losses. Listening, I am reminded of how little I can do. I cannot restore my patients' losses, either past or current. All I can do is create an empathic bond, a connection with my patients in which they can feel understood and no longer alone. It falls far short of fixing things, but it can make a great difference.

I've come to believe that feeling helpless comes with the territory. It is the paradox and the tension at the center of doing psychotherapy, of being a parent, probably at the center of every relationship of helping and caring: what we can do for one another feels so limited, and we so often feel impotent; yet what we offer in caring and in the assurance that the other is not alone is the strongest, truest help we can give each other.

These are the convictions that have shaped my therapeutic work. Not surprisingly, much of that work has been with people dealing with major losses in their lives: deaths of parents, abuse and sexual molestation in childhood, disasters both natural and man-made. I had to rethink and retest my convictions when I began to see parents and families who had lost a child.

I was deeply impressed by the severity of their loss. A mother myself now, I could imagine all too clearly what losing a child would feel like. I also began to feel that the usual psychological formulations about loss were simply not adequate to describe these families' experiences. As I talked to other psychotherapists, particularly several who had themselves lost a child, and as I read the clinical research, I heard my hunch confirmed. Losing a child is a different kind of loss. Its dimensions are more profound, and the swath it cuts across families' lives is much broader than that of any other loss.

Two groups of people seem to know about this worst of all losses: the researchers and therapists who work with families, and the families themselves. Many of the former have written with great understanding and compassion about the psychology of child loss, but they've written for their professional colleagues. If such phrases as "internalized object representation" are not part of a reader's vocabulary, the value of the professional literature is sharply limited. Over the years I often wished that that which the professionals had learned could be more widely available.

Parents who have lived with their child's death and have rebuilt their lives are the other great experts. Every week they share their expertise, and their considerable capacity to help, in meetings of Compassionate Friends, Candlelighters, Survivors of Suicide, and other self-help groups. Often I thought that what they knew and the models they offered could help parents and others beyond their immediate group.

I began to think about a book that could put psychological

constructs into shirtsleeve language, that could tell families' stories, share their painfully gained knowledge, and model their remarkable courage. I wanted to write a book that could help families know what they were facing, understand what they were feeling, and appreciate their own needs and timetables. I wanted a book that professionals also could turn to, so that they could better understand the experience of the families they were trying to help.

From the start, I knew that families' voices must be heard, and it is their stories that shape this book. I have had my own losses and have read widely. I have treated a number of parents and siblings and listened to many more, shared their pain and empathized with them. But I have not lost a child. I have not walked in the dark country of their grief. The voices of those who have experienced this loss should speak the clearest; they are truly the experts in living through the worst loss.

The people who speak are not my patients. Practicing psychotherapy, I have heard many stories. But my compact with my patients requires that their stories remain in my confidence.

The people whose stories I tell are from northern California, the Midwest, and New England. They learned of my research, through Mothers Against Drunk Driving (MADD), through hospices, Compassionate Friends, AIDS support groups, police chaplains, and a variety of personal channels. Their names and the identifying details about their lives and their children's deaths have been altered sufficiently to protect their privacy. Some stories reflect a composite of several families' experiences. Every person understood when we talked that I expected to write a book. Their candor and generosity have amazed me. I thanked them each when we talked. I thank you all again. Without you, this book could not have come to be. Together we have fashioned a guide for other families who must travel that dark country you know too well.

Part One

~

The Torn Canopy

A young child plays contentedly by herself. She is serene, focused on her play. Above her, invisible to her, arches a bright canopy of safety. Erected by her parents, it enables her to play and to grow.

The canopy is the protection and love that as parents we provide for our children. Without it they will not survive, neither physically nor psychologically. Its arching fabric is woven of many elements: our recollections, conscious and unconscious, of our own parents' treatment of us when we were children; our hopes and fantasies for our children; who they are to us and what we hope they will become; our commitment to care for them, to all the daily drudgery as well as to the pleasures of their care. It is organized around our vision of ourselves as parents and shaped by our continuing interaction with them.

Woven through the fabric are the shining threads of illusion. The world is a safe and orderly place. Our family is especially safe. Nothing bad will happen to you. We, your parents, have the power to keep you safe. Time and experience will fray these threads, and our children will part with their illusions. But for a time in childhood these illusions are essential to children's growing up whole. Before their own resources are sufficient to rely on, these essential illusions make it possible for children to feel safe.

The canopy we furl over our children keeps us safe too. The illusions we weave for them sustain us as well. The knowledge that *we have constructed a safe canopy for our children becomes a source of deep personal satisfaction and a pillar of our self-esteem.*

A child's death tears the canopy wide open. Parents and siblings stand robbed of the child, bereft of their illusions, exposed, overwhelmed, alone. In the first three chapters, we examine what happens to parents and to children when their bright canopy no longer protects them, when a child dies.

· 1 ·

A Loss Like No Other:
What Parents Lose

*"When you lose a child, your
losses are just beginning."*
—Tom

Patrick was fifteen, and he savored every moment of his summer. His job at the pool gave him a chance to see all his friends. He'd brought his times down in the freestyle. He'd gotten up the nerve to ask Rosemary out, and now they'd been going together for a month. At the end of August he and his brother and his dad were going to canoe in the Boundary Waters wilderness for a week. On an evening in July, just at dusk, Patrick and Rosemary were sitting on the curb in front of her house, talking. A drunken driver careened around the corner, going 50 mph. His car hit Patrick and dragged him eighty feet. When the car stopped, the driver wheeled it around and backed over Patrick as he sped away.

The death of a child is a loss like no other. The *Diagnostic and Statistical Manual of Mental Disorders,* psychiatry's diagnostic bible, does not overstate the case when it calls the death of a child a "catastrophic stressor." It robs parents of what they love most, isolates partners from each other, and deafens them so that they cannot hear the cries of their other children.

3

It is four months after Patrick's death.

"I'm in the middle of a hurricane, in a tiny life raft. My raft's leaking badly; some days I'm sure I'll go down." Elaine is Patrick's mother. She speaks in a low, flat voice. Suffering has drained all the light from her face. "I can see Tom, my husband, out there. He's hanging on to a raft of his own, but he's too far away to reach.

"The day-to-day stuff undoes me. Patrick would come grocery shopping with me sometimes. He'd goof around, pick up a box of detergent and do these loony commercials, right there in the store. He made me laugh until my sides ached. Now I walk past some detergent he'd gone off on, and I realize I'll never see Patrick do a commercial again. Last week Tom came with me. He had the cart, and I'd gone to a different aisle to pick up some silver polish. I came back to where he was, in the cereal aisle. He was holding a box of raisin bran. Patrick's the only one in our family who ate raisin bran. Tom held the box in both hands, and his shoulders heaved. I knew he was crying, and I didn't have a thing to give him. I couldn't even go and hold him. I walked to another aisle and waited.

"Jeremy, our youngest, has always had this way of taking stairs three at a time. He sounds like a herd of elephants. I used to yell at him to keep it quiet. Since Patrick died, he climbs the stairs one at a time, very slowly. Like an old man. Annie, my daughter, said something about it yesterday. I hadn't noticed. My own son, and I hadn't noticed."

To Annie, seventeen, the sadness in her house is nearly palpable. "All the light and the color drained out of our family when Patrick was killed," she says. "We sit at dinner, and it's like we're lost in this fog; nobody hears, and nobody can touch each other." She hesitates, then adds, "A lot of the time I feel like I've lost my dad too. He just sits and stares, and he doesn't want anyone to say Patrick's name. Mom's pretty much of a wreck, but at least she'll talk about him."

When you lose your child, there are no precedents. Nothing prepares you for your loss, or for the intensity of your grief. "It's like someone reached inside and wrenched out a part of my body," Elaine says. "I really feel like some vital piece of me is missing. I'll never get it back, and I'll never be whole without it. I know all the theory of grieving, and I'd even worked with parents who had lost a child. But since Patrick died, I hurt so much I've felt my grief must be different. Nobody can live with this kind of pain."

Grief for a child is wrenching and disabling. It hits harder and lasts longer than anyone anticipates. In *Maternal Bereavement*, Linda Edelstein describes the sweeping disruption that occurs in all areas of a survivor's life. She calls it disorganization. "Disorganization is a form of adaptation to trauma, the symptoms including listlessness, depression, startle reactions, recurrent nightmares, fears, and unsteadiness in relationships and in work."[1] A mother who prided herself on her cooking finds she cannot plan what to have for dinner. A father who played eighteen holes of golf every Saturday now stares at his clubs and wonders what the point was. Tom remembers his disorganization in the weeks after Patrick's death as "like watching myself on television. I'd see myself walking through the motions. I did what had to be done, made funeral arrangements, talked to lawyers and the police. I went to work. But I was on autopilot. Completely mechanical."

As the immediate disorganization subsides, the long haul of mourning begins. Mourning consumes your energy for the first year. As you struggle to come to terms with the finality of your loss, you have very little left to give your partner, or your children, or yourself. Your grieving will take longer than you or anyone around you expected. Your loss will be with you every day, casting a shadow on all that you do. Your life, and those of your children, has been permanently altered. Nothing will ever be the same again.

To understand how a child's death so devastates a family, we need to look at the special nature of the bonds between parent and child and between siblings. As we understand what a child means to parents and to brothers and sisters, we begin to take the measure of all that they have lost. Here we will explore the special connection between parent and child. In chapter 2 we will look at bonds between siblings.

The Child-Parent Bond

The ties of love and hope that bind parent and child are the most powerful in human relationships. We can tease apart the strands and identify five factors that charge that bond with its special importance.

Children Invite Our Love, and They Return It Richly. From infancy, by their physical helplessness and their intense need for interaction, our children invite us into a mutually loving relationship. Many parents freely acknowledge that the love they enjoy with their child is the richest, most satisfying, least ambivalent in their lives. Young children adore and idealize their parents. Preschoolers know that their mommy is the prettiest, sweetest, wisest mommy and their daddy is the strongest, bravest, kindest daddy. Children's experience with our actual shortcomings does not shake their conviction. This kind of unqualified, no-strings-attached love is heady stuff for parents, one of the sweetest rewards of parenthood.

Remembering her son, Elaine says, "I had a relationship with Patrick that nothing will ever replace. We sang show tunes together, and he talked to me about his swimming, school, whatever was on his mind. When he got into junior high I sort of stepped back a little and let him figure out how close he wanted to be to his mother. But he still wanted to talk. And play Chinese checkers. I taught him Chinese checkers when he was six, and that was always our game. Even that summer, he was getting to be such a big guy, with a job and a girlfriend, and still, once in a while he'd find me and say, 'Hey, Mom, how about Chinese checkers?' "

No matter how much we love them, and they us, our children do things we do not approve of. They hurt us. They disappoint us. Sometimes they become people we cannot like. Yet no matter who our child becomes, no matter what the years bring, some piece of our early, intense love persists.

Harry knows more than he ever wanted to about the persistence of his love. He is thirty-eight. As we sit in the October sunshine in a park, he looks too young to have an adult son, and yet he looks very old. He scuffs the yellow leaves at his feet as he tells me how his son Ray died.

"Ray walked into a gas station at about ten o'clock at night. He waved a pistol at the guy behind the counter and told him to empty the cash drawer into a bag. The guy was the owner, and he'd been robbed before. He reached under the counter, grabbed his gun, and came up shooting. He shot Ray twice in the face, point-blank range. Ray died before the police got there."

Harry's large palm presses hard against his eyes, as if he could wipe away the scene he visualizes. Several moments pass before he speaks. "What Ray did was flat wrong. He'd been messing up his life that whole year: drugs, hanging around with some pretty bad company. I wish I could say it was his first robbery, but it wasn't. He and I were on the outs, because he knew what I thought of his life. I knew he came over to the house when I wasn't there, to see his mother, and I never interfered. There was still a lot of good in that boy. I figured he'd work things out for himself and then he and I could work it out. He ran himself out of time."

Harry leans away from the bench and pulls his wallet out of

his back pocket. He extracts a worn photograph, and his hand shakes a little as he holds it for me to see. A blond boy of nine in a baseball uniform smiles up at his father. "This is the Ray I remember."

Our Children Carry the Hopes and Aspirations That Are Most Precious to Us. A child embodies deeply valued parts of the parent's self. Helping his child grow, watching his potentials unfold, fulfills a parent's hopes for himself. *She will have long legs and run effortlessly. He will learn from me all I know about animals, and he will come to love them as I do. She will grow up knowing she's smart, and she'll go to college.*

"Children are a second chance," goes the saying. A child offers us the opportunity to set right what went wrong in our own childhood. Rebecca is an articulate woman of thirty-four, a pediatric nurse practitioner whose daughter Kate died at five months of the mysterious cessation of breathing called sudden infant death syndrome. Rebecca grew up with a very disturbed mother, who abused her physically and violated her sexually. With considerable effort Rebecca extricated herself from her family, went to college, married, and started a family. Although she loves her young son, nothing could match her pleasure and her hope when she learned she was pregnant with a daughter.

"That was cake and ice cream and the Fourth of July," she remembers. "My pregnancy and the time I had with Kate were the happiest time in my life." Her face lights up, confirming her memory. "Having a little girl helped me begin to heal some of the awful stuff from my childhood. When I took care of her, I felt like I had a shot at finally putting that stuff behind me. Doing right by her was the deepest satisfaction of my life. I guess taking care of her was taking care of me. I keep going now, for Rick and Charlie. But when Kate died, some of my hopes died with her."

We Create Our Child in Our Mind. A child exists as a real and separate person. Equally real is the child we create in our mind, a part of our self. Even before a child is conceived, parents have fantasized about it, endowed it with their hopes and longings. Our sense of our own self, both good and bad aspects, interweaves with our growing knowledge of our child to form this internal image. Our child becomes an intimate part of our self-image and our self-image an integral part of our internal vision of our child. Psychiatrist Beverly Raphael describes the child we create: "The image each parent holds of the child will be constantly modified and molded by the real interactions with him. It will be a complex amalgam of the thoughts and feelings, memories that encompass the relationship's past as well as projections for the future. It will include both positive and negative aspects, and will encompass mutually dependent needs of both parents and children."[2] Most of the time our real, external child and our internal image blend seamlessly. All unconsciously we create this complex synthesis of self and other, revising it as the child grows and changes. Only when the private, inside version of the child parts company too sharply from the outside, observable child do we notice there are two. Every parent will remember times when the child he saw did not fit with the child in his mind.

A mother remembers such a time with her young son: "Once, as I drove up to preschool to pick up Jared, I saw a little kid with skinny legs, mousy brown hair that stuck out, and food on his face. I thought, 'What a grubby little kid.' Then I realized it was Jared. Boy, was that a jolt. I was looking at him the way someone who wasn't his mother would see him." She recalls the moment with a rueful smile. "But I always remember that picture. It gives me a little better balance; it sort of offsets my adored-beautiful-son routine." This mother's jolt when she saw her son as someone else was one of those occasions when a parent becomes aware of the two images. Just noticing the difference prompted some correction of the internal version.

This constant unconscious interplay between the real child and the internal one contributes to the importance the child holds for the parent. Our child exists in the world; he also exists as a kind of continuous psychological creation, a blend of the actual child and our hopes and fantasies. We see in our child our best hopes embodied. Some pieces of our picture will fit; more will have to be cast aside, or recast to fit the reality of the child.

Jack, a newspaper reporter, a man who values verbal skills very highly, talks about his son, now in high school. "He can't spell, he doesn't really like to read that much, and he can't always say what he means. For years I thought he wasn't that bright. It wasn't until he got into junior high and started making As in math and science and did a project on ecosystems that wowed everybody that I began to understand that he's very smart. He's smart on his terms, not on mine. I really had to rethink who I thought my son was. I had to give up my idea of a kid with verbal skills, who could talk and write and do the stuff I love. But when I did that, gave up my idea of who he ought to be, I found I could enjoy who he actually is."

It is the real child, in all her unique particularity, that drives the dialogue between inner and outer. When you lose your child, you are left with this richly elaborated creation, the product of your own efforts, conscious and unconscious. With the real child gone, the dialogue cannot continue. Not only have you lost the real child; you have also lost the interplay that has enriched your internal life. Because this process goes on for the most part out of awareness, it is hard for you to name this painful aspect of your loss. When you say "I feel like I've lost a piece of myself," you are speaking of this loss of the interplay between your internal experience of your child and the child herself.

You want to talk about your child. Talking about him revives that interplay. Harry: "People assume that if your kid dies, it would hurt too much to talk about him. They're wrong. I don't talk to everybody, but with our friends, people who knew him, it really helps. When we talk about Ray, I feel like I'm keeping him alive. Not literally, don't get me wrong. But talking about him helps my memories of him stay stronger, especially the good ones. It's like watering a garden."

With a living child, the interchange between inside and outside, real child and the child in your mind, simply continues, as constant as breathing and as unnoticed. Only when your child dies and the dialogue ends do you become painfully aware of its absence. Talking about him, remembering him with people who knew him, helps you to hold on to him. Talking and remembering restores the interchange that death derailed.

Your Child Gives You a Job and an Identity. There is no question that raising a child is a job. Especially in the first six years, children require enormous investments of time and energy from their parents. No matter who works outside the home, no matter what the child care arrangements, parents are the bottom line. In society's eyes, and in our own, we have committed to the job of caring for our child. Mundane, unpaid, the job of parenting rests on that nonnegotiable commitment.

Early on, parents learn the costs of their commitment, in difficult choices and sacrifices. "I was offered an assignment in Bosnia last year," says Phil, a free-lance news photographer. "It was a great opportunity, and I hated to turn it down. But I've worked too much in war zones to delude myself about the dangers. After Betsy got pregnant, I started thinking seriously about how I wanted my child to grow up. What would it be like for my kid if I was gone half the time? Or if I was dead? Some days I read about what's going on, and I really wish I was over there. But that was a trade-off for having Sarah."

For mothers the sacrifices and hard choices are constant.

Even after thirty years of women's liberation, in most families mothers organize their lives around their young children's needs to a far greater degree than fathers do. Being the person most responsible for a young child means surrendering a significant piece of your life. For a mother with babies or toddlers, sleep, free time, even the simple luxury of a cup of coffee and reading the paper for fifteen minutes are put on hold, sometimes for years. Being a mother becomes a central fact of your identity, an identity you affirm and earn every day.

The daily work of parenting and the sacrifices we make in order to do it make our child precious to us. Tedious, fatiguing, demanding: The work of caring for our child becomes the crucible in which we mold our identity as parents. The knowledge that we are meeting our child's needs, fulfilling our part of a sacred trust, makes that identity valuable, a deeply rooted source of self-esteem. The daily evidence of our child's flourishing confirms the worth of our efforts.

By becoming parents, we also expand our whole sense of who we are. We watch amazed as we become more patient, more empathic, more attuned to the needs of another. We become kinder and somehow tougher. What we become in caring for our child inevitably makes us grow in every part of our lives; it alters who we are and how we see ourselves in every sphere.

Phil knows himself as a dedicated photojournalist, a professional who puts his life on the line to bring in the story. He admits to having trouble integrating his nurturant feelings with his hell-for-leather war correspondent version of himself. Thinking about Sarah, he recovers a memory. "When I tried to put this together, I remembered my dad. He died when I was eight, so I don't have too many memories of him. But once he helped me build a hutch for my rabbits. We sat on the back steps, and he held my mother rabbit and stroked her. I've got to be there to build a hutch for Sarah."

From the Day Your Child Is Born, You Commit to Protecting Her. In no other relationship do we feel such a strong commitment to taking care of another. When our child comes into the world, we enter a compact with our newborn. We promise her and ourselves that we will keep her safe and provide her with all she needs to grow up. Our commitment has nothing to do with class, or income, or race; it is simply what parents do. Talking about parents' commitment to their children, the English psychoanalyst D. W. Winnicott said, "There is no such thing as a baby." He meant that a baby does not exist alone. Without her parents' fierce and daily commitment to her care, no baby or child would survive. Not physically, not psychologically. Our commitment to our child guarantees the child's survival. Our compact with our child is part of the bright canopy that we raise over our family, protecting our child and ourselves as well.

Ask parents about the rewards of parenthood, and they will talk about how deeply satisfying it is to be able to take care of their child. "I love it that, when he's hurting, I can make it better." "I know what she needs, and I know I can give it to her. That just feels good." Providing for their children, keeping them safe, confirms for parents that they are honoring their commitment.

The canopy of love and protection parents erect above their children also covers tears in the fabric of their own childhood. "There's something real satisfying for me when I talk respectfully to my kids," Lee observes. He is a machinist, the sixth of seven children. "My dad knew every curse word in the book, and he used them all on us. I grew up on 'you're a dumb fuck,' and 'you're chickenshit.' I can't undo how my father talked to me, but when I make sure my kids hear different from me, I'm fixing something for myself as well."

Under the canopy we erect to keep our children safe, our

own illusions bloom. *The world is a safe and orderly place,* our assurances run, *and our own family is especially safe. We, your parents, have the power to keep you safe.* Spoken or simply felt, this is the litany and the illusion all parents share.

These five strands of love, hope, the child in our mind, identity, and protection help us understand what we already know: that children stand at the center of their parents' lives, desperately important, deeply loved. They claim our present, and they shape their future. We turn now to ask what parents lose when they lose a child.

What Do Parents Lose When a Child Dies?

A child's death is a dark stone dropped in the pool of your life. Ripples spread everywhere; no part of you is spared. "When you lose a child," Tom laments, "your losses are just beginning. You lose a piece of yourself. You lose your illusions. You lose reason and predictability; all the order falls out of the universe. And you lose your future."

The Loss of a Piece of Yourself. Our time, our efforts, and our hopes—these are our most precious commodities, the materials of our selves. We invest them lavishly in our child. The more we have invested, the more we lose. How much of ourselves we have invested is not measured by how many months or years the child lived. A stillbirth or the death of a newborn is as great a loss as the death of a young adult. As Linda Edelstein reminds us, "The death of a child is an event that occurs in the [parent's] inner and outer worlds." To take the measure of your loss, we must appreciate the unique place your child occupied in your inner world.

We have seen how intertwined a child becomes with your self. Your child's death robs you of a central piece of your self, part of what is most you. "Judy was developing a real eye for color and line. She'd started to design outfits for herself. She'd draw them, and I'd help her figure out how to sew them." Martha remembers her fourteen-year-old daughter. "Helping her make a design into something real was one of the most satisfying things I've ever done. When we were working together, I couldn't even tell you where it was her and where it was me."

After Judy was killed, Martha did not sew again for years. "I lost so much of myself, I just couldn't. When I got back to it, it was like starting over. I had to find a way to sew that let me connect with Judy but that I could do without falling apart. That took awhile."

The Loss of Illusions. Our belief that we can protect our children too often turns out to be an illusion. We elaborate other illusions as well: "If I behave right and play by the rules, bad things won't happen to me." "Cancer happens to other people." "This is a good neighborhood; my kids are safe." These ideas sit in the back of our minds, seldom invoked, yet powerfully reassuring. Illusions indeed, as any reading of the daily paper proves. But they are necessary and helpful ones that even the most sophisticated and cynical of us weave for ourselves. They enable us to get about our lives.

When you cannot protect your child, you lose the canopy of illusions that has sustained you. Your child's death delivers a staggering blow to your self-esteem. Your job as parent was to protect your child, and you could not. No matter what the circumstances of his death, no matter how impossible to prevent or beyond your control, you hold yourself responsible. If what happened to your child happened in another family, you would not hold those parents responsible. Yet you hold yourself to a different measure.

Joan and Ed had two adolescent sons and were experienced

foster parents when they adopted Tess. She was a drug baby, born to an addicted mother, still withdrawing at two months when she came to them. Her medical chart revealed the chronic irritability and frequent seizures that ravage an infant in withdrawal. She'd been with the Gibsons for fifteen days. "She was calming beautifully," Joan remembers. "Her color was better, and her movements weren't so jerky. We were really getting somewhere with her." Joan put her down at nine o'clock, checked her at eleven before she went to bed and again at two thirty. Each time Tess was sleeping comfortably, and her breathing was easy and regular.

Joan woke up at six and immediately went to check on her. Tess was cold. She died between three and four A.M., according to the autopsy report. There were no signs of distress; she had simply stopped breathing.

As foster parents, Joan and Ed knew the risks that attend a drug baby. They understood that a nervous system that was awash in toxic chemicals as it formed is vulnerable during the stress of withdrawal. They knew that sleep apneas are always a risk. None of what they knew could change how Joan felt. She held herself responsible. "It didn't matter to me that she'd been ours such a short time or that she was still withdrawing. The minute I took her, she became my child." After Tess died, Joan's confidence unraveled. "For months I didn't do much of anything except get through the day and think about Tess. If you can't protect your own child, what are you worth? That's how I felt.

"One night a few months after Tess died, I couldn't sleep. It was way after midnight. I got up and walked into her room. Her yellow bunny was still in her crib. This was one of those stuffed animals with something inside that pulsed like a heartbeat. They're just a godsend for addicted babies; they soothe them and help them sleep. When I'd found Tess that morning, her face was up against the bunny's stomach. I had to know whether she'd suffocated—if the bunny I gave her to help her sleep had killed her.

"I pushed that bunny as hard as I could against my face, over my nose and mouth, and I held it there. I could still breathe just fine. I must have stood there ten minutes, sobbing into the bunny. It was sadness and relief all mixed up. Until then I didn't know how much I'd been holding myself responsible for her death. It was still a long time before I could feel whole. But that night with the bunny I got it straight that I hadn't failed her."

With any disaster—earthquake, death, car accident—the trauma arises not only from the event but from its power to rip away our illusions. We stand pitifully exposed to our own help-lessness: All that we have done right, all the good we've been has not availed us. When parents whose child has died talk about what they have lost, they always mention the loss of their comforting illusions. These sustain us, and they are a lot to lose. Life goes much harder without them.

The Loss of Order in Our Universe. Parents are older, children are younger. Children will grow up, parents will grow older and die, and their children will bury them. The order of the generations is deeply embedded in our thinking. It is how things are, the way they ought to be, natural and inviolable. A child's death violates this order. Every parent who has lost a child feels that violation. Age offers no statute of limitations.

"You're not supposed to bury your children," Fred whispers. He is eighty-three, a retired railroad engineer, confined to bed by the emphysema that is slowly killing him. Two years ago his son died suddenly, of a cerebral aneurysm, at fifty-four. "When Pete died, it just knocked all the stuffing out of me," he says. "We didn't talk all that often, but we were close. I was there for him, and I knew he was there for me. Your son dies before you do, it's just not how it's supposed to go. Not a day goes by I don't think about him. I miss him terribly."

The Loss of the Future. A child's death robs you of your future. Your child is woven through the tapestry of your future, an integral part of the design. When death rips your child from the tapestry, the design is changed, damaged past repair. You lose the pleasure and pride that comes from watching her life unfold and her potentials flower. You lose the pleasure of her company. Holidays and birthdays turn into hollow, exquisitely painful reminders of her absence.

Parents hold on to fragments of their tapestry. Your child grows up in your mind. Martha's daughter Judy was fourteen when a drunken driver locked his brakes and his pickup skidded into her. Seven years later Martha remembers Judy's love for clothes and her growing design sense. On the first warm day in April she drinks her coffee at a sidewalk café. As young women pass her on their way to work, talking with their friends, she watches one who looks to be twenty-one, the age Judy would be. She thinks about what her daughter would be wearing.

In the spring of his freshman year, Ted's son Jamaal ran the 400 meters, until a stray bullet found him on the way home from practice. "He was one of the fastest freshmen on the team," Ted says. "The coach was really excited about what he was going to do. I'd run with him on weekends, just conditioning workouts; when he decided to take off, he could blow me out." Ted and I stand on a hill and look down at the high school track where Jamaal had run. "He'd have been a senior this year. Wonder what his time would be."

Coaches and runners know the tall, pensive man who comes to practice, clocks practice laps for them, and listens quietly to their fears and complaints. "I just listen," Ted says. "I want to tell them 'Be glad you're here, and you can run.' "

When your child dies, you lose simultaneously on so many fronts. You lose the embodiment of your special hopes, and you lose your second chance. You lose someone who loved you and whom you loved, perhaps more extravagantly than anyone else in your life. In your own eyes you have failed, because you could not protect your child. You lose a job and a piece of whom you know yourself to be. You are cheated of the natural order of time and generations. The tapestry of your future has been torn and forever altered.

Facing the awful catalog of your losses, you still must look to your other children, who still need you and need your help to grieve. A mother remembers: "After Jordy died, sometimes I hated Janelle for still being there and needing me. I also know that a lot of the time, her needing me was what made me keep going." In the next chapter we hear from surviving children, as they tell us what they lose when a sibling dies.

· 2 ·

The Family Undone:
What Children Lose

*"Mom got the flowers, Dad got the money,
and everyone told me to be good."*
—Melissa, age seven

*F*or ten years Judy Davis has been listening to children who lost a sibling to sudden infant death syndrome, or SIDS. As director of the Sibling Project, she meets with families around California who have lost a child. She invites children to talk with her about their brothers and sisters who died, what they remember, how they feel. Her office is cozy, a small, bright cave. It would be a comfortable space for a child. The wall behind her chair holds shelves and cubbyholes filled with tiny dolls, animals, puppets, dinosaurs, vehicles, houses, furniture— all the furnishings for a miniature world, at children's disposal to help them reveal their inner world. Her body spreads into the chair, and her feet do not quite reach the floor. A nimbus of gray hair surrounds her face. Her eyes are intensely green; their color deepens as she talks.

"Children lose so much when a sibling dies," Davis says. "When they lose their brother or their sister, they lose their family as they know it. They lose their parents, at least temporarily, because parents are so disabled by their own grief.

20

Their place in the family is forever changed, and so is the family itself. And they have fewer tools to handle it with than adults." Her eyes go a darker green. "I saw Hallie when she was nine, in a family of stair-step kids, one of the steps missing. She was five when her brother died. Her parents did what a lot of parents do. They told her that her brother was dead, that he was with God, in heaven. They didn't shut down or refuse to answer her questions, but they didn't talk about the baby themselves, at least not around their kids.

"I told Hallie I knew she'd lost her brother, and I asked her what she remembered. Hallie answered by telling me about her dog: how pretty he was, and how smart, and how much fun he was to play with. After a while I asked where her dog was now.

"She started to cry. She said her dog died last year. Then she said, 'They did the same thing to my dog that they did to my brother. They took him away and didn't tell me what happened.'

"I asked her, 'What do you want to know?'

" 'Where's my dog, and where's heaven?'

"I suggested that maybe she and I could talk together with her parents. She asked them the same question, and they gave her some good, straight answers. When their baby died they'd done what they'd been told to do, which was answer questions if their children asked, but don't volunteer a whole lot, so as not to confuse the children. But when you're five, you don't even know how to ask about the things you don't understand. And if nobody talks about it, then you never figure out how to. That's what I mean about tools."

The Bonds Children Share

Brothers and sisters share a special bond. After the connection with you, the parents, the bonds children share with their siblings are the strongest and most constant in their lives. Especially for young children, siblings are a continuing daily presence. They are playmates, confidants, competitors; they may also be protectors, tormentors, or special responsibilities. Siblings know each other more intimately than anyone else. Siblings know, as no one else in the world does, what it is like to grow up in your particular family. Relationships with a brother or a sister help children know who they are and how they fit in the family. The bonds between siblings are woven into the fabric of each one's life. As we did with parents and children, we can examine the fibers that make up the bonds between siblings, to understand what children lose when a sibling dies.

These bonds are so much a part of your family's life, so self-evident that you may not even speak of them. But they are worth restating here because when a child dies and the bond is severed, all the fibers are left hanging. To understand what your surviving children have lost, it helps to look again at what they have had.

A Constant, Daily Presence. Especially when children are close in age, a child may simply never have known a life without brothers and sisters. Preschoolers eat together, play together, fight together, take baths together, and go to sleep together. Although differences in gender and temperament and changing developmental needs soon place them on diverging paths, children see their siblings as ever-present and an important part of their lives. A four-year-old watches for his sister to get off the school bus; her return is a marker in his day. A high school freshman comes home from basketball practice and even as he heads for the refrigerator, he asks where his ten-year-old brother is. A sibling is so much a piece of the family and a part of a child's life that life without him or her is unimaginable.

Playmate, Confidant, Competitor. Because brothers and sisters are there, they are a child's first and most constant playmates. They share toys and compete for them, and they collaborate in weaving the stories and fantasies that shape so much of children's play. Siblings introduce each other to new skills and songs, new friends, to off-limits places and forbidden games. They keep each other's secrets, stand together against parents.

As in any intimate relationship, the bonds between siblings are threaded through with ambivalence. Ever-present, a sibling competes for parents' affection, both directly and in the surrogate forms of privileges and praise. As a child sees the other(s) getting what she also wants, jealousy and anger are inevitable. Children face the task of balancing these disruptive feelings with the affection they feel for a sibling. This is a hard task at any age. How well your children manage ambivalent feelings toward siblings has much to do with the way you, the parent, deal with those feelings. When you treat your children's feelings respectfully and empathically, they come to treat their own feelings in that way. They learn to tolerate their anger and jealousy, keep them in control and in perspective.

If that anger and jealousy are not dealt with empathically, you will see less of these feelings. Children will struggle with them alone, with their more limited resources. They are more likely to suppress unacceptable feelings, only to have them erupt unpredictably. Their relations with siblings may come to be burdened with painful ambivalence, compromising their ability to enjoy one another. When ambivalence makes relations difficult between siblings, it becomes a formidable barrier to children's making peace with a sibling's death.

Siblings Know Each Other Better. Growing up together, siblings come to know each other without pretense. Of this intimate knowledge that siblings have of one another, the psychologists Stephen Bank and Michael Kahn write:

The core of one's identity is sometimes valued, sometimes hated, but is rarely exposed to others, and then only to a very few. A sibling and, later, a spouse, a best friend, or a psychotherapist are usually the only ones ever trusted enough to be allowed a glimpse into the core of one's self. Although all parents might wish to peer deep into the inner recesses of their children's minds, children, as we know, often hide their true feelings from their parents. A brother or a sister is much more likely to know one in this most basic sense.[1]

To have another person know you that well is indeed a form of intimacy. To lose the person who knows you that well is to lose a piece of your self.

Alice is in her early forties, the mother of four, and a junior high principal. She remembers her sister Louise, who died of leukemia at eight. "There were seven of us, five girls, each about eighteen months apart, so my parents sort of clumped us all together. Louise was five years younger. We had two sisters in between us, but she and I were always the closest. I used to take care of her a lot, but I realize she also took care of me. I'd talk to her about who I liked at school and what I wanted to be. She really knew me better than anyone. After she died, I changed so much. I was thirteen, and after that, I was just never at home. I couldn't bear to be there, because no one else in my family really knew me the way Louise did, and I couldn't let them. I couldn't get close to anybody for years; not until after my daughter was born. Not the way Louise and I were close."

Only a Sibling Knows What It Is Like to Grow Up in That Family. Children share the inside view of their parents and the private knowledge, both good and bad, of what life is like in their family. Annie, Patrick's older sister, talks about her brothers: "Patrick and Jeremy are the only other people in the world who know how weird Mom gets when she starts on Latin roots. We'd just sit at the table and roll our eyes. Or how Dad loves us but has such a hard time showing it, and makes speeches instead. Jeremy and I have lost a witness. We feel like we're the last survivors of some tiny tribe."

Annie's tribe still has another member. Today's families are smaller; many children have only one sibling. For such children to lose their sibling makes them an only child, a sole survivor. The child they grew up with, who lived through their childhood with them, their witness, is gone.

Relationships with Siblings Help Children Define Themselves. Through their interactions with brothers and sisters, children come to define their place and their value within the family and in their own eyes. Kenny's experience reveals much about how a child benefits from this relationship with a sibling and how much he loses when that sibling dies. For Kenny, his sense of himself as a capable and worthy young man was organized around his self-appointed role as Gail's protector. When he could not protect her, the bottom fell out of his life.

Kenny lounges against the fender of his car in his neighborhood in Oakland. "I was four when Gail was born. When Mama brought her home, I said, 'This is my baby.' She always was. Even when I got mad at her or she got into my stuff, I was always like, I'm her big brother, and I'm gonna take care of her. Day she started kindergarten, I was the one that walked her to school.

"It happened in August, in the late afternoon. Mama told me to go to the store. I said, 'C'mon, Gail, come down to the store with me and help me carry this stuff, and I'll buy you a Popsicle.' She loved grape Popsicles.

"That car, I never saw it coming. Folks said he was doin'

sixty. He just come whaling down the street and up on the sidewalk where we were walking. I pulled her hard as I could, but he just coming too fast."

Behind his silvered sunglasses, Kenny's eyes fill with tears. His mouth sags, his scowl crumbles, and the twenty-three-year-old gang member weeps softly. "I was eleven when that guy killed my sister. I tell Mama I was on the right track till Gail died. Ain't nothing gone right for me since."

Gail lived for eight days, unconscious. All Kenny remembers of that time was missing his mother, who stayed at the hospital. Gail was in the intensive care unit, and children weren't allowed to visit. The day Gail died, their mother flew back to South Carolina, where all her family lived. "She never even come to tell me Gail died. The lady who was keeping me told me."

Kenny flew alone to join his mother the day of the funeral. "I hadn't seen Mama but a few minutes in almost two weeks, and now there's all these people around her sayin', 'Don't bother your momma, she's having hard enough time as it is.' So I kept to myself and tried not to bother her. We didn't talk much about Gail, and when we got back home I guess we never got around to it.

"I used to see Gail a lot. Clear as day. She'd be in the room with me. Not saying anything, just standing there, with light all around her. I told Mama about seeing her, and she sent me to my auntie in South Carolina. I missed Mama and I wanted to go home. They said, 'You still seeing your sister?' I said no, so they let me go home.

"Junior high, it just got worse. I'd just know that my teachers were talking about Gail, saying bad things about her. I couldn't keep my mind on school. I just quit going. Mama took me to a doctor. I talked to him once, and he said Mama should come too, but we didn't go back."

Kenny hung out with older boys who stole cars, and sometimes he helped them. At fifteen he was arrested and charged with accessory to auto theft, and spent two years at the California Youth Authority. He has served time for possession of stolen goods, driving without a license, failure to appear in court, and resisting arrest. Although he earned his general equivalency diploma (GED) in jail, he has few job skills; the longest he has held a job is five months. He feels his life is going nowhere.

Kenny's experience is extreme, but not unusual. His sister's death robbed him of his adoring friend and companion. It convinced him that he had failed in his highly valued job as Gail's protector, and his sense of his own worth collapsed under him. It left his mother so profoundly bereaved that she was unavailable to him. Without her help, he was unable to grieve; he blamed himself for Gail's death, withdrew from people, and maintained an hallucinatory bond with his sister. His grief overburdened him, depriving him of the psychological energy and staying power that normal adolescence requires. With each passing year, Kenny fell farther behind kids his age in academic learning and social skills. He fell in with the gang because their badness fit with his view of himself and because they tolerated him.

Not every child whose sibling dies sees his life plunge so precipitously downhill. But every child who loses a sibling does face a painful array of losses. In the next section we examine those losses and their consequences for the child's future.

What Children Lose

When a brother or sister dies, your children's loss is profound. The losses come on many fronts, touching all the important areas of their lives. They lose the easy assumptions of invulnerability and immortality that make childhood a safe place. Often they hold themselves responsible for their sibling's death. Their loss isolates them from other children; no matter how much they care about your children, before late adolescence age-mates cannot bear to talk about your children's loss. Worse, as Judy Davis reminds us, children who lose a brother or sister may also lose their parents. Overwhelmed by their own grief, for a time parents are likely to be unable to help their children. Contending with the most painful and frightening event of their lives, children may be abandoned to their own insufficient resources. To take the full measure of children's bereavement, we will look at each of these losses in turn.

Childhood Is the Kingdom Where Nobody Dies. This wishful pronouncement by Edna St. Vincent Millay is an illusion— one of the essential illusions children require to grow up psychologically healthy. Although these ideas are not always consistent with the facts, they provide young children with a sense of comfort and safety. *I am safe, and my family is safe. My parents will always take care of me. Nothing bad will happen to any of us. Nobody I love is going to die.* As the canopy of illusions arches over children, it furnishes them with the raw materials and time they need to build their own internal sense of safety.

Over time, these illusions crumble under the weight of children's own experience. The loss of illusions, necessary losses, as Judith Viorst calls them, always hurts. But if the canopy has lasted long enough and the children have had time to establish reliable internal structures of their own, then the crumbling of illusions will not undo them. In children for whom those illusions are never fostered, however, the internal structure does not get built. Children who lose their illusions too early and too harshly will have significantly damaged the capacity to feel safe.

Part of feeling safe is the conviction that people you love don't die, at least not until they're old. Children don't die. Least of all your brother or sister. When a sibling dies, the whole bright canopy over children comes crashing down. They feel exposed, endangered. Amanda was four when her baby sister died of SIDS. Before, Amanda had gone to bed without much fuss. After Carrie died, though, her mother couldn't get Amanda to settle at night. She fought against going to bed, would get out of bed repeatedly, and when her parents returned her to bed, she would play and sing to herself for hours before she fell asleep. Finally, months later, when her mother found her awake at midnight, sitting up in bed and staring into the dark, Amanda said that she was afraid that if she went to sleep she wouldn't wake up. When her mother reassured her that she would, Amanda asked, "How do you know? Carrie didn't."

Reuben was sixteen when his four-year-old brother was diagnosed with leukemia. "I was okay when he was just in the hospital for a few days at a time. My mom would be over at Children's Memorial with him, and that was kind of a pain, but my dad and my sister and I kind of took over. We all learned to cook and do our own laundry, and then in a few days they'd be home.

"It got bad a couple of years later, when Asher got really sick. I was down at Purdue by then. Every morning I'd drive over to campus, and I'd sit in my truck, listen to the radio, and then I'd say, 'Nope. Can't do it today.' I'd go over to the union and get a coffee and talk to people I knew, but I just couldn't go to class. I had a job, and I couldn't ever get there on time. It's like, anything that required any concentration or any responsibility I just couldn't do. Like, if a little kid could just die, what was the point of doing anything?

"I played in a band, and a couple of the guys did a lot of coke. When I used it I felt so much clearer. In control and empowered. Asher was going downhill pretty fast. When I was using was the only time I didn't hurt. I managed to land myself a pretty hefty drug problem.

"After he died, I stayed wasted all the time. I left school, which was just a formality, because I hadn't seen the inside of a classroom for months.

"My friend Neal probably saved my life. He'd known all along what I was doing. He just glommed onto me. He said, 'You've got to get off of that shit.' I knew he was right.

"He'd come over every day and make me talk about Asher. Everything I could think of, everything I could remember. Silly stuff I used to do with him. I talked so much about Asher with Neal that when I wasn't with him I didn't need to think about him.

"He'd call just when I was getting in from work, and we'd go out together and talk some more. We'd have a couple of beers, nothing else. In a week I was clean, and I knew I could never mess with that stuff again. He stuck with me like that for a month, and by the end I could see my way back toward my life. I wrote two songs in that time. One was about how Asher died and how all of us came out of it.

"I was still very angry. I couldn't see how Asher dying should ever be allowed to happen. I stayed angry, some part of me, for years. It wasn't until Jane, my wife, was pregnant that it really went away. At first when she was pregnant I was terrified; what if our kid had leukemia? I wanted her to have an amniocentesis. Jane's doctor was great; I think she knew how scared I was. After I could feel the baby moving I kind of calmed down. The last trimester I was really calm and mellow.

"Rachel's a wonderful little girl. She kind of reminds me of Asher, with her smile and her curiosity about everything."

Kenny, Amanda, and Reuben all lost the shelter of invulnerability and, with it, the safety and the sense in their lives. The car that killed Gail also shattered Kenny's life; he lost his connection with his mother, and he held himself responsible for his sister's dying. For Amanda, even falling asleep carried a lethal risk. Overwhelmed by grief, raging at a universe that would allow his little brother to die, Reuben could see no purpose in his life. He looked for anesthesia in cocaine.

They each recognize the impact of their sibling's death on the way they look at their own lives. Kenny looks back at his growing up: "I was on the right track till Gail died. After that, I just couldn't see the point of doing nothing. Still don't sometimes." Now eight, Amanda plays with stuffed animals, but never with dolls. She likes babies, but she's not sure she'll have any when she grows up. "Babies can die sometimes," she says, "and then everybody is very sad." Reuben stayed angry for years; only the birth of his own child soothed the wound. "Even now," he observes, "when anything happens to Rachel, I get much more scared than Jane. I think when she gets past six and a half—that's how old Asher was when he died—I might calm down. But I know I'll always see life differently. It's more fragile than people know. You can't count on things lasting."

The Burden of Guilt. Kenny believes that he is responsible for Gail's death. "Seems like it was my fault. I'm her big brother, I was supposed to take care of her. I even told her to come with me. Afterward I felt so bad I pretty much kept to myself. I'd think about it every day; couldn't think about much else. I had nightmares. The car'd be coming straight at us, and I'd wake up screaming."

Although the nightmares stopped, Kenny's guilt stayed with him. Talking about his life after Gail died, he reveals a pervasive conviction that, because he allowed his sister to die, he deserves to be punished. After the accident he began to ride his bicycle recklessly; more than once he rode straight at an oncoming car. He injured himself frequently, including two fractures. He picked fights with larger, older boys, fights that guaranteed he would get beaten up. Although he did not steal, his pattern of carelessness and bad judgment ensured that he would get arrested and charged. By seventeen, when he left the Youth Authority, he saw himself as bad and helpless to change.

Even children who were not directly involved in their sibling's death will feel magically responsible. Brothers and sisters quarrel. They fling insults and angry words. They feel envy and hate. When a child dies, the living siblings, left with their angry words and secret wishes, may believe that their anger caused the death. Even adults easily slip into believing that angry thoughts cause harm. Usually our capacity for reality testing is sound; we check ourselves and remember that our thoughts don't make things happen. The younger children are, the less their life experience and the less established their reality testing, the more susceptible they are to their own guilty conviction that their thoughts killed their sibling. When a child's death is violent and sudden, the odds are high that the surviving children will hold themselves responsible.

Children who believe that their thoughts or actions caused a sibling's death carry a crushing burden of guilt. They are unlikely to reveal their belief directly; it is too awful. Their guilt will show up in changes in mood and behavior. They may isolate themselves from friends or deprive themselves of activities and pleasures they once enjoyed. Like Kenny, they may behave in ways that invite punishment. They may become thin-skinned, short-tempered, explosive.

In the fall after his brother Patrick was killed, Jeremy, eleven, did not go out for soccer. A fierce defender, he'd played for four years, and the boys he played with were his closest friends. All he would say was "It's just a dumb game, and I don't feel like it." He had been an easygoing, affectionate boy. Now little things set him off; he would fly into a rage and retreat to his room. One night he exploded at dinner because he got a cheeseburger instead of a hamburger.

Elaine found him lying facedown on his bed in the dark. He deserved to die, he told her finally, because he'd made Patrick die. Ever since Patrick had started going out with Rosemary, he hadn't had any time for Jeremy. Despite the difference in their ages, the boys had always enjoyed each other's company and spent time together. Patrick's move into dating that summer had left Jeremy hurt and lonely. The night Patrick was killed, it was his and Jeremy's turn to do the dishes, but Patrick had left before they were done. Patrick said that he was going over to Rosemary's and that Jeremy would have to finish by himself. Outraged and hurt, Jeremy stood at the kitchen door and shouted at his brother's back, "Dumb ass! I hope you never come home!"

When Jeremy told his mother what he had said, he began the complicated work of unraveling his guilt. If he had not told her, he would bear his burden still. No child or adolescent can work out this kind of irrational, self-imposed guilt alone. Children need to talk with an adult who can appreciate their pain and can help them sort out the underlying mix of love and ambivalent wishes that give rise to distortions. In *The Sibling Bond*, Bank and Kahn state emphatically, "These distortions must be exposed if the living sibling is to mourn completely."[2]

This sorting out is not the work of a single conversation; it takes place over months and years, as your children go about their lives and live with their memories. The movie *Ordinary People* shows us this process in exquisite detail. After the death of his older brother, Buck, Conrad's picture of his family and of his place in it is shattered. We watch as the events of Conrad's daily life force him to reevaluate his feelings about his idealized brother. To build a new picture he can live with, Conrad must reexamine his feelings, including the painful feelings of envy and rivalry, and question just what he was guilty of.

You may be able to help your children yourself. Providing opportunities to remember what happened, and for your children to talk about what they wished or said or did, may be sufficient. The trick is to be able to hear them when they want to talk. For every dramatic explosion like Jeremy's, there are a hundred subtle indicators, the nearly invisible signals children send when something is on their minds. You won't catch them all; no parent ever does. But by creating a climate that acknowledges that people have painful feelings and that talking about them helps, and by talking about your own painful feelings, you increase the odds that your children will feel safe enough to share things with you.

When rivalrous and angry feelings have colored the relationship, or when one child's actions actually may have contributed to a sibling's death, the work of sorting out guilt and ambivalence and responsibility becomes more complicated. The surviving child may benefit from psychotherapy. In chapter 8 we look more closely at therapeutic help with grieving, and how and when it can be useful.

No One to Talk To. A sibling's death isolates children from their friends. Although they care about the survivors and can empathize with their sadness, usually friends cannot talk with children about what they are going through. The younger the children and their friends, the more this is so. Death is frightening, and young children do not seek out their painful and uncomfortable feelings. Whatever happened to the child who died might be contagious. Even adults think so—often adults force their children to avoid a bereaved family. When the cause of death was leukemia or a car accident or drowning, this notion seems irrational, but it is how young children think.

Friends can comfort children, and they can offer relief from grieving that young children need and welcome. But children cannot look to other children for help with their grief.

Bereavement groups for children are different. A bereavement group recognizes the isolating effect of grief and counteracts it by inviting children to share their stories. "Hearing other kids talk is enormously valuable," says Liz Sumner, a pediatric nurse who helped develop the children's groups at San Diego Hospice. "Especially for young children, who feel like they're the only person in the world who's lost a brother or a sister. They get in there and hear other kids talking about what happened, and you can practically see them starting to think.

"After they've come a couple of times, their parents start seeing changes. A dad stopped me in the hall after group last week and said, 'This is really helping Susan. After her sister died she just clammed up, and her mother and I have been kind of worried. She came home from the last meeting and I don't think she's stopped talking since. She's asked some really tough questions about her sister's illness. It hasn't been easy for any of us. But I think she's doing what she needs to do.' "

Older children who have lost a sibling speak of their sense of isolation. A year after Patrick's death, Annie reflects: "My friends all know about it, and they care about me, but I feel like they can't possibly understand. What happened to Patrick has made me think about what really matters. Sometimes when one of them gets steamed over something at school or something somebody said, I kind of shake my head. Like it just doesn't matter. My family really matters, and being with the people I love. A lot of the rest is just not important. That kind of makes me different."

More disabling than the isolation from peers is the isolation from their parents that children frequently experience.

A Double Loss. When a child dies, parents and siblings are stricken at once with the same grief. Although the fantasy is that they will cling to each other and comfort each other, what happens is often sadly different. As mentioned earlier, Elaine, Patrick's mother, sees herself alone on a tiny life raft. She can see her husband and her children, each on their own rafts, battered by the same storm. But she is so close to sinking herself that she must focus all her energy on staying afloat; she has none left to help them. Parents are so overwhelmed by their own grief that they cannot comfort their children or help them grieve. In such situations the surviving children suffer a second loss. Not only has a sibling died, but they have lost their own connection with their parents.

The younger the children are, the more devastating this loss will be and the more profoundly it will affect their development. Young children's sense of safety and well-being arises from their sure ties to the people who take care of them. When an important caretaker is absent, as Kenny's mother was while his sister was in intensive care, or when she is physically present but absent emotionally, as Alice's mother was after Louise died, the surviving children feel abandoned to their own resources.

Alice: "Last year my mother told me that for two years after Louise died, she'd get up in the morning and get us all off to school, and then she'd go back to bed and stay there all day. Her sisters and the neighbors came in and took care of the two youngest kids and the house. By the time we got home from school, she was up again. When she told me, it made a whole lot of things make sense. You see, she was there, and the house was nice, and she and my dad said all the right things, but nothing felt good anymore. I couldn't ever put that feeling into words back then. I blamed myself that I ran around and never stayed home. But now I see that my instincts were right. There wasn't anything there for me, not any help with missing Louise or with how I was feeling. There sure wasn't any room to talk about it."

Preschoolers, unable yet to comprehend the irreversibility of death, feel the depth and breadth of their loss primarily through the change in their caretakers and in the quality of the relationship with them. By trying to hide your grief or making no mention of it, you do *not* protect the surviving children. Instead you deprive them of your help. You help them more when you allow them to see your grief. Expressed and explained in ways your children can understand, your own grief holds no terror for them. In fact, what you do will serve as a model for their own efforts to grieve.

Children of grade school age and young adolescents feel their sadness so intensely that they cannot bear it alone. If they do not have an empathic adult to talk with, they may suppress it. While they may push their grief out of consciousness, it does not go away. They struggle with guilt and ambivalence, and, more often than parents realize, confusion about the facts: what actually happened to the child who died. The parents' withdrawal from their surviving children and their reluctance to hear their children's pain and to help them make sense of what they feel, leave youngsters feeling abandoned and at risk.

A Climate for Children to Grieve

As a parent, you want to help your children deal with the loss they have suffered. The last thing you want is to compound the loss. Yet three factors conspire to make it possible for parents not to see the extent of their children's grief. One powerful factor is our adult reluctance to know that our children feel terrible pain. To know how much our children are suffering brings with it the obligation to help. If you know that your children are hurting as badly as you are, then you must do something. When you are immobilized by your own pain, you simply may not have the strength to help anyone else. It may be easier to believe that the children are too young or don't understand.

Children's more limited capacity for verbal expression is a second factor that makes it easier not to see their grief. Children are simply not as articulate as adults; the younger the children, the less capable they will be of putting their feelings into words. Young children may feel their loss as intensely as their parents do, yet never speak of it. If, like Hallie's parents, you do not speak of the dead child, the events surrounding the death, or of your own feelings, surviving children may feel forbidden to speak. Or they may simply be unable to find words for what they feel.

Children also take breaks from grieving; they can play with their friends or become absorbed in a television show, or beg to go to the circus even in the midst of their own intense grief. What for children is a necessary respite from overwhelming sadness may look to their parents as evidence that they simply do not feel the loss.

A third factor that tends to obscure children's grief from their parents is children's exquisite sensitivity to their parents' tolerance for painful feelings. If children sense that a parent cannot bear to hear their feelings, then that parent will not hear them. The children will suppress their feelings, even at considerable cost to their own well-being.

Children can begin to deal with their own loss when you, as parents, grieve, allow your children to know of your grieving, and can hear your children's feelings. In chapter 8 we look more closely at how children experience grief at various ages and how you can help your child.

It is essential that grieving children maintain their connection with their parents. In her essay "Loss and the Family: A Systemic Perspective," family therapist Monica McGoldrick speaks to the healing potential of connectedness: "When families can come together and share the grief experience, quite positive changes are likely to accompany the distress, strengthening the family unit and all members . . . Families can develop a clearer sense of life priorities, an increased valuing of relationships, and a heightened capacity for intimacy and empathy."[3]

Achieving these positive changes requires time and hard

work; grieving is indeed a long haul. Part Two helps you understand what is involved in living through your loss.

The next chapter discusses the ways children die. It is intended chiefly for professionals who deal with families who have lost a child; if you do not wish to read it, you can proceed to page 47.

· 3 ·

How Could It Happen?
The Ways Children Die

*"He lived but a fewe days,
and then he was gonne."*
—Seventeenth-century diarist

A child's death has always been a violation of the natural order. Even in the Middle Ages, when infant deaths were commonplace and when, in the words of historian Phillipe Aries, "one had [many] children in order to keep just a few," parents mourned their children and remembered them. Aries describes a triptych from 1610 of a couple in their sixties. Between them stands a five-year-old boy. He is their son, who had died decades earlier. When the parents commissioned the painting in their old age, they included their son, a still-remembered, still-cherished member of their family.

In nineteenth-century America, mortality rates for children remained high. Massachusetts was the first state to keep statistics on deaths, starting in 1850. That year there were 131 infant deaths per thousand live births; twenty years later, in 1870, the figure was 170 deaths per thousand. As recently as 1900, the principal causes of death for children were infectious diseases: typhoid, scarlet fever, diphtheria, whooping cough, measles, pneumonia, and influenza.

Parents' diaries document their pain. Mary White, writing in 1844 about the death of her daughter Fanny, observes that "I am just beginning to feel her loss & each day as I see the group of little ones around me & hear their cries raised in tuneful praise I feel that one is absent, that our sweetest singer is gone & can scarcely realize that it is forever but seem to feel that she will soon again be here & mingle her voice with those who are sad without her. But I know that these are vain thoughts. She will no longer return to us, but we shall go to her . . ."[1] Although frequent and expected, children's deaths were still profound losses.

The great drop in childhood mortality rates in this century reflects two great advances in scientific knowledge: an increased understanding of how diseases are transmitted and the discovery of antibiotic drugs. As researchers figured out how communicable diseases spread, the public health movement grew. Clean water, flushing away sewage in cast-iron pipes, and the Pure Food and Drug Act all reduced the transmission of disease and greatly increased children's chances of growing up.

In 1931 a chemist at I.G. Farben, the great German chemical firm, discovered sulfonamide, the first of the antibiotics. A simpler metabolite, sulfanilamide, was developed in 1935 in France. Lewis Thomas, M.D., later president of Memorial Sloan-Kettering Cancer Center, was an intern at Boston City Hospital in 1937:

> I remember the astonishment when the first cases of pneumococcal and streptococcal septicemia were treated in Boston. The phenomenon was almost beyond belief. Here were moribund patients, who would surely have died without treatment, improving in their appearance within a matter of hours of being given [sulfanilamide], and feeling entirely well within the next day or so.
> . . . For an intern it was the opening of a whole new world. We had been raised to be ready for one kind of

profession, and we sensed that the profession itself had changed at the moment of our entry. We knew that other molecular variations of sulfanilamide were on their way from industry, and we heard about the possibility of penicillin and other antibiotics; we became convinced, overnight, that nothing lay beyond reach for the future.[2]

The drugs that opened a new world for Thomas and his peers also transformed the world that parents lived in. As the practice of medicine was transformed, so were the basic assumptions and deepest fears of parenthood. Children born after 1940—the war babies and the postwar boomers—became the first generation ever to grow up whole, their ranks undecimated by childhood killers. Like Thomas, their parents had been raised to be ready for one kind of parenthood, which included the certainty of serious infectious diseases and the real possibility of losing a child. Now the assumptions had changed. Fifty years later the wonderment still echoes in the voices of these parents.

"It used to be, when I was growing up, that strep throat was two weeks in bed, and my mother scared the whole time that it would go into rheumatic fever," says Margaret. She is sixty-eight, with three sons, all now in their forties. "Then, when my boys came along, and they got the strep, the doctor gave them a shot of penicillin. They didn't much like getting the shot, but I could see how they started getting better the same day. That penicillin really was a wonder drug."

These children who grew up with antibiotics are now themselves parents. They have little memory or experience of childhood deaths; for them and their families they did not happen. Consider the inoculations their children now receive as infants: polio, diphtheria, whooping cough, tetanus, measles, rubella. These are the diseases that killed children in 1900.

The gains of twentieth-century medicine bring an unanticipated side effect: Because medicine has been so successful in preserving so many lives, expectations have risen. We expect physicians and their breathtaking technology to save every life. In the face of medicine's successes, the death of any child becomes all the more unexpected and outrageous.

And yet babies and children do die. In 1989, the most recent year for which the Census Bureau has data, the death toll was 92,355 infants, children, and adolescents. A virulent strain of influenza drives the number up by several thousand; a mild flu season brings it down by the same amount.

Infants under one year old die chiefly from congenital anomalies (genetic problems), sudden infant death syndrome, respiratory distress syndrome, disorders related to short gestation and low birth weight, complications of pregnancy, and accidents. (See table 3.1.)

Between ages one and fourteen, the principal killers of children are accidents, cancer, congenital anomalies, homicide and legal intervention (killings by law enforcement in the course of pursuit, arrest, and detention), heart disease, and pneumonia and flu. Older adolescents, fifteen to twenty-four, die of motor

TABLE 3.1

Causes of Infant Deaths, 1989

Total	**39,655**
Congenital anomalies	8,120
Sudden Infant Death Syndrome	5,634
Respiratory Distress Syndrome	3,631
Short gestation, low birth weight	3,931
Complications of pregnancy	1,534
Accidents	996
All other causes	15,809

SOURCE: *Statistical Abstract of the United States* (Washington, D.C.: U.S. Department of Commerce, Bureau of the Census, 1992), p. 80.

vehicle accidents, homicide, suicide, cancer, heart disease, and
HIV infection. (See table 3.2.)

The tables tell us how children die. What they cannot reveal
is the experience of the 92,355 families that have lost a loved
one. There is no easy way for children to die, no circumstances
of death that diminish the pain parents and siblings feel. Each
child's death is unique, an incalculable loss to his or her family.
Each family's efforts to heal are that family's alone.

The circumstances of the child's death greatly influence the
ability of parents and siblings to deal with their loss. Time is a
critical variable. Families that receive a diagnosis of a fatal
disease have months, sometimes years to live with the fact of a
child's impending death. They have time to prepare themselves, time to value each day with their child, time when the
end is in sight to begin to grieve, even to make funeral arrangements. Although helpless to change the course of the disease,
they take some comfort from their ability to care for their child,
to arrange what they can in his final days.

TABLE 3.2

Leading Causes of Death in Children and Adolescents

Cause	Age 1–14	Age 15–24
Total	16,200	36,500
Accidents	6,900	16,700
Malignant neoplasms (cancer)	1,700	1,900
Congenital anomalies	1,400	—
Homicide and legal intervention	900	6,200
Suicide	—	4,900
Heart disease	600	900
Pneumonia and influenza	400	—
HIV infection	—	600
All other causes	4,300	5,300

SOURCE: *Statistical Abstract of the United States* (Washington, D.C.: U.S. Department of
Commerce, Bureau of the Census, 1992), pp. 83–84.

By contrast, other deaths—stillbirths, deaths of newborns, SIDS, drownings, car accidents, falls, murders, and suicides—cheat families of time. Suddenly, with no warning, their child is dead. They are left with the pain of misunderstandings undealt with, plans unfulfilled, the future abruptly broken off. For them there is no chance to prepare, no time to say good-bye. The overwhelming shock and utter helplessness felt after unexpected deaths add extra complexities to the difficult work of grieving.

When the death has been violent, survivors suffer the additional horrors of imagining the child's experience, pain, and aloneness. Here grieving staggers under additional, unimaginable burdens of fear, rage against the perpetrator, and desire for revenge.

Each death carries with it unique problems for the surviving family. At the same time all families face similar concerns and one common, continuing question central to all grieving: What of the child can be kept in memory and what must be let go? In the chapters that follow we look at the work of grieving: why we must do it, its expectable tasks and stages, how children grieve differently, and the barriers to healing that families may encounter.

Part Two

~

The Work of Grieving

*E*xpected or sudden, long feared or newly learned, your child's death forces you on a journey, one you would have given anything not to undertake. An unwilling pilgrim in the country of grief, you stumble through a nightmarish landscape. Weeks and months pass in a painful blur. Over time in this dark country, parents report that they begin to find a path. They encounter guides who know firsthand the depth of their sorrow. They discover maps; often they make their own maps.

Parents who have lost a child so frequently use the metaphor of a journey that I have borrowed it here to illuminate the process of grieving. Although each person's journey is unique, enough commonalities exist that we can chart the terrain and describe some expectable stages and tasks.

Grieving is the hardest work we do. Simply put, grieving is the work of coming to terms with the fact that the person we loved is dead. The person who loved us back, whose needs gave shape and focus to our days, is dead. No longer here. We will never have her back. What we most want we cannot have.

It is terrible work, and utterly necessary. Freud observed, "The unconscious gives up nothing willingly." As human beings we give up nothing easily. When we lose someone we love, our own lives stop. Our loss immobilizes us. If we do not grieve, we stay frozen in pain; only by grieving can we enable our lives to continue.

Grieving, families learn their own measure. What they once felt they could not bear for a day parents find they can bear every day, only because they must. Acute grief, with its disorganizing symptoms and loss of function, slowly gives way to the long, long haul of mourning. This long haul is the work, simultaneously, of building a life in which the child does not live and in keeping the child alive in your heart.

In this section we learn how grief, in each of its phases, serves us and how differently from adults children grieve. We also look at barriers to grieving and timetables for healing that make sense.

·4·

Why Must We Grieve?

"If you don't grieve, you'll go under."
—Karen

I didn't know anyone could hurt this much and still keep on living. The pain when I think about him, and what happened, is just unbearable, and yet I can't *not* think about him." Gene speaks softly and looks around the room at the quiet faces. Three months ago Gene and his fourteen-year-old son Will were snorkeling off the California coast near where they live when they got caught in heavy surf. The current pulled Will away from his father, toward the exposed rocks. Gene watched, helpless, as the waves threw his son against the rocks. Will was knocked unconscious and drowned as the waves tossed him like a scrap of driftwood. This is Gene's second time at the Compassionate Friends meeting.

Other parents murmur in understanding. Karen, who sits next to Gene, lost a daughter in a car accident eighteen months earlier. She pats Gene's arm and says, "Grieving hurts. It's about as bad as it gets."

"How do you stand it?" Gene turns to her and asks.

"Not much choice, is there?" Karen answers. "If you don't grieve, you'll go under. Oops, sorry about that metaphor."

Gene stares at her for a moment, and then, for the first time since Will drowned, he laughs. "I've had more going under than I can take," he says. "I guess I'll have to grieve."

49

Grieving is the most painful work that human beings have to do. Karen is right that the choice we face is to grieve or to "go under" ourselves: If we do not grieve, we stay frozen in pain, immobilized, our lives stopped where our loss left us.

When your child has died, you may feel that your life has indeed stopped, that there is nothing worth going on for. That feeling may stay with you for a long time. To you grieving, the coming to terms with the reality of your loss, may sometimes seem to make things worse, as if you are immersing yourself even deeper in your pain. But the immersion is necessary. Only by allowing yourself to grieve—what Gene later called "leaning into the pain"—can you move toward a time and a place where the pain does not consume you. This is a paradox: Only by allowing yourself to feel the most intense and shattering pain can you move toward a life in which pain is not the center. It is paradoxical, yet it is simply how human beings are built. The spiritual "Rock of My Soul" reflects this understanding:

> So high, you can't get over it,
> So low you can't get under it,
> So wide you can't get around it,
> You must go through that door.

Parents who have grieved for a child tell us that the only way out of the pain lies straight through it.

If you are reading this very soon after your child has died, straight through may not feel possible or right for you. You may want to come back to this later.

As you lean into the pain, it helps to know something of what lies ahead. The rest of this chapter explains how grieving works and what it accomplishes, and offers you some idea of what you might expect. Although your grief is your own, unique to you and to your loss, and your ways of coping with it will

reflect your own life and experience, you share with every bereaved parent some common tasks.

When you lose someone you love, your world changes forever. When you lose a child, it falls to pieces. Nothing can ever
be the same again. Through grieving you must reassemble a
world in which you can live. This new world is not built in a
day or a year. Parents say they work with these tasks intensely
for two to four years and, one way or another, for the rest of
their lives.

I list the tasks in linear order only because print and speech
unfold like that. Life itself happens all at once, and these tasks
will come at you sometimes all at once, seldom as simply as one
at a time. When a child dies, bereaved parents must:

- face the finality of the loss;
- remember past memories and experiences with their child;
- sort out what aspects of their child they can keep and what
  must be let go;
- deal with a sense of failure and personal diminishment; and
- build a life for themselves without their child.

The list is daunting. Perhaps it looks impossible. Perhaps as
you read it you felt a surge of pain, or rebellion, or sheer
unwillingness to give up so much that has been a part of you.
Keep in mind that this is not a list for a month or even a year.
These are not items that get checked and put behind you. The
work goes on intensely for the first two years and then off and
on, as you need to, for the rest of your life. People take each
task up as they must, as the flow of their lives demands. They
work on one or several until they find a measure of resolution,
enough room to go on. Their grief recedes for a while as other
pieces of their lives claim them. They will return to the same
tasks again and again. Imagine climbing a spiral staircase. You

come again and again to the same point on the spiral, but each time you reach that point, you have moved to a new level, and you see the point from a different perspective.

Facing the Finality of Your Loss. Immediately after a child dies, especially if her death was unexpected, you simply cannot face the loss all the time. You find yourself in periods of denial. There has been a mistake. It can't be true. Parents bob and weave with what they know. Gene: "For months, every morning I'd wake up, and I'd feel fine for a couple of minutes. Then it would come back to me, like an anvil landing on my chest: Will is dead. When I'd remember, all the life just drained out of me." Karen, who has lived a year and a half longer with her loss, told the group one night about the fantasy that drifts across her thoughts once or twice a week. "As it gets dark, I find myself getting annoyed with Linda. She should be home by now. And then I have to tell myself, 'Linda won't be coming home.' " Wayne, her husband, adds, "When she told me about it, I understood it right away. I've found myself thinking she's on a trip. She's been gone for a long time, but when the trip is over she'll be back."

Is Karen's fantasy that her daughter is just out late a pathological failure to grieve? What about Wayne's, that she is away on a trip? Is he refusing to face the facts of his loss? Probably not. When people must live with a horribly painful reality, they need to retreat from time to time. As we will see in chapter 8, "How Children Grieve," young people often need to lay down their grief. They step away from it, play and party, and quite genuinely forget their loss. For adults, too, the burden is simply too heavy to carry all the time. Fantasies provide a retreat, and so do dreams. Many parents report dreams about their child, often in which their child is the age he would be in the present. "I love it when I dream about Linda," Wayne says. "I wake up feeling better."

Denial and fantasy become problematic only when they interfere with a person's ability to get on with his life. If Wayne and Karen are living with their loss and working to rebuild their lives, the relief from their pain that fantasy affords is simply that: a very temporary relief from their pain. In chapter 9 we will look at the problems that develop when the retreat becomes more than temporary.

Remembering Past Memories and Experiences with Your Child. Remembering is the work of a lifetime. Sometimes pleasurable, sometimes intensely painful, usually both, remembering your child is the very essence of grieving. Three-quarters of a century ago Sigmund Freud, trying to describe the work of mourning, put it this way: "The task is now carried through bit by bit, under great expense of time and cathectic energy, while all the time the existence of the lost object [person] is continued in the mind. Each single one of the memories and hopes which bound the libido to the object is brought up and hypercathected, and the detachment of the libido from it accomplished."[1] Although the language is dated, the task is clear: Every memory of the child who has died must be summoned up, with all its feeling, and reworked with the new and painful knowledge that the child is now gone. This is one of the most painful aspects of grieving, the releasing of your love. We love the dead differently from how we love the living. As you live with the reality of your loss, your love must recognize the changed reality and change itself. You will never stop loving your child. But in order for your life to move again, for you to be able to welcome any good thing into it, you must release some portion of your love from your child who has died. Remembering, bringing up feelings and memories, is what accomplishes this painful task.

Remembering comes in many ways. Most troublesome are the waves of memory and feeling that sweep over you, unexpected and unbidden. This happens most in the early months after your loss, as mind and heart and memory still grapple with disbelief. Sometimes the triggers are obvious, as in the grocery store, when Tom picked up the raisin bran that only Patrick had liked. Others triggers are less clear; one may simply be unstructured time, when your mind is free to wander. "I came to dread long traffic lights," says Rebecca. "I'd be sitting there just fine one minute, and the next I'm seeing Kate in the ER, so still, already growing cold. Or I'd see myself the night before, putting her down in her crib." Over time, as you live with your loss and your life shapes to the fact of it, the floods of memory come less often. Their intensity will diminish also.

Holidays, your child's birthday, the anniversary of his death all will bring memories flooding back. Because your child continues to grow up in your mind, times that mark what would be a new piece of his life will be especially poignant. Maria's son died a stillbirth, a week before his due date. He would be five this year, starting kindergarten. "The first day of school is going to be a hard day for me," she anticipates. "Things that remind me what should have been for Luke bring back my sadness very fresh."

Often you will remember your child when you choose to, spending time that is both comfort and pain, replaying the time you had together. Sometimes you will want to remember her in the privacy of your own thoughts and alone, and sometimes you will want to share your memories of her, especially with the people who knew her. Your child's possessions, photographs and videos of her, songs and smells and special places all bring back the memories. Take the time. Spend the hour in her room. Look at the things that remind you of her. The remembering helps you with the work of releasing love and of holding on to what you can keep. In the first year or two after your child has died, remembering her will be the center of your days and of your life. It needs to be this way. It is through the remembering that, slowly, you will allow your head and heart to know what has happened to you. This is the central work of grieving. Only as you do a great deal of this work, over more time than you imagined, can you lift your eyes to what else might enter your life.

Conversations with parents who have lost a child inevitably come around to their experiences of their child's continuing presence. Your child may appear to you in dreams, once or many times. "In the first year after the accident, I had a lot of dreams about Daniel," Martha remembers. "At first, they were awful. He'd be covered in blood, and I'd wake up screaming. Then they changed. I'd see him a day or two before the accident, and he'd be trying to warn me about something, and I wouldn't get it. I'd wake up feeling so cheated. For several years he wasn't there at all. Then he appeared the age he'd be now, twenty-three. He was smiling, and he radiated a contentment. I had the feeling he wanted me to know that he was all right. He wanted me to be all right too. I woke up feeling more whole than I'd felt since he died. I mark that dream as the beginning of my being able to think about what I could do in the world."

Phillip, two, and his family battled his illness, a rare leukemia, for fifteen months. A month before he died, a family friend wrote and illustrated a book for him. A bluebird flew across many of the pages—a messenger of hope, the book explained. Phillip loved the bluebird and insisted his mother read him the book every day. The day after Phillip's funeral, a bluebird appeared in the family's backyard. It has been there, constantly, daily, for seven months. "You can think of it what you will," Phillip's father says. "We are sure it is a messenger from Phillip. I feel stronger when I see that bird, less alone."

If you have sensed your child's presence, or felt a message from her, or seen her in a dream, you are not alone. Most parents reported these experiences. They had no explanations for their experience and sought none. They echoed Phillip's father, saying that their experience of their child's presence had comforted them, helped them feel less alone.

Sorting Out What You Can Keep and What You Must Let Go. You keep the child in your mind. He is yours for all your life. What you cannot keep is the child in the real world who has now been taken from you. While your child was alive, the distinction between the two seldom showed and hardly mattered. Now, when one is gone and the one who remains feels like a pale shadow and poor consolation, it becomes all the more important to find out what is left to you. Closely interwoven with remembering, the work of sorting becomes a way to claim all that you can of your child.

Parents report that they find themselves taking on some aspects of their child, usually aspects that they admired and shared. "For a year after Patrick died, I couldn't stand to hear any of the music we'd listened to together. It just hurt too much." Elaine talks about how she reclaimed a part of her life that she and her son had shared. "But one day I found his tape of *Phantom of the Opera* in a pile of stuff behind the stereo. He loved that show. I played it and cried most of the way through it. But after that, something changed. Now I can sing and play the music that he and I used to sing. It comforts me. It's a way of holding on to Patrick."

What parents describe so frequently as their child's growing up in their mind, we can also understand as a vital, active holding on to the child who lives in their mind. Just as with a child still alive, the internal image changes, reflecting what would be the child's current age and size and staying faithful to his character.

Dealing with a Sense of Failure and Personal Diminishment. A child's death leaves parents with a profound sense of failure. As a parent, your first commitment has been to maintain the bright canopy of love and protection arching over your child's life. When that canopy fails, no matter what the reason, you feel it as your personal failure. The blood clot that drifts blindly into the placental artery, the white cells' insane multiplication, the driver so drunk she lurched across the center divide, straight into your child's car: they are events out of your control, and you would never hold another parent accountable for not preventing them. But because you could not protect your child from them, you may feel yourself less capable, somehow less reliable, guilty of some unspecified failure.

You feel a terrible helplessness. You could not stop the clot, slow the white cells' reproduction, change the path of the car. Nor could you keep your child always at home or always out of the path of every dangerous thing.

If other people's carelessness or viciousness led to your child's death—if indeed it might have been prevented—then rage and outrage compound your helplessness. If your child's judgment, or your own, was unsound, you are likely to turn the torment and rage against yourself. "Every day of my life," Gene says, "I live with the fact that I led Will into a section of the cove where I didn't know the currents."

For many parents, feeling that they failed to protect their child and feeling the helplessness that comes with their child's death combine to create a sense of personal diminishment: the conviction so many bereaved parents voice that they are not very good or competent or worthwhile people. This is one of the most painful aspects of mourning and, for many parents, it is one of the slowest to resolve. What seems to help the most is your own decision that you will sit with your pain, even the pain of your own self-reproach, and not attempt to avoid it. You must go through that door.

At times parents' sense of personal diminishment gives rise to thoughts of suicide. For some it is a fleeting thought; for others, a preoccupation that haunts them for months and years. Other parents speak of their thoughts of revenge on the people whose actions led to their child's death. These are powerful feelings, and frightening. They claim your time and your thoughts; no other work of grieving can occur when you are held in their grip. You should know that in the first months after a child's death, such thoughts are not unusual; if you find them persisting, or if you think seriously about acting on them, that is cause for concern. You may want to look at chapter 9, on barriers to grieving, and you may want to consult a mental health professional.

Although you may not believe it, you will not always feel the way you do now. As you grieve and find your ways to live with loss, your sense of personal worth will slowly rebuild. You likely will find things you can do that help you feel less helpless and, in fact, help you feel like a worthwhile person. Often these take the form of a memorial to your child or work you may do in your child's memory.

Building a Life for Yourself Without Your Child. Your design for your future never included the possibility of your child's death. You had no contingency plan, no instructions. For the first year or more, you will not know how you can even imagine a life for yourself. Parents who have preceded you in this dark country say that the future is not the first concern. The more urgent tasks of reckoning with finality and with memories will claim you. "For a long time, it wasn't even a question," says Karen, who lost her daughter in a car accident. "I was so blind with grief, I couldn't see past the end of the day I was in. I didn't think about where my life would go for close to a year."

The other claims on your life tend to continue: partners, other children, jobs, other family. Although the demands that these make are frequently more than you can meet, they also provide a structure that your life desperately needs. Parents who have been there caution you to preserve the relationships you have and make no decisions hastily.

If you have a partner, you both will have to find a way to support and respect each other's grieving. Your styles of grieving will differ. Men frequently keep their grief to themselves. Your partner's obvious sadness or her request that you talk about your grief may feel like an assault on your all-too-tenuous hold on yourself. For women, your partner's reserve does not necessarily mean that he does not care, but rather that he was schooled to deal with his feelings very differently, much more inwardly. In the next two chapters, on acute grief and the long haul of mourning, we will explore the issue of grieving styles more fully.

It is inevitable that you will be out of phase with each other. One of you will be ready before the other to resume aspects of your relationship that gave you pleasure: meals together, sex, social life, sports, vacations, and the like. Whether you are ahead of your partner or behind, working out what you will do and when requires tact and a willingness to hear each other's needs.

The shape your life will take emerges slowly. It will come from your gradual understanding that you look at your whole life differently since your child died. "I take nothing for granted anymore," Harry says. "When Ray was shot, he and I hadn't talked in months. I've got three more kids coming along, and I don't care what they ever do, I'll keep talking to them. I've told them that. Family is the most important thing there is. That's what's different for me since Ray died."

Other parents say much the same things. After a child's death they feel that their priorities have shifted, in the direction of relationships, connectedness, making a contribution in the lives of the people they value. Conventional markers of success—money, promotions, possessions—come to matter less. Many parents search for a way to honor their child by making a difference in the lives of other people. Wayne talks about how his life may evolve: "It's too soon to say what I'll do for Linda. I'm just now to the point where the stone isn't on my chest all the time. I kind of figure it'll be something through our church, maybe some way of helping a kid. I don't know yet, but since Linda died, I've learned there's a lot I don't know. I'm learning how to keep myself open. If I do, I believe something will come."

Facing the finality, remembering, holding on and letting go, dealing with your personal sense of failure, building a life for yourself without your child: the work of grieving for your child is a long haul, work for a lifetime.

Leslie Swager qualifies as an expert in this field. A clinical social worker and former director of Bereavement Services for San Diego Hospice, she has lost two children of her own. "What I always stress to parents is to take care of themselves and to give themselves time. Most people's timetables for grieving are ridiculously short. Allow yourself two years to get to where your child isn't at the center of your awareness all the time . . . that's if you're straight with yourself and let the feelings come. If you try and suppress it, it'll take you longer. Then for most people it's another two years before they feel their lives are reliably back on track. The track is usually somewhat different, especially as to their values. It is a long process, but I haven't seen any way to speed it up."

You must go through the door.

The door opens with acute grief, which we take up in the next chapter.

·5·

Acute Grief

"For months after Ira died
I saw him everywhere."
—Martha

*E*mily and Dan remember the afternoon their son died.

Dan: "I'd just gotten home, and I was standing in the kitchen talking to Emily. She was getting dinner. Robin, our daughter, was watching TV. She was seven then. Pete was due home from baseball practice any time. Their practice field was pretty near our house, and that time of year it was light after practice. Pete had just turned twelve, and he liked being able to ride his bike home instead of having to be picked up. The doorbell rang and Robin answered it, and then she was in the kitchen doorway. Her face was very pale. She said, 'There's two policemen at the door, and they want to talk to you guys.'

"I remember looking at them and thinking how serious they looked. Even before they spoke I knew it was bad. The older one asked our names. Then he said, 'Your son was hit by a car while he was riding his bicycle. When we got there he was already dead. I'm very sorry.' "

Dan looks at Emily and says, "You'd better take it from here."

"Dan sort of staggered, and then he sat down hard, like he'd been poleaxed. Robin ran over and grabbed me. I held her in front of me, and I started talking like a maniac. I asked the

61

police a million questions: How did it happen, where was the accident, who was the driver, where was Pete now, are they sure he was dead, did they have a doctor examine him—a million questions. I guess I was practically shouting. And Dan's sitting there, totally out of it.

"I went into some kind of overdrive. I insisted that the police take me right then to the morgue. I had to see him. Robin came with me. I didn't even think what it would be like for her. When I got home, Dan was still sitting there, staring. I went into the kitchen and cleaned it all up and put the food away. I don't know why I did that. Then I called my sister and my parents and Dan's mother and our pastor. People had heard, and they were coming over. The phone didn't stop. It's eleven-thirty at night, and our living room is full of people, Dan's out of it on the couch, and I'm talking nonstop. Finally I said, 'You all have to go home. We've got to go to sleep.' Somebody had called our doctor and there was something for us to take. Dan went out like a light. Even with the medication, I didn't sleep. I'd fall asleep and then I'd dream about Pete. He'd be riding his bicycle, all covered with blood. Then I'd be wide awake.

"The next morning I was sitting at the breakfast bar in the kitchen, and Robin walked through and went into the family room and turned on the TV. Her brother died last night, and she's watching cartoons! I screamed at her to turn it off." Emily winces. "Poor Robin. Poor all of us. We were wrecks."

Dan: "I slept until noon. I'd wake up, and then I'd remember about Pete, and I'd fall back asleep. When I finally woke up and stayed awake, I told myself, 'Come on, you can't leave Emily and Robin hanging out there with this.' I came downstairs and held Emily, and we all sat and cried together."

Emily: "That's when my Wonder Woman stuff unraveled. When Dan came downstairs, I'd been talking to my sister and making funeral plans, very detached. Businesslike. After Dan held me, I lost it. I couldn't think straight. I'd start a sentence and I couldn't remember what I wanted to say. When Dan held me, that was the first time I knew for sure I wasn't all alone with this. Then I could finally collapse. Not being able to think was really scary. It went on for weeks like that. Even when it got better, sometimes it would come back. I was sure I was going crazy."

Robin sits next to her mother. Her eyes shift to the parent who is speaking. She listens intently. Now she pulls her mother's arm around her. "It was awful," she whispers. "I miss him so much."

All of Dan and Emily's reactions are typical of acute grief. In these first weeks especially you may find yourself thinking and behaving in ways that feel so strange, so unlike your usual self that you wonder if you're going crazy. You have a lot of company. During this first phase, which Linda Edelstein has called "disorganization," most people do believe they are going crazy. If you can recognize the expectable reactions and understand the purposes they serve, their strangeness will lessen. Even in the worst throes of acute grief, you are acting to take care of yourself. Your reactions serve to protect you, help you gather your strength, and move toward healing.

The ways people react during acute grief vary widely. You will not see yourself in all the reactions and responses described here. But your own experience likely includes some of them. As you recognize your own responses, perhaps you can appreciate how much, even in the early stages, you have already begun the work of healing.

Emergency Responses

Shock. For most people the first response is shock. Shock is a physical and psychological emergency reaction, a way of slowing everything down, of warding off facts too horrible, too overwhelming to take in. It is an involuntary response. Shock is no more under your control than is running a fever in response to infection. A person in shock cannot "snap out of it," or will the condition away. It will dissipate within hours or days. It can take the form it did with Dan, of a physical immobilization. He sat because he couldn't stand; his legs would not support him. In shock you may be unable to move or speak coherently; people report that they cannot think. Shock responses may also be active and intense; you may have screamed, or run from the room, or physically attacked the bringer of the news. All of these behaviors are means of shutting down, of distancing yourself from a reality that you do not yet have any way to deal with. As you look back, your behavior may seem bizarre and totally out of character for you. Remember that all your world had been knocked out from under you. You were in free fall, and your first task was to find a way to stop the fall.

Numbing. Like shock, numbing is an emergency response to a reality too painful to deal with. Unconsciously imposed, it buys some time until you can take hold of your loss. After a death, many people report feeling in a fog, doing what is required of them with no connection to their feelings. Their numbness may last for a few days, or it may persist for weeks. The numbness may cave in suddenly, or it may ebb slowly and return from time to time when the full measure of the loss becomes unbearable. Protected from pain, you may believe that you are handling things rather well. As the numbness ebbs and you begin to realize fully that your child is gone, the realization can come like a second blow, a psychological aftershock.

Gene, whose son drowned, remembers that morning and the next few days in a kind of fog. "I was there when it happened. I never disbelieved it. But it was as though it happened to someone else. Someone else, very far away, had seen his son drown, and I was watching it on television." He can remember the two lifeguards bent over Will after they'd pulled him to shore, one pinching his nose shut and breathing into his mouth. "I thought about how grossed out Will would be, to have him doing that, if he were conscious. The towel underneath him had red and purple hibiscuses with lime-green leaves. I can tell you the pattern and colors on the trunks of some guy who was watching. Crazy details."

Denial. As shock fades, and your mind and body reclaim their control, you start to take in the news. But it still may be too much; you may move in and out of denial. Lasting for hours or sometimes days, denial is another way of retreating from a reality too painful to bear. Denial says that it cannot be true. Someone is lying. There has been a horrible mistake. The phone will ring, the door will open, and he will be standing there, grinning his wonderful grin. At any moment the doctor will step back into the room with new test results, and you can all pack up and go home together.

As irrational as it may seem to others, denial serves a necessary purpose. It is a psychological emergency measure, a temporary forestalling. You are not yet ready to confront your loss head-on. Denial is a fragile and temporary respite, a warm hut where you seek shelter briefly before plunging into the arctic night. It buys you some brief time in which to gather yourself for the awful work to come.

If your partner or a child has relied on denial, you know how uncomfortable it can make you. You also know that it doesn't do much good to challenge denial directly. Denial is brittle but remarkably tenacious; people cling to it for as long as they need it. To the person denying, challenge feels like an assault on the only comfort he has. Time and events will work to erode it. Donald, who found his five-month-old daughter Kelly in her crib, a sudden infant death syndrome victim, remembers: "I said to my wife that maybe she was just cold, and if I wrapped her in a blanket and held her, she'd wake up. She didn't say anything, but the look on her face said it all. By the time the paramedics came, I didn't say anything to them about her being cold, although I still half believed it. By the time we'd sat in the ER watching the line on the oscilloscope, I knew that I knew. Over the next day or two, the idea [that she was just cold] would float in and out of my mind, and I'd go with it for a few minutes, but I knew it was just a way to protect myself."

Brittle, unreal, denial still serves an important purpose. It cushions your mind and heart against truths too horrible to face all at once. Even as you deny what has happened, at some level you know it is so. Gradually the denial gives way, crumbling, as Donald described his experience, under the weight of its own unreality. Gradually you find the strength to look into the awful face of your loss.

The Experience of Acute Grief

Changes in Perception, Concentration, and Memory. When the emergency measures of shock and numbing and denial give way, you are left with the most painful of all human experiences, acute grief. In the midst of acute grief you cannot concentrate or make decisions. Reading a newspaper is beyond you. Memory fails; you forget the simplest things. Thoughts of your child crowd out everything else in your mind. Every chore and act you perform evokes memories of her. Every person you meet, every place you go floods you with reminders of her presence and of your loss. You see her in the next aisle in the supermarket, at the movies, in a car passing you. These experiences of mistaken identity, of seeing your child, can be so intense, feel so real, that they make parents fear they are going crazy.

You are not going crazy. You are hard at work. Your mind is

actively, intensely engaged in the hardest work that human beings must ever do: coming to terms with loss. As we saw in the previous chapter, the essential work of grieving is the facing, day by day, memory by memory, the new, awful reality that your child is gone. This is the agony and the inescapable task. When you find your mind flooded with thoughts of your child, know that you are at work, taking care of yourself, doing what you must do. When you see her on the street, you are not crazy, you are at work: remembering, longing visually, doing the work of grieving. When you cannot think clearly, cannot remember the simplest thing, you are at work. Like a computer churning away at a huge, complex equation, your mind has focused all its energies on the painful, multifaceted, exhausting work of grieving. You don't think or remember very well simply because all your processing capacity is in use. There isn't enough left over for the requirements of routine concentration and memory.

Increased Dependence. Because you are overwhelmed, the ordinary routines of your life now feel like staggering chores. What you did automatically before now requires concentration and energy, exactly what you do not have. You may find yourself relying on other people to do things that you would usually do for yourself: planning meals, getting the car serviced or clothes washed, making routine arrangements for yourself and for your other children. Interactions with other people are the most difficult. Even the simplest interactions—greeting them, making conversation, telephone calls, seeing friends and co-workers—feel like more than you can manage. A relative or a close friend who can step in and help with these will be of enormous value. You are wise to let that person help.

Lowered Expectations. You will not always feel the way you do now. The first six months are the worst, the most disabling, for this is when you are struggling so hard to get your heart to accept the worst of all losses. In this period all your psychological energy is consumed just with coming to know that the loss is real. You live in constant, severe pain. During this period you must lower your expectations of yourself.

Elaine looks back on the first months after her son Patrick was killed: "There were a lot of days when I got through the day fifteen minutes at a time. My chest hurt so much that I truly believed I was going to die. I'd tell myself that if I'd just sit here and breathe, and think about Patrick, the hands of the clock would move. I decided that if I got myself showered and dressed each day, and got Jeremy his breakfast and put something on the table for dinner, that I was doing all that I could. I was like that from July to about Thanksgiving. I remember that I actually did do Thanksgiving; by then I had periods for as long as two hours where I could think and function."

Physical Symptoms. Acute grief is an intensely physical experience. If you have previously had trouble falling asleep, it now becomes ten times worse. When you do sleep, dreams of your child haunt you and wake you. Later on dreams will become a source of comfort and a connection to your child. But now, as you are struggling to accept the new reality, dreams are more likely to be filled with images of his death.

Or you may sleep ten hours and awake as tired as if you had not slept. Your strength and energy desert you. Walking up a flight of stairs becomes a taxing chore. Everything you lift feels heavier; the simplest tasks leave you fatigued. Chronic fatigue and exhaustion become constants, often for as long as a year. You hear yourself sighing. Breathing hurts. You may lose all interest in eating and even lose awareness of hunger. Food has no taste. You eat only because someone tells you to. Swallowing may become difficult. Your stomach may feel empty, or it may feel full and your whole digestive tract, slowed down.

Your whole body misses your child, aches with your sadness.

You may have a generalized, all-over aching or a localized pain. Grief seems to lodge in the chest and the gut: a strong, dull ache like an iron band around your chest or a hollow pain in your stomach. Localized pain will give way to a more diffuse but still intensely felt sense of emptiness that may last for a year or more. Mothers who have lost a baby or a very young child frequently get "aching arms," a heavy ache, especially in the upper arms. Their arms cry out for the child they can no longer hold.

Searching. You may find yourself searching for your child. Many parents remember from the early weeks and months a driven, unfocused restlessness. You wander from room to room, especially to your child's room, not knowing what you are searching for or even that you are searching. You walk past your child's school, visit his playground, the places where he hung out. You may drive to where the accident occurred, or maybe you just drive. "I couldn't stay in the house," says Harry, whose son was shot. "Especially late at night. I'd just have to get out and walk. I covered every part of town, but more often than not I'd find myself somewhere near the gas station. Sometimes I'd be gone until midnight, or later. I didn't understand it. One night about ten I was heading for the door and Paula, she's next oldest after Ray, said, 'Dad's going looking for Ray again.' And I realized she was right. I didn't know it, but I was looking for Ray."

Guilt and Self-blame. Guilt and self-blame occupy much of your thinking. Thinking about the days and weeks before your child died, you fix on the things that you did and on what you failed to do. Joan brooded for weeks about the toy bunny she had given her daughter to help her sleep; could Tess have smothered from it? At breakfast the day Pete was killed, he and his father had gotten into an argument over homework. Dan blamed himself. He was sure that Pete was upset about their quarrel and less attentive to traffic as he rode. If you were listening to other parents talk about what they did, you would want to hush them, reassure them that nothing they did, or failed to do, could have changed what happened to their child. But when it is you, and you have lost your child, always in the first months there will be the guilt.

It has to do with helplessness. The worst thing is that nothing you did or failed to do could have changed what happened. This is the most painful part: For all your love and caring, for all the times you protected your child and taught her how to protect herself, for all you did to preserve the bright canopy over her, still she died. It is easier, in the first months, to find yourself guilty of some sin of omission or commission than to know how helpless you truly are.

Anger. You may also find yourself getting angry with and being rude to the people who most want to help. Their very presence becomes an irritation; what you most wish is that they would leave you alone. Your feelings puzzle you, scare you, make you wonder if you're losing your mind. You are not. You are so spent, so depleted, that you have nothing left, even for friendship.

It is worth saying again: You will not always feel like this. The same symptoms and behaviors of acute grief that claim you and make you someone you hardly recognize are working to help you. They are protecting you as you take in the news. They are the evidences that all your energies are concentrated on getting the painful reality into your head and your heart.

Making Decisions

Your child's death disables you psychologically and simultaneously confronts you with tasks and decisions and demands for action. What is to be done with the body? What kind of funeral do you want? When? Where? How will you let people know? If your child died violently, police want to talk to you. Right behind the police come the reporters, print and television, who will insist you talk to them. What to do with her clothes, her possessions, her room? You are blind with pain and you can't even breathe. You do not know how you will get from now until lunchtime. How can you deal with all this?

Well, you can't. And you shouldn't have to. You need a triage. In a hospital emergency room the triage officer is the physician or nurse who looks at every patient coming in and sorts out who needs what, by urgency. You need someone you trust, who knows you well, to help you triage. Together, you sort all these demands with a simple triage system of four Ds: Delegate, Defer, Decline, and Decide. Every question, every request for a decision, every demand for action should be triaged by 4-D.

• Is this something I can delegate? You don't have to do everything yourself. Times like this are what friends and family are for. Someone you trust, who knows you well, can shoulder many pieces of the load.

• Is this something I can defer? Other people's sense of urgency should not be your obligation. Many things can wait. Many should wait. Especially about your child's clothes and possessions, you need to allow yourself time.

• Is this a request I would rather decline? Some things you must do, by law and by dictates of religious practice. Beyond these, there is very little that you are required to do. If you do not want to talk to the media or support a cause, you do not have to. You may change your mind later on. But now you have every right and reason to decline what you do not feel up to.

• Is this something I must decide or want to decide? For some issues the answer to this question will be yes. Here is where you focus your efforts. Let the people who care about you deal with the rest.

Practical Matters

After you have delegated, deferred, and declined, in the midst of your grief you still face some decisions that only you, as parents, can make. Chief among these are decisions about your other children and about a funeral. You know your family and your particular needs, and you alone can decide what will work best. The ideas that follow reflect what other parents and brothers and sisters have said about their experience.

Brothers and sisters say that no matter their age, no matter how awful the death, they want to know what has happened. They desperately need their parents to talk straight to them. They want to be with their parents. Being sent away doesn't feel like protection; it feels like being shut out of their own family. Their own parents, even in shock or in tears, are far more comfort than anybody else. Almost always they want to attend their sibling's funeral. Always they want to have that choice. Even toddlers who barely understand what death means know that something terrible has happened. They need to be with their parents. You may need help in caring for your young children, and you may need to have them away from you for some periods. But siblings need to know that even when things are bad, *especially* when things are bad, they are still part of their family.

Your decisions about funerals will be shaped by your religious convictions and your own experience with funerals. For many parents, planning their child's funeral, deciding about music and readings and who would speak, became the first counter-measure they could take against their helplessness. A funeral or memorial service allows other people a chance to show you that they care. When their son Ray was shot committing a robbery, Harry and Susan were deeply ashamed. Their first impulse was to have a private service, with only the immediate family. Their other children insisted that Ray's friends needed to come. They did, more than fifty of them. "There were kids there I never met, and a lot of adults too. Teachers and a guy he used to work for. It helped a lot," Harry said, "to know that so many people cared about Ray." Particularly if the circumstances of your child's death have been violent, allow people the chance to comfort you.

How Long Does This Go On?

How long will your acute grief last? It will last as long as you need to get through the first coming to terms with your loss. For many losses, a six- to eight-week period of acute grief is expectable. For the loss of your child, this is grossly inadequate. Your timetable must be your own. How long your acute grief lasts will have to do with the facts of your child's death, your relationship with your child, the quality and strength of your other relationships, your own life history—especially your prior experience of loss—and the circumstances of your current life.

Many parents remember some shift in their grieving at around four to six months. "After Patrick died, it was like a flood," Elaine says. "I was swamped, under ten feet of water all the time. Then it receded, so slowly that I didn't notice for a while. One day I looked at the calendar, and it was near the end of October, and I'd decided I'd better get some candy for Halloween. That was the first time I'd even seen the calendar or thought about a date. And on Halloween I actually kind of enjoyed myself, handing out candy and talking to the really little kids. For a while that night I didn't think about Patrick.

"After that I began to feel my grief more like a tide. It would rush in, and I'd be swamped again. I'd feel like nothing would ever be different, and I'd drown in my grief. Then it would slip back, and I'd have a few hours or a few days where I felt like someone had given me my brain back. I could read and think, and I'd have more energy, and the pain in my chest let up. Then the tide would come back in. But I began to see that each time it went out, I'd be a little bit more my old self. My new old self. I'll never be who I was again."

Elaine describes a gradual change, and this is in fact how most people experience the change in their grief. Acute grief, with its intense, unrelenting pain and it losses of function, slowly begins to ebb. Although the pain is still the center of your days, you find that you are given respites: first minutes, then hours when you can breathe, and think, and focus on other pieces of your life.

The dark time is a long way from over. You still live with pain so intense it blots out the sun. Your body still aches, and the problems with thinking and memory come back again and again. Where your child was, where your life was, there is a bombed-out crater. You do not know how you will live, and some days you can't think why you'd want to.

But a day comes when you notice that the breeze feels cool on your face. Or you smell the pavement after a rain. Your own capacity for response surprises you. It is like opening the door to a room in your house that had been shut for so long that you'd forgotten what was in it. You do not know yet how you will live with your loss. But for the first time you believe that you will. Acute grief begins to recede, and the long haul of mourning has begun.

·6·

The Long Haul: Mourning

*"The hardest piece of my grieving was that
all my efforts, all those years of taking
care of him, went down the drain."*
—Victor

*R*ebecca sits across from me in the booth at McDonald's. It is
late summer, and there's been a brief letup at the clinic where
she works. She has time to take a lunch hour. In October it will
be three years since she found her daughter Kate dead in her
crib, at five months old, from sudden infant death syndrome.
She talks about what has happened to her since that time.

She stares into her coffee cup and rotates it slowly in her
hands. Looking up, she says, "Losing a child isn't something
you get over, ever. What you do is find a way to live your life
without your child.

"Some days I feel like I've learned to do that. I'll go along
pretty well for a week or so. Then something will come up. Like
last week. I took Charlie, my son, to buy some new sneakers.
In the shoe store there was a little girl about three and a half,
the age Kate would be, and she had strawberry blond hair, just
the color of Kate's. It washed over me all over again, as though
it had just happened. It must have showed on my face. Charlie
looked at me and said, 'Mom, what's the matter?' I told him,
and he understood. He's eight. He was five when Kate died,

75

and he remembers a lot. We bought his shoes and got out of there, but I wasn't worth much the rest of the day, or the next day either.

"Then it kind of fades. It comes and goes like that, but lately I notice that when it comes it's not so intense as it used to be. The bad times don't last as long as they used to. But there isn't a day of my life that I don't think about her. I figure that won't ever change.

"For about six months after she died, Rick and I were train wrecks. We walked and talked and went to work, and I guess we got Charlie to kindergarten, because he says we did. I worked in the OR then, mostly cardiac surgery. It was very high pressure. The surgeries would sometimes last eight or ten hours, and that was fine with me. I'd get in there and I'd get so absorbed that I couldn't think about anything except what we were doing. Work was a relief; it was the one time I didn't think about her.

"The next spring some things began to change. My arms stopped hurting so much, and I wasn't tired all the time. After Kate died, I'd been really short with Charlie; at five, he was usually messy or noisy or both. I noticed that his stuff didn't bother me as much.

"Rick had planted sweet peas along the fence in our side yard. They have the loveliest scent. I'd go out in the morning to smell them, and I'd cut some to take inside. One morning I had my nose in a bunch of blossoms, and I said, 'Hey, I'm doing something for pleasure. I'm enjoying this. That's a change.' I mention all these things like they happened at the same time, but it was very gradual. A lot of small changes that gradually piled up.

"Very slowly I began to realize that I was going to live. For months I'd hurt so much that I wasn't sure I wanted to.

"Even knowing that was good news and bad news. After Kate died, I felt like I was living in a landscape flattened by a nuclear blast. Everything was deadened and gray, but it didn't matter, because I was either deadened or in such horrible pain that I didn't notice anything around me. Now, if I cared about the way sweet peas smell, I'd have to think about how I was going to live. That felt very scary, because I didn't know how I would do it."

Rebecca describes her gradual shift from acute grief toward the long haul of mourning. Her life, which had felt as bleak as ground zero, three years later is becoming a place she wants to inhabit. Parents say that the measure of successful grieving is the renewed ability, in the face of your loss, to find pleasure and rebuild meaning in your life. Psychologist Linda Edelstein agrees. She talked extensively with sixteen women who had lost children. Reflecting on how these mothers have grieved, she writes, "Mourning is letting go of the past as it was, allowing a productive life in the present."[1]

Holding On and Letting Go

To move toward a life in the present requires you to find ways both to hold on to your child and to let her go. It is a long haul because getting it through your head and your heart that your child is no longer here is such a huge and awful task that it cannot be accomplished quickly. It is slow work, accomplished a day at a time, a memory at a time. It is painful work because it is facing the reminders of her absence that drives your work. Reminders of her are everywhere.

Your Child's Room and Possessions. Practical questions force the issue. What will you do with his room and his things? What will you keep that reminds you of your child? How will you use his room or his space? How soon will you move to sort out his things and decide what to do with them? If space is tight

in your house, the question of what to do with your child's room
will come up sooner.

No single approach works for all families. Your family may do
better keeping everything just as it is, untouched, for months.
Or it may feel right to give away things slowly, as you feel ready.
What helps, parents say, is to open these questions to everyone in your family, from toddler to parent. When all of you
talk together about what to do, you may find significant differences among family members about timing and what feels
comfortable.

It will probably take more than one round of talking to get
everyone's wishes and feelings heard. Decisions may not be
unanimous. Like most matters in families, parents' views will
probably carry more weight than children's. But the experience
that each family member's feelings and wishes were invited,
were listened to respectfully by everyone else, and were considered in arriving at a decision helps everyone's grieving.

Every member of your family faces the task of sorting out
what she can hold on to of your child and what she must let go.
Your child's clothes and books, sports equipment, games, tapes,
things he made, trophies and prizes and souvenirs, photographs
of him—anything that was his—have the potential of helping
the people who loved him come to terms with their loss. His
friends will also welcome things that belonged to him.

"Remember Charlie and the blanket?" Rebecca's husband
Rick has joined us. He explains.

"It was a couple of months after Kate died. We hadn't done
anything with her room, or her things, because we just couldn't.
It was a Saturday, Becky was working, and I was home with
Charlie. The house was quiet, and I realized I hadn't seen him
for a while, so I went looking. The last place I looked was Kate's
room. The door was open just a crack, but I could see him in
there. He was in her rocker, hugging her pink blanket, rocking

and singing 'Swing Low, Sweet Chariot.' Becky used to sing that to Kate when she put her to bed.

"I opened the door, and when he saw me he got this real scared look on his face, like he thought he'd done something bad. I couldn't even speak. I gathered him in my arms and sat in the rocker and held him. We sang 'Sweet Chariot' together, and we just sat there a long time.

"When I could talk again, I said, 'Maybe you need that blanket.' He said, 'Yeah.' End of conversation. He's kept Kate's blanket ever since. We used to find it in his bed, and then for months we'd see it in the back of his closet, wadded up. He never mentions it, and we don't either. I just figure it's helping him work out what he's feeling about Kate."

Rebecca adds, "After that, we figured we'd better deal Charlie in on whatever we decided to do about Kate's room and her things. One night at dinner I said, 'We're thinking about what to do with baby Kate's things, and we wanted to know what you wanted to do.' "

"He said, 'I want her rocking chair.' He listened to Rick and me talk about what we'd do, and he didn't say anything else. That's Charlie, always a man of few words. But I think it helped him that we asked him what he wanted to do. I know it helped me. When I go into Charlie's room and see Kate's chair, I'm always glad we asked him."

The Feelings Are in the Details. Feelings get lodged in the details and the daily routines of our lives. You can talk about large, abstract topics such as loss and parenting and grieving and not feel a thing. But talk about when you were folding a load of clothes and there were your son's jeans, and your feelings well up.

Sorting through your child's possessions is the kind of practical task that brings up feelings, requires you to think about what has happened. Folding his jeans, stacking his tapes, you are reminded again and again of what will never be. In the face of these hands-on reminders, the most tenacious denial gives way.

Sometimes, months after the rest of your family is ready to go ahead, you or your partner refuse to allow any change in your child's room. You may refuse because you can't bear to face her sneakers in the closet or the scrunchies on her bureau that tell you how things are now. If your refusing to allow change in your child's room is part of a larger refusal, or inability, to deal with the new reality, then you have cause for concern. In chapter 9 we talk more about interferences with grieving, including the inability to accept what has happened, and how to deal with them.

Holidays and Anniversaries. Holidays and birthdays sharpen our vision of our families, focusing our awareness of what we have together. As we go about our familiar observances and rituals, we contrast what we do this year with what we have done in past years. Doing what we have done before reassures us in our own eyes, confirms that we are still here. When you have lost a child, holidays remind you with a terrible acuteness of all that you have lost. You remember how she made the apple pie last year, with only a little help from you; how he practiced so he could ask the four questions at Passover.

The calendar is relentless. Christmas shows up every December 25 no matter what you feel like. So do Passover and Thanksgiving and Ramadan, and so does your child's birthday. What will you do on his birthday? What will you do this Christmas? There are no packaged answers; your family and your loss are unique, and only you can work out the solution that fits. What helps the most is for parents and children to talk together and listen to each other: what you're feeling, what you want to do.

As parents, you acknowledge that things are painfully different this year, and because of that you all need to think and talk together about what you want to do.

The first year, the first time through each holiday without your child, is the worst. You are in a place you have never been and never wanted to be. Reminders of your child crop up constantly: her favorite foods, the placemat she wove, the rituals she loved, the presents you would have bought her. Over and over you stumble into things that remind you of your loss. Know that the first time will be hard, and awkward; keep your expectations low.

"Thanksgiving was always our favorite holiday," Tom says. "We'd do dinner on Thanksgiving day and the next morning we'd drive up into Wisconsin. We'd go to the same place, a cabin near Lake Michigan. Usually the weather would be pretty awful, but the cabin's winterized. We'd hike, or cross-country ski if there was enough snow, and have a big fire going. We'd play games with the kids, and Elaine and I would veg out and read.

"After Patrick was killed, I couldn't ever see myself enjoying anything again. Sometime that fall Elaine said she'd gotten a call from the people who own the cabin and did we want it this year. I just stared at her like she'd gone mad. Patrick is dead, and you want to talk about Thanksgiving?

"She said we needed to talk with Jeremy and Annie too and hear what they wanted. I wasn't having any part of it. When she brought it up again with the kids there, I got up and walked out of the room. That week was the worst time in our whole marriage."

"It was awful," Elaine concurs. "There were the kids, needing to talk, and their father walks away. I was furious, and scared, and I've never felt so alone. Finally I told Tom that I needed him to be part of our family and that if he couldn't, then

I couldn't be part of his life any longer. It terrified me to say it, but I knew it was true. I couldn't go along with his rule of silence about Patrick any longer."

"I was torn apart. If I didn't do what she wanted, I knew I'd lose her, and probably the kids as well. If I did, I'd start crying, and I knew for a fact that if I started crying I'd never stop. They'd find me in a puddle on the floor. That sounds melodramatic, I guess, but I really believed it. I'd held myself together hard ever since Patrick died, because I was sure that it would kill me.

"So, great, here I am, three months after my son's death, when people at work are expecting me to be pulling it together, and I lose it completely. I spent a week just about immobilized. I didn't go to work. I stayed in bed until noon, and then I'd get up and sit in Patrick's room and look at his stuff, and cry. I was a basket case, just like I thought I'd be. But somehow I wasn't scared.

"Once I let it happen, it was better. The worst part was before, all those months teetering around on the edge of the cliff, scared to death I'd fall off. Being in free fall hurt like hell, but now I knew where I was.

"It was like that for me and the kids too," Elaine adds. "Here's their father, the old stalwart, sitting in Patrick's room, sobbing. But they were relieved too. They kind of understood that he was doing what he needed to do."

"And they didn't have to mop me off the floor. Somewhere toward the end of that week I shaved and dressed and showed up at dinner. I said we needed to talk about what we were going to do for Thanksgiving. Jeremy and Annie stared at me like I was from Mars, but eventually they got their mouths open. They both said they wanted to do what we always did, do Thanksgiving dinner and then go to the cabin.

"We went. The weather was awful, as usual. We had a sleet storm. We were stuck inside for a couple of days. We talked about Patrick, and sang a lot, all the stuff that Patrick loved to sing. There were a lot of tears, but a lot of good memories too. The second night we were there, the storm broke. The temperature dropped, and everything froze. In the morning the whole world was dazzling: The sun came out, the sky was an intense blue, and every twig, every leaf was covered in silver. We walked to the edge of the meadow and stood together. I can't explain it, but we felt Patrick was with us.

"I don't know what we'll do next Thanksgiving. We'll have to talk about it. I get indications from the kids that they might like to do something different. Annie starts college next fall, so that'll be a big change. I think I'd like to do something different too."

Blindside Reminders. Blindside reminder is Dan's term for the unexpected, unforeseeable event that seizes you unaware and floods you with memories. Sometimes the trigger is clear: a child who looks like yours or a song on the radio that you always associated with him. Sometimes you cannot explain why the way the grass lies flattened after a rain or the display of hand tools in the hardware store window crushes your chest and leaves you gasping. You feel exposed; you do not know how to protect yourself from these unbidden memories. Every parent will tell you it has happened to them.

"People at Compassionate Friends say you're never the same person after you've lost a child. Where that really hits home for me are the blindsides. Those things make me feel so damned vulnerable," Dan says. "Losing your child makes you realize how helpless you are. Some things I know are going to hurt, like driving past the ball field where he played. I can change my route, or I can brace myself if I go that way. But nothing rubs it in my face, the helplessness, worse than those zingers, where something completely unexpected brings up the memories. It makes me wonder if the wound can ever close."

Over time, the blindsides seem to come less often. Most parents find that by the third or fourth year, as they are rebuilding their lives, the blindsides have subsided. "It still happens," says Martha. "But I don't feel so exposed all the time, the way I used to."

It is not simply the passage of time that makes the blindsides happen less. Your efforts to rebuild your life are what make the difference. The blindside reminders arise from your own awareness of the huge hole that the loss of your child has left and how helpless you feel. Whatever you do to feel less helpless works toward rebuilding your life. Everything you do toward rebuilding your life reduces your sense of helplessness. As you rebuild, the blindsides happen less often.

You will never recover the easy comfort that was there before the canopy fell down. But you can get to a place where your memories come more often when you want them to and less often when you don't.

Holding Your Child in Your Mind

Although your child has died, he stays intensely alive in your mind. Part of what makes grieving such a long and painful haul is this jarring discordance. In your mind he is a vital presence, and you love him more than ever. Yet every day a hundred things remind you that he is not here. How to make sense of these two? How can you possibly sweep up the heart and put love away?

From your experience of other losses, you know that the person you loved stays forever with you but slowly recedes from center stage. As time passes, you find ways to hold on to what you loved best about the person, notice the ways in which he has become a part of you. As these shifts occur, you gradually recover your capacity to invest in relationships, to allow an-other person onto center stage.

The way your child stays with you, woven through your thoughts and your imaginings, marks the loss of a child as different from any other loss. Resolving your grief and moving toward healing will take longer than with any other loss. Your child was so much a part of you—all that she inherited of looks and temperament, all your hopes and plans for her, all the hours and nights of caretaking, all your pride in what she had done and what she would become—that losing her has meant losing a large piece of yourself. "Gail came from me. She was a part of me. There's no way to put it back," Melanie says. You do not let go of so much in a hurry.

You will find ways to keep your child. You will find ways to keep the parts of you that have wrapped themselves around her. She will grow up in your mind. You will see who she would have become. You will sense her presence, find her in your dreams, talk to her. In your mind you will fashion a bright room where all that you loved of her still lives, where all that was good about her can become a part of you. Slowly, as you are ready to have it happen, you will move her from center stage. But she will never be unseen. You will have her for all of your life.

Kenny's sister Gail died in the hit-and-run car accident twelve years ago, when she was seven. Since then his mother, Melanie, has married again and had another child, a daughter. "Day she died, when she and Kenny were walking out the door, Gail reached down and picked up an onion that had fallen on the floor. She said, 'This for you, Mama,' and she gave it to me. After I come back from the funeral that onion was still sitting on the counter, and it had sprouted. I planted it, and it grew and flowered, and made little onions. I kept it going for years.

"About a year after she died I was out in the yard, by her

onion. I felt a hand on my shoulder, very light, the way she used to reach up and pat me. I didn't see anyone, but I *knew* she was there with me. She was trying to tell me, 'Don't worry about me; I'm all right.'

"After that I didn't cry so much. I always thought about her, and at first with my daughter Christine every time I looked at her I'd see Gail. But I'd have times where I'd just get away from everybody, maybe just a few minutes, so I could think about Gail.

"Every year on her birthday I call her father. He's back in South Carolina, and otherwise we don't keep in touch. But he's the person that understands the most what I've been going through."

Talking About Your Child. More than anything else, what helps you hold your child in your mind is talking about her. With your partner. With your other children. With your family and friends who knew her, and if your child was older, with her own friends.

"If there is one thing I would tell people," Elaine says, "it's that when someone's lost a child they need to talk about the child. People seem to think it'll be upsetting to me if they mentioned Patrick. Do they really think that if they didn't mention him I wouldn't be thinking about him?

"When someone I know mentions Patrick, it's like a gift. It helps me know that he mattered to other people. It's a kind of assurance that he made a place for himself in the world and that he won't be forgotten.

"It's a double gift, really. Because the person who speaks is also recognizing me and what I'm living with. If you talked with a person about their child while he was alive, then talk with them about their child after he's died. Not just at the funeral, but six months later, and a year later, and five years later. He's still their child.

"When a child's alive, parents get a million chances to talk about him. When your child dies, all that talk goes silent. You lose that interest, and caring, and the recognition that your child matters. It compounds what you've lost."

Talking with Your Family. The people you live with, who know you best and knew your child best, are the people you most need to talk with. Like you, they also hold your child in their minds, and like you, they are groping their way toward what they can keep of him and what they must let go.

Even though you all feel depleted and helpless, you have within you the capacity to help each other hold on to the child you have lost. You don't have it every day or all the time. Remember that living in a family is a percentage game. You don't have to bat a thousand to make it work. If you muff an opportunity—and given how you're feeling, you're bound to muff some—a dozen more will present themselves.

The talking that helps the most will probably come out of your daily routines and the reminders they bring. "[My daughter] Robin had started to set the table a few months before Pete was killed. When we got back into a regular routine and were eating dinner together, she still set a place for him. The first time she did it, I just removed the mat and the silver before we sat down." Emily winces at the memory. "She did it again the next night, and I removed the things again. The third night she got between me and the table and said, 'Don't take Pete away.'

"I said to myself, 'My God, what does she have to do to make you see?' She started talking about how much she missed him and what she wanted to tell him.

"That got to be a time, when I was getting dinner, and Dan was helping if he'd gotten home, and she was setting the table, when she'd talk about Pete. She remembered all kinds of funny details about him, things that Dan and I had forgotten or hadn't ever known. Not every night, and sometimes not for days or weeks. In fact, she stopped setting his place a few months back. But it's still a time when we remember Pete."

How Groups Help

Groups for parents can make all the difference. As you live with your pain, you realize that very few people in your life can understand the magnitude of your loss. A child's death is such a profound loss, one that so disrupts and changes your life, that the people who can best understand what has happened to you are other parents who also have lost a child.

Another bereaved parent understands how much you need to talk about your child, how you need to remember him aloud with people who care about you.

Another bereaved parent knows how much pain you feel and understands why you can't stop remembering.

Another bereaved parent doesn't require any explanations.

Groups for parents are usually one of two kinds. Bereavement groups, run by a hospital, mental health clinic, a church, or a hospice, are led by a professional or by a volunteer trained in bereavement work. Usually they are open; bereaved parents can come or not as they wish and attend for as long as they want. A call to a local hospice or mental health association can help you get connected.

Self-help groups are run by members, with the assumption that bereaved parents can help others most knowledgeably. They are open meetings, usually once or twice a month, with parents serving as elected group leaders and policy makers for the group. Sometimes there will be a speaker or a specific topic; usually there is opportunity for parents to talk and remember their child with others who know their need.

Compassionate Friends is the largest and best-known self-help group for parents who have lost a child. It was started in

Coventry, England, in 1969 by two couples, both of whom had lost their young sons. Meeting by chance, they found that grieving and talking together helped them bear their pain. They approached the Reverend Simon Stephens, assistant to the chaplain in the Coventry and Warwickshire Hospital, and asked him to work with them to establish an organization "which could offer understanding, friendship, support and care to other bereaved parents."[2] The first American chapter was organized in Miami in 1972; at this writing there are 675 chapters established in the United States. The national headquarters is in Oak Brook, Illinois:

> The Compassionate Friends
> PO Box 3696
> Oak Brook, IL 60522-3696
> (708) 990-0010

Volunteers staff the phone at national headquarters, and they will be happy to tell you the chapter nearest you and how to get in touch.

You and your partner may decide to go to a group together. Or you may go by yourself, because your partner refuses. You may need the group especially because of what is happening, since your child's death, between you and your partner. A child's death affects every area of your life, and none so dramatically as the relationship between you and your partner.

· 7 ·

You and Your Partner

*"We wanted to help each other, and we finally had
to realize that we grieved on such different timetables,
and in such different ways, that most of the
time we had to turn to other people."*

—Joan

*F*or a long time after Jamaal was killed, Susan and I weren't on the same page. If I was feeling better, she was down. If she wanted to talk, I didn't." Ted turns to his wife, sitting next to him on the couch in their family room. "Isn't that about right, honey?"

Susan smiles and arches an eyebrow. "I'd call it a gross understatement, but at least you're talking in the right direction." She reaches over and squeezes his hand. "Looking back, I really don't know how we got through it. Force of habit, I expect. And for me, I guess, a feeling that I just couldn't take any more losses."

"The worst of it was the first year, when we were both so torn apart we didn't have anything to give each other." Ted grimaces at the memory. "I'd come home, and Susan would be right here, stretched out on this couch, with her eyes closed, and I could see she'd been crying. I'd go to hold her, and she'd push me away. I started staying later at the office."

"The more he stayed away, the more I thought he didn't care, and then I couldn't stand to have him touch me."

90

Ted and Susan's experience has a sadly familiar ring. One of the myths about loss is that a shared loss brings a couple closer together. The painful fact that parents discover is that losing a child can isolate them from their partner just when they need each other most.

Your child's death irrevocably changes your relationship with your partner. As the two of you make your way through your grieving, together and alone, you will see your partner in ways you had not. Your relationship may end up weakened, or it may become stronger. But it will never be the same as it was.

Your Loss Hits You Both Simultaneously

Usually partners do help each other with losses. Your wife's brother is severely injured in a car accident, and you're there for her, consoling and supporting her through the surgeries and the convalescence. Your husband's best friend has a heart attack and dies a week later. You're by his side through it all, and you're patient and understanding as he grieves for his friend. When your partner is hurting, you're there to help.

When you lose a child, however, you both suffer the same profound loss at the same time. Acute grief disables you both. Although your particular styles of response are different (one of you may be numb and one of you frantic), you are both undone. Grief cuts you off at the knees, drains and depletes you. You have nothing inside, nothing to give. Like Elaine, you can see your partner on his life raft, but you are yourself so near to drowning that you cannot help.

At the same time, you desperately need your partner to help you. Susan remembers, "I'd say to Ted that I needed him to be with me. I needed to know he was in the house, where I could see him. Sometimes I'd want to talk about Jamaal. Not about what happened, but good times, when he was little, things we'd done together."

"Every time I'd talk about him, or look at his picture, I'd get so angry I wanted to kill someone," Ted exclaims, slamming his fist into a pillow. "The guy who shot the bullet, or the D.A. who was dragging his heels on the case. I could not, *could not*, sit and talk about Jamaal. I knew it was what she wanted, but I couldn't do it."

"And I knew he wanted me to hold him, and make love, and there was no way in the world I could do that."

When you desperately need your partner's help and she cannot help you, you get angry. You feel hurt, and un-understood, and unloved. These feelings compound your grief and leave you even less able to help your partner.

You Lost the Same Child, but Your Loss Is Unique

You both lost the same child. But each of you had a unique relationship with your child. He held a special importance in your heart. Because he had become a part of your self, you lost not only your child but a piece of yourself. He was equally a part of your partner's self, and your partner has also lost a piece of himself. Your loss is as profound as your partner's, but what each of you has lost is unique to you.

Tom: "Everyone knew that Patrick and Elaine were soulmates. The same love for music and parties, the loopy humor, and that passionate loyalty to friends. It's easy, or people think it's easy, to see what she lost. But I lost just as much. It was subtler, but he and I always knew how much he was my son too. As he got older, I could see aspects of myself emerging in him: how good he was with his hands, and something about how he goes—how he went—at a problem, low key, but bulldog tenacious."

It does not matter that one of you felt closer to your child than the other or that one of you had an angry or an estranged relationship with him. Anger, distance, ambivalence—none makes your partner's loss any less. A more conflicted relationship tends to leave you with even more pain and a harder job of coming to terms with your loss.

The differences in what each of you did as a parent also affect how you feel your loss. The difference will be sharpest when you have a stillbirth or lose a newborn. Because mothers are physically so involved—the baby is still within you, or newly separated but still nursing, intimately with you—you feel your attachment to her and your loss in a more total and physical way. As a father you did not love your baby less, but you could not know her as intimately as your wife did. Aching arms, the persistent pain in the arms that many mothers experience for months after their baby's death, reflects the physicalness of their involvement with their child.

For many fathers, the sharpest pain comes from the fact that they could not protect their child. Although mothers and fathers both share the commitment to protect their child, men have been taught that keeping their family safe is their first and most important task. Never mind that so many children's deaths are simply not preventable; who can stop cancer or sudden infant death syndrome, and who could get every drunken driver off the road? When your child has died, as a father you feel the particular shame and helplessness that comes when you cannot do what you believe it is your job to do.

You and Your Partner Will Grieve Differently

How each of you deals with your grief, and what you need and expect from your partner, will be shaped by a number of factors, including gender, the family you grew up in, what other losses you have been dealt in your life, and what else is going on in your life. As we look at each of these, perhaps your differences with your partner will begin to make more sense.

How Men Deal with Feelings. Boys grow up with a different set of expectations from their parents than girls do, and how they handle their feelings is one of the significant areas of difference. If your partner does not respond in the same way you do, it is for a good reason: he is doing what's expected of him.

The comments that follow are generalizations, based on the ways that most boys and girls are raised and how they are taught to deal with feelings. They apply to many men, but not all. Some women will find themselves in the description as well.

Most men were brought up to focus on tasks more than on feelings or relationships. Getting the job done is what counts, they've been taught. When that is what counts, attending to feelings, yours or someone else's, will be secondary, even a hindrance. Men have learned to suppress feelings, not express them. When your wife asks what you are feeling, and you answer "I don't know," it is probably an honest answer. The ability to know what you feel and to know how to put your feelings into words are acquired skills; you learn them only if you are encouraged to. If, on the contrary, when you were growing up feelings were a hindrance or a sign of weakness ("big boys don't cry"), then you were less likely to pay attention to yours.

Men learn much more about soldiering on and much less about how to ask for support or how to give it. What your wife sees as an appropriate and helpful expression of feelings may look to you like a dangerous loss of control, prelude to a breakdown. If you asked for help the way she did, you'd feel you were being weak. Tom's experience—that allowing his feelings to well up wasn't nearly the torture that suppressing them had been—was a revelation to him. He has a lot of company.

The way people, even your own family, treat you after your child dies shores up the be-strong-don't-feel imperative. Harry: "People always said to me 'How's Virginia taking it?' Nobody ever, ever asked me how I was taking it. You get the message pretty clear: They're allowed to cry; your job is to be strong." Elaine corroborates: "Those days that Tom spent in Patrick's room, I knew he was doing what he needed to do, but still it made me really scared. Tom doesn't cry, I do. What was he doing, coming unglued like that? I was as caught up in what we expect of men as he was."

Women Deal with Feelings More Directly Than Men. Most women have been raised to believe that relationships are the framework of their lives. Maintaining those relationships then becomes their obligation and commitment. To honor this commitment, it is essential to be attuned to feelings—your own, and those of the people around you. To perform the continuing work of maintenance that relationships require, it helps to be able to talk about feelings, and to listen to others talk about theirs. Women talk about their feelings far more than men do. They are often more comfortable than men are about revealing what they feel.

For many more women than men, revealing that they feel scared or sad or inadequate is a statement of fact; it is not an admission of failure. Asking for support is a practical response, not a defeat.

When your partner seems not to notice what you feel, when he does not speak his feelings, much less ask for help, it's easy to believe he doesn't feel. It takes self-restraint and patience—as usual, required the most at times when you have the least—to consider the other possibility: that he is behaving the way he feels he is expected to, every bit as much as you are.

Grieving and Sex. You and your partner are likely to be in different places on the subject of sex. Women tend to experience sexual desire arising out of their feelings toward their partner and how things are going in the relationship. To feel like having sex, a woman needs to feel fairly comfortable with her own body and with her partner. She also needs to feel some freedom to set aside the concerns of the day and what's on her mind. Grief interferes with all of these conditions. Grief leaves many women sexually numbed, uninterested, and unable to respond.

Even when the capacity to respond sexually starts to return, women are more likely to feel reluctant to have sex. "My baby died two months ago, and there I was making love. It just felt wrong," says Rebecca. "Like I shouldn't be enjoying myself; I felt somehow disloyal to Kate." You may feel as if having sex, having pleasure, means your child's death matters less. If you lose yourself in the experience or have pleasure, you may feel you have somehow let go of your child. You are right. Enjoying yourself sexually does require a letting go, a temporary setting aside of your grief. Your grief is a link to your child. By setting it aside you may feel that you are compounding your loss.

Or you may be worried that you could get pregnant. Before, pregnancy was a happy outcome; now it looms as a reminder of your child's death.

Men more often see sex as a way to seek comfort and to lose themselves for a while from their pain. After a loss, men report a resurgence of sexual desire far sooner than women. A respite from grief and pain, sex also becomes a way to reconnect with their partner. Your partner's refusal or lack of interest may leave you feeling hurt and even more alone.

Men also may have difficulties in resuming sexual activity. The feelings of worthlessness and inadequacy that so frequently come with grief can make a man feel unable to function sexually. Or he may simply feel so depleted by his sadness that he loses interest.

Sexual interest and desire will return. When, and how soon, will vary from one individual to another. Sex and getting back to it are issues that the two of you need to talk about. You need to hear out your partner's feelings. Equally important, you need to tell your partner what you feel. There are no national standards on what people in your situation should do. What matters is that each of you talks and each of you feels that you have been heard. You don't have to understand why your partner feels as he or she does, but you need to respect his or her right to feel that way. A climate of mutual respect is the essential beginning from which you build a new sexual relationship that will work for both of you.

What you do should reflect both of your wishes. One of you may end up waiting longer than you'd like to while your partner sorts out her feelings. Or you may decide to have sex with your partner even though you don't feel one hundred percent ready or comfortable. Sometimes your partner's stance that "we've got to start some time" will make sense. "I didn't feel that ready when we started having sex again," Rebecca says. "I felt weird, the first few times, like I was betraying Kate. But it mattered a lot to Rick. There's a saying, 'Fake it till you make it.' I didn't fake anything; Rick knew how I felt. It just means that sometimes you've got to go ahead with something, even when you don't feel all there. Both of us found that out about a lot of things after Kate died. One of us had to push the other back toward life."

Other couples confirm what Rebecca says. In many areas of your life together, such as socializing, family activities, holiday observances, one of you will be readier to reengage than the other. If your partner wants to do something and you feel unready, you may need to push yourself. There is a balance to be struck in your effort. Your child and your loss will always be with you. But giving up your life with your partner and the pleasures you have had together will not make your loss less. Your balance has to do with holding on to your child yet finding a way to live your life, for yourself and with your partner.

Your balance will not be arrived at quickly. Expect false starts and uncertainty. You need your partner's patience and your own. Let your partner know what you're feeling.

Family Influences. One thing you can count on in this long haul is that your partner will not grieve the way you do. The family your partner grew up in, how that family dealt or did not deal with loss, will influence how she grieves, or what he feels he should be doing.

"My family's Irish," Tom explains. "That meant a stiff upper lip, and the only way a man can show anything is to get loaded and yell and throw things. I've done my share of getting loaded, God knows. I'd been sober three years when Patrick died, and I vowed I wasn't going to lose that. But I did just what I'd seen my father do: silence and distance. Oh, I'd learned a lot of ways to handle feelings since I quit drinking, but now, push come to shove, the old ways were all I knew how to do.

"Elaine kept wanting to talk about him, or she'd start to cry. Every time she did that I wanted to walk out of the room. Sometimes I did. Or else I wanted to throttle her. I felt like she was undermining me. When she started in about the cabin, I was sure that was the end of us."

Your partner is too expressive, like her mother and her aunts. Or she is too remote, like her parents. He can only get angry and blame everyone else, the way his father does, or he sits and broods all the time, the way all the men in his family do. She wants to plunge into socializing because it makes her feel better, and you can't bear to see people. He wants you to get back to fixing dinner because his family always sat down to dinner no matter what.

What feels like appropriate, "right" ways to grieve and what feels peculiar are shaped for each of us by our experience grow-ing up: how our parents and other adults around us grieved and the models they offered us. All the patience and tact you can muster will serve you well here. The more you know about your partner's family, what losses they have suffered and how they dealt with them, the more you can understand why your partner behaves the way he or she does. You don't have to agree with your partner's way of handling feelings, but if you understand how he or she came to be that way, you're more able to allow the necessary latitude.

Earlier Losses. Your child's death sets off resonances of other significant losses in your life. If you have had many losses, especially when you were a child, you may well have unfinished business: unresolved feelings about your earlier losses that leave you with a residue of sadness and anger. Too many losses early in your life will leave you with less resiliency with which to face this one. You may feel overwhelmed.

When Gene's son drowned, he was flooded with memories. His father had left the family when Gene was ten. His mother remarried; his stepfather was an abusive man who had beaten and terrified him. When he was sixteen, his mother was killed in a car accident. His grieving for Will was long and painful, not only for itself, but because, in the process, his undealt-with sadness about his mother bubbled up. His sense of responsibility for what happened to Will became entangled with his feeling that, even at ten, he should have been able to protect his mother.

To understand what your partner is dealing with, it helps to know who else he or she has lost in life and how well he

or she has been able to make peace with those earlier losses.
If you don't know, ask her. Ask him. It may take a while for
you to move beyond your own pain to the point that you can
reflect on your partner's experience. But when you can, the
rewards for both of you can be considerable. Knowing more
about your partner's experience of loss will make him or her
more intelligible to you. Your interest and concern are likely
to make your partner feel more connected to you and cared
about.

What Else Is Going On in Your Life. Your child's death
seizes your attention and blots out everything else in your life.
Yet as the acute shock and disbelief begin to fade, everything
else in your life will reassert a claim. How you grieve, or flee
from grieving, and what you can offer your partner will be
influenced by these other claims.

When his daughter Tess died, Ed was orchestrating a major
expansion in the family business. The day after her funeral, Ed
went back to work. "I'm the oldest, and I'm the only one with
the financial know-how. My brother and my sisters were depending on me," he remembers. "We were doubling our floor
space, dealing with the banks, expanding production, all at
once. I went flat out for close to a year. The business was all I
thought about. I don't know how Joan put up with me. Once
things settled down, I just crashed. I'd thought I was doing fine
with Tess's death, but the business had just distracted me. I
hadn't touched it."

Life's timing isn't always good. Sometimes it's down-
right rotten. A new baby or business problems or a thesis to
finish or another family member's medical emergency may demand your attention and energy. Sometimes one of you will
be unable to grieve until you deal with something else. The
other one may have to wait, feeling alone and very much out
of sync.

When You and Your Partner Are Out of Step

Sometimes when you and your partner are out of step, you need to leave her alone to work things out on her own. Sometimes you need to nudge him gently and tactfully. Sometimes you need to speak and act forcefully. You are the only one who can decide what you need to do. Here are some approaches to your partner that other couples have said were helpful for them.

Let Your Partner Know What You Feel. You do not have to grieve exactly as your partner grieves. Your loss is yours alone, and no one can prescribe how you will feel or how you will express your grief. But if you can find some words to let your partner know what you are feeling, she will feel less alone, and so will you. She cannot read your mind to know that you stay late at work because you can't bear the heaviness in your house when you come home. She will take your absences to mean that your child didn't matter that much to you and that she doesn't either.

Especially at first, you may not have the words or the ways to comfort her. You may not know what will help, or how to ask for it. But letting her know what you're feeling, even a sentence or two, begins to open a channel between you. "It started to get better between us when we started doing that," Ted remembers. "It wasn't anything much; most days, a one-line status report: 'I'm totally in the pits today. How you doing?' But doing it helped. It made me feel like I knew her better. Saying something to her helped me know what I was feeling."

Give Your Partner Room. After Ray died, Virginia remembers the walks Harry took, every night, for months, in all kinds of weather. "I didn't have a choice about leaving him alone. He left me alone. It was real hard for me to watch him open the door and walk out and leave us. I needed him at home. I felt like he was letting the other kids down. They needed him too. Sometimes when he was gone, the kids and I talked about Ray. Nothing all that special. But we were putting the family back together, and he wasn't there to be part of it. I was worried he'd lose that connection with the other kids, and he'd never get it back.

"Still, I knew he needed those walks. I never asked him anything about what he did, but I knew he was doing what he needed to do."

There are limits to how much you can help your partner. You are limited by your own grief and depletion. You are limited by your partner's style of grieving, which will determine what she can accept from you. You are limited by the unavoidable and perverse fluctuations of mood that accompany every couple's grieving: You feel better today, and he's in a blue funk; he's got more energy, and you can barely drag yourself through dinner.

You help each other when you can. But sometimes the best thing you can do is leave him alone. This will not and should not become a permanent condition between the two of you. But for many couples, time alone and apart is necessary. You cannot get back together without it.

Seek Sources of Help Other Than Your Partner. Especially early on, both of you are so overwhelmed that, much as you want to help each other, you simply don't have much to give. You want comfort and empathic concern from your partner; he may be in too much pain to give you anything. If you were both seriously injured in a car accident, neither would expect the other to be nurse and caregiver. Your emotional trauma has disabled you as extensively as physical trauma does. At times both of you will do better if you turn to others for some of the help you need.

"Very soon after we lost Will, I realized I couldn't look to

Gene," says his wife, Allie. "He was coming apart. We went to Compassionate Friends together, and that saved us. When we broke into small groups we'd each be in different groups. I made a friend there who became my mainstay. She helped me through the worst of it, and we've stayed very close.

Gene: "So much stuff started bubbling up in my head about my mother that I did start coming apart. I wasn't crazy or self-destructive, but I sure wasn't much use to anyone. Someone in Compassionate Friends gave me the name of a therapist, and I got started with her. For a long time, she's been the main person I've turned to. I don't fault Sherry. She's my wife, and Will's mother, not a psychiatrist. I think when I get more of my old stuff worked out, I'll be in a better place to get closer to her again."

Let Your Partner Know What You Need. What you need may be to get back to having dinner every night. Or taking a vacation together. Or having sex. Or doing something about your child's room, which has sat untouched. Or being able to talk freely about your child. What you need may be more than your partner feels able to do. But she needs to know where you stand and what you want of her. If you tell her, she may or may not come through. Always, in relationships, you face these risks. Your asking may expose some painful areas between you, issues that were there before your child died. Your telling your partner what you need of him will probably force both of you to look harder at your relationship. You both will need to make some changes.

But if you do not speak up, you face a guarantee. If you don't make your needs known, you are guaranteed not to get them met. You can count on staying stuck in the painful status quo.

Elaine had come to this realization when she told Tom she needed him to be part of the family. Doing so scared her. "I was pushing all my chips into the center of the table. I really didn't know what was going to happen, what he'd do. But I meant it. I truly couldn't go on living with him the way he was." What she said was not a threat but a statement of fact.

Your child's death forces your relationship to change. Neither of you is the same person you used to be, and your lives will never be the same. The relationship you used to have cannot stay the same either. The same loss that forces the need for change also renders you, for some time, unable to do much about it. Changes in how you are with each other evolve slowly, as you grieve and as you rebuild your life.

When one or both of you founder in grief, you may begin to think of divorce. Getting away from your partner and your disappointments may feel like a way to get away from your pain. Couples who have come through their grief together and those who have divorced all offer the same counsel: Take it slow. Grieving is a bad time to make major decisions. Both of you are depleted, your relationship is in flux, and you cannot predict how you will feel a year from now. Give yourself to time to heal, they say, and to see how each of you and the relationship evolves.

Later on you may decide to divorce. If you do, you are likely to be glad you gave yourself time to make a careful decision. Molly and Steve lost their only child to leukemia when she was five. A year and a half later they separated, and now their divorce is close to final. "We married pretty young," Steve reflects, "and as we both grew up we changed a lot. Even before Angie got sick, we both knew that she was the main reason we were still together. I think even if she hadn't gotten sick we'd have divorced sooner or later.

"I give Molly a lot of credit; well, I guess I give us both a lot of credit. We worked together really well the whole time Angie was sick. We just put all our differences on hold. After she died, we both crashed. Everything that had been on hold between us came back. That time was sheer hell. I felt like leaving about twice a week. But we stayed together long enough to figure out that it was our basic differences that made it so hard for us. When we separated, we'd worked out enough between us that neither of us felt like we were just shipping out. I feel better now, making a life apart from Molly. But I know I'll always have a bond with her, because we are Angie's parents."

When Your Partner's Reaction Is Destructive

People don't always handle their feelings in ways that are helpful to them. In the face of a loss as devastating as your child's death, you will not always behave well. Tempers flare. Hard words and accusations fly. Judgment falters. You do unpredictable, erratic things. All of this comes with the terrible disruption of your life. Over time, you will recover your self-control.

Sometimes, though, you or your partner continue to deal with your grief in ways that are damaging to your relationship and to your whole family. One of you may blame the other for your child's death. Or one of you may turn to alcohol or other chemicals to anesthetize your grief. Feeling uncared about and un-understood, one of you may have an affair. You may retreat into your work so much that your partner and your children lose you when they need you most. In chapter 9 we will look more closely at barriers to grieving: what interferes with a person's capacity to deal straightforwardly with loss and what leads to maladaptive responses.

When your partner's behavior undermines your relationship or threatens to damage his or her health, you must, for both your sakes, speak up. You need to tell your partner of your concern, plainly and clearly. Stay away from scolding, accusations, and threats; they only muddy the waters. As you talk with your partner, focus on what *you* need and where the limits of your own tolerance are.

A single conversation does not guarantee that your partner will respond and change in the ways you want. But this approach offers you both an opportunity to begin to talk to each other.

Whether your partner decides to change how he or she is dealing with the pain is up to your partner. You cannot make him or her change. What you can do is clarify in your own mind what you need and where your own limits are. As you sort these things out, you move toward a clearer understanding of what your relationship with your partner needs to be.

You may decide to consult a psychotherapist, someone who can help you look at what has happened to you and how it has changed you. You and your partner may want to work together with a psychotherapist, sorting out how you have changed and how each of you needs things to be between you now.

The changes in your relationship after your child dies will affect not only the two of you, but your surviving children as well. Their capacity to deal with their loss will be shaped by the models you and your partner offer them, for living with loss and for building a relationship that supports a partner. In the next chapter we take a closer look at how children grieve and what they need from their parents.

· 8 ·

How Children Grieve

"I'm so mad at you, Charlie.
You left me here alone."
—Timothy, age nine

J oan Hoff lives and works daily with children's responses to death. A counselor with more than two decades' experience, she serves as program director for the Dougy Center for Grieving Children, in Portland, Oregon.

The Dougy Center is named for Doug Turno, who, at age nine, developed an inoperable brain tumor. He dealt with the news in ways that characterized his whole life. Wanting to know more about dying, he wrote to Elisabeth Kübler-Ross, "Why aren't there any books for children about dying? If you're old enough to die, you're old enough to read about it." Over the next four years, he visited other children in hospitals, sharing his own message of life and hope.

After he died, Beverly Chappell, one of the nurses who had cared for Doug, determined to start a place that could help children who were dealing with loss as well as the adults who were part of their lives. In 1982 the Dougy Center offered its first support group, for children living with a recent loss. A decade later, the center's comfortable frame house now houses seven full-time staff members and twenty-six support groups. More than 150 volunteers extend the professional staff's work.

Children are assigned to a support group of other children their age. Each group will have eight to fifteen children, one professional staff member, and enough volunteers to maintain a one-to-four ratio. This generous ratio means that children will have someone with them as they move around the house according to their needs: from the talking room, to a painting area, to the Volcano Room (lined in carpet and padding, and containing a giant hanging punching bag), to typewriters where they can type a letter to the person who died.

Dr. Donna Schuurman, the executive director, explains the center's philosophy. "We operate from four principles," she says.

- Grief is a natural and expectable response to loss.
- Each individual carries within him an innate capacity to heal.
- The duration and intensity of grief is unique for each individual.
- Caring and acceptance are helpful to a person in resolving grief.

Inherent in these principles is the conviction that grieving children know what they need. "We don't heal them," Schuurman explains. "Kids heal themselves; we just provide a safe place for them to do their work."

Much of the staff's work involves helping adults understand how children grieve. "People just don't know much about how children grieve," Hoff observes. "There's a lot of confusion and misinformation out there. They want to help but often don't know how. Sometimes parents' assumptions about how their child should be reacting actually get in the way of the child's being able to deal with his loss.

"Adults may assume that their child will respond to a loss in the same way that they, the adults, do: on the same timetable, with the same intensity, and in the same style. That child is probably grieving just as deeply as his parent. But, depending on his age and developmental level, and his own personal style, his grief can look very different. He may be much more physical, or much angrier, or much more inward. When we work with parents, we emphasize the unique nature of each child's efforts to come to terms with his loss. Usually it's a relief for parents to see that their child is indeed grieving and that his reaction, even if it isn't exactly like theirs, is valid, and his own."

Three Perspectives on Your Child's Grief

Hoff's observation that children's development levels affect how they grieve is central to understanding your children's experience. As you try to understand your children's responses, you will find yourself sighting down three lines simultaneously: the maturational level of their thinking processes, their relationship with the adults who care for them, and your children's unique temperament and particular history.

The first two lines arise from the fact that your children are, by definition, works in progress. Their abilities to understand and to deal with their experiences are incomplete, still evolving. The younger your children are, the larger a part you must play in helping them understand what has happened and in creating a psychological climate in which it is safe to question and to feel.

Cognitive Maturation. Children's cognitive capacities—how they make sense of the information they have, how they understand time and the irreversibility of events, what distinctions they make between feelings and fact, between fantasy and actual event, and how large their fund of information and life experience is—all of these aspects of their thinking will shape how they understand what has happened.

As they mature and their cognitive capacities expand and change, their understanding will change. A child who is five when her baby brother dies makes sense of her loss as best she can, given what she knows about death and how she thinks. Five years later, this same child will have used the significant changes in her thought processes that occur between five and eight years, her increased fund of information, and greater verbal skills to rethink what happened, ask new questions, and come to a more refined and elaborated understanding of her loss.

A Safe and Helpful Climate. Your surviving children's relationships with the adults who take care of them—how safe they feel to reveal their feelings, what kinds of support they need and what they can feel hopeful of getting, how much they believe they must take care of you, the parent, or spare you pain—shape what you will see of their grief. The quality of support and understanding your children receive from you and the other important caretakers also will determine how safe it is for them to feel.

"Just this week I met with a couple who said their two surviving children had never grieved for the death of their brother," Joan Hoff recalls. "Upstairs, at the very same time, one of my colleagues was talking with those two girls, and they were in tears and feeling a lot of pain through the whole hour. When we got together, we figured out that the girls had been hurting for a long time, but they felt that they had to protect their parents from their pain."

The younger children are, the more their own intense emotions threaten to overwhelm them. For children to feel that they can safely allow their sadness and anger to emerge, they must feel that they have a reliable, understanding adult to help them. If children do not feel that safe presence, they cannot allow themselves to feel. It is too dangerous. Instead, their intense feelings will lie unexamined and un-understood. They may find expression in chronic anger and aggressive behavior, or in depression, or, as Kenny's did, in unconsciously driven self-punishing behavior.

Your Children's Individual Responses. Who each particular child is and how she responds to events is the third line, the one you know the best. Whether a child is quiet and introspective or tends to show and magnify her feelings, whether she must seek a reason and an explanation for everything that happens or can accept events as unexplainable, whether she sees the world as full of hope or danger, whether in the face of stress she withdraws or gets active: characteristics like these are aspects of temperament. They are innate, part of who your child has been since the day she came into the world. From your experience as a parent, you know that although what you do can amplify or tone down aspects of children's temperament, you cannot change who they are. Each child's unique way of dealing with life also will shape how she grieves.

Children's Understanding of Death Changes as They Grow

Here is a chronology for children's understanding of death. Like any developmental timetable, the ages are not absolute, but consist of ranges. Some children will show the thinking skills and kinds of understanding described at the early end of the age range; for others, these capacities will develop over the span of time.

Zero to Two Years. Although at this age children do not understand death, they are aware of the absence of a familiar sibling. If they can talk, they may say the child's name, asking for him. They experience loss most sharply through the change they sense in caretakers: their grief and withdrawal and in shifts in the emotional climate: who is gone, who is available, and the quality of their involvement with them. Lacking words to frame questions, they will express their awareness of the changes through behavior. They may become fussy or harder to calm, or develop sleep problems, including nightmares. They may become more clinging or fearful, especially about separations from you.

Maintaining your children's usual rhythms and routines, within the limits of your ability, will reassure them. Be prepared to offer more physical comfort: rocking, holding, whatever soothes them. Keep separations brief; you are their source of comfort and well-being; your absence for more than a day will increase their anxiety. See the remarks about separation in the next section.

Remember that as they develop language, children's comprehension runs far ahead of their ability to speak. They understand much of what you say, even when they cannot frame the words themselves. Use simple words that you have used before, and explain in a way that makes sense for a child: "Mommy is crying now. She feels sad. Aaron is gone, and Mommy is so sad."

Three to Five Years. Young preschoolers have some concept of death but do not understand its irreversibility. Because, in their eyes, adults are omnipotent, they see death as temporary, an inconvenience that the grown-ups can fix. You will see your children wrestle with the concept of death's finality again and again. This is the nature of all learning at this age: the repeating, the going over and over an idea. Just as your children love to hear a favorite story every night or like to watch the same video over and over, they need to ask you the same questions about what happened and think and talk about it again and again.

Your children's questions will be very concrete. They will want to know about the facts and the practicalities of death and burial, of what happens to bodies. For example, four-year-old Jane knew that her sister had been buried. She asked, "Did they throw dirt on her face?" When you provide your children with straightforward answers, you help them to know what happened. When they know what happened and know you will help them make sense of it, you have helped them begin to find a way to live with their loss.

Because their life experience is so limited, preschoolers need continued clarification and reassurance that what happened to a sibling will not happen to them, or to you. They probably know that you can catch colds and the flu from other people; they need your assurance that they won't catch heart disease or sudden infant death syndrome or a car accident. They need to know that their parents will be there for them and will continue to take care of them. Your assurances and your patience with their need to go over the facts with you, again and again, are the threads from which they will reweave their own protective canopy.

In the best of times, caring for preschoolers is hard work. When you are overwhelmed by your own grief, especially early on, you may very well want a brief respite from the tasks of caring for young children. As you make your plans, try to look at things from the children's perspective: Something terrible has happened to their brother or sister, and it could happen to them. Nothing feels right. Mommy and Daddy are sad all the time. They say the children will be at Aunt Peggy's for a week, but what does a week mean? To children of this age, leaving the family feels as if they will be lost forever.

At three to five, children's sense of time is very different from yours. Amanda, four, conceptualized time as most four-year-olds do. She used the term "last night," but it could mean anything from last night to a week ago to before she was born. When she said "next week" she meant some time in the future; it might refer to any future time, close or distant. She did not have the same sense that an adult has, of what seven days are, how long a day and a week feels, and how you count them off. A month after her baby sister died, Amanda's mother decided she needed some time all alone, and her sister offered to take Amanda for a week. Amanda loved her aunt Peggy and her cousins, and she had visited with them often. But she remembers the week at her aunt's as endless, and she believed it meant the end of her family. "I was scared my Mom and Dad had died too," she remembers.

Five to Seven Years. This is a time of enormous change in children's thinking capacities. Between five and seven—roughly between the beginning of kindergarten and the end of second grade—your children's thinking shifts from a primarily magic and fantasy-based mode, in which wishing makes things happen and the world is populated by ghosts and dragons and dream figures, to a more reality-based mode, organized around time awareness, rules and expectations, and a greater interest in how the world works. A seven- to eight-year-old doesn't think like an adult, but the outlines of adult thinking are taking shape.

These changes are reflected in children's understanding of death. They now understand that death is irreversible. Their life experience now includes the deaths of insects and birds, of a pet, and perhaps the deaths of people they have known. They know that death brings sadness and a sense of helplessness.

Their emerging moral sense makes them question the fairness of death. They may voice their anger and outrage or express it in explosive physical activity. Conscience develops in this era, and it tends to be harsh and inflexible. Children are likely to examine their own actions and may well hold themselves responsible for a sibling's death.

Peter, seven, had always envied his younger sister Anna's privileged status as the baby. He avenged himself occasionally by snatching Anna's toys or her beloved blanket. Anna caught a cold, which escalated into pneumonia. By the time it was accurately diagnosed, she was desperately ill; after a long week in the hospital, she died. Peter was grief-stricken and crushed with guilt. He believed that he had killed his sister: if he hadn't taken Anna's blanket that day, she wouldn't have gotten pneumonia.

Eight to Eleven Years. In these years, children refine and develop their understanding of cause and effect and their skills in logic and problem solving. Their store of information and experience expands, including their knowledge of death. They have learned enough about disease and accidents and violence that they conceptualize causes of death much as adults do. Yet elements of magical thinking persist in the tendency to believe that one's thoughts and wishes can cause harm. Jeremy's conviction (reported in chapter 2) that his shouted curse had caused his brother's death was a piece of magical thinking.

"Children of this age see death as all-powerful, something that can come to get them," writes Janice Harris Lord, director of victims services for Mothers Against Drunk Driving (MADD). "This is evidenced by children's fascination with the power of evil forces at Halloween and at the movies."[1]

At the same time, their thinking is still sufficiently self-centered and magical that they hold themselves responsible for failing to stave off death. "If I'd said my prayers every night it wouldn't have happened," Jessie, ten, theorizes about her brother's drowning. Kenny believed he killed his sister

Gail because he asked her to come to the store with him. Frequently children of this age will see their sibling's death as their fault. Inaccurate as this conviction is, it causes them great pain, and it seems impervious to parents' efforts to convince them otherwise.

What helps children more than reassurance or than dismissing their idea is simply to ask them to tell you more about it and then to listen respectfully. By understanding that you take them seriously and appreciate how bad they feel, children gain the room they need to rethink things. "Jessie wasn't even there when Will drowned," Gene remembers. "She and Allie were way down the beach, looking in tidepools. When Allie and I found out she thought her not saying her prayers was what caused it, we were dumbfounded. I charged in with a whole bunch of explanations, but Allie had the good sense to shut me up. She just let Jessie talk about how much she missed Will and how important it was to say your prayers and that you let God down if you didn't."

Allie: "I didn't say much, because I didn't know what to say. After that time she clammed up for weeks. Then one day we were driving to gymnastics, and out of the blue she said, 'Maybe Will would have drowned no matter how much I prayed.' I said, 'I'm afraid you're right, honey. We don't know why God took him, but I don't think it was a punishment for you.' I wanted to make a whole speech, but I bit my tongue. I think what helped her was the chance to think it through herself and talk to me when she needed to." Allie's comments echo the Dougy Center's principle that caring and acceptance enable a person to resolve her grief.

Between ages eight and eleven, children's capacity for empathy expands; they are able to see their parents and others as specific individuals, with specific strengths and needs. Children learn to attune themselves to their parents' feelings, often reading the adult's moods with astonishing sensitivity.

Children's increased empathy is a double-edged sword. At best, it indicates a new level of maturity and the development of a vital means of connectedness between people, a trait to be valued and cherished. At worst, in combination with an immature and still often inaccurate reading of your needs, children's empathic sense of your pain may make trouble for them: If they feel that you are too much awash in your own grief, they may protect you more than you wish or need. Sensing your pain, they may decide that you could not bear to hear theirs. They may be right. But they may misread you and shut down the connection with you that they need in order to sort out their own feelings.

There is a balance to be struck. Children need to see your grief. If you were to deny it or suppress it, they would know that there was something desperately wrong and that you were not dealing honestly them. Your expression of your grief, and your efforts, over time, to come to terms with your loss and your life, offer your children powerful models. The balance—and it is not a one-time thing, but a continuously evolving equilibrium— has to do with letting your children see enough of your sadness that they feel they know and share your experience, but not so much that they fear for you or feel overwhelmed. You will not get it right every time. No one does. But if, over time, your children know both the measure of your pain and that, most of the time, you can table it and be available to them, then you have taken a significant step toward creating the safe climate they need.

Eleven to Fourteen Years. In this age span, children gain the capacity to think about ideas and abstractions as adults do. They understand death as adults do and now struggle to integrate this understanding with their emerging religious and philosophical concerns, such as causality, eternal life, good and evil. Many young adolescents find this kind of mental activity very attractive, because it enables them to use their developing powers of abstract thinking. When they have experienced a loss as painful as a sibling's death, adolescents also find that philosophical discussion helps them distance themselves from the pain they feel and their unbearable sense of helplessness.

Early adolescence is also the time when children are beginning the natural but demanding process of detaching themselves from the family. In order to grow toward psychological independence, they must loosen the ties of dependency that have bound them to parents all their lives. This is a long process, one that proceeds by fits and starts over the next ten years. As they begin to pull away, the prospect of sharing with you the intense and painful feelings that the death of a sibling stirs up may feel dangerously regressive: It threatens to pull adolescents back into the very dependency they are working so hard to outgrow. They need and want to talk about their feelings—but with anybody but you!

Your children very likely may find another adult, or a friend of the same age, and do much of their grieving and soul-searching with that person. They may or may not let you know that they are doing this. As a parent, you may see a child who is aloof and remote with you, who gives you no clue about her efforts to grieve. You face a complex question: Does your teenager's refusal to grieve with you mean that she cannot grieve, or simply that she does not grieve with you? Her withdrawal from you and her refusal to make use of the help you offer may well feel like yet another loss, and your feelings may be hurt.

If that last statement sounds to you like a description of the facts of life for parents of young adolescents, you are right. In many areas besides grief, youngsters of this age seek their supports and discuss their concerns anywhere but home. It takes a good supply of self-confidence and a bottomless well of tact to watch as your children spurn your best efforts to help. As a parent, you are now called upon, and will be increasingly so, to give up the familiar pleasures of caretaking in favor of the less predictable rewards of watching your children seek their own way. When normal development proceeds on course, it inevitably brings with it losses.

Time will be your ally in determining whether your child is grieving her loss. As the weeks and months pass, if she returns to her usual level of functioning in school and with friends, and if you see she finds pleasure in her accomplishments, it's likely that she is finding ways to come to terms with her brother or sister's death. The shadow of that death will not be dispelled lightly, or soon; as with you, her life will never be the same again. But if you see, in general, a return to her old strengths and pleasures, it's likely that she is doing what she needs to do.

On the other hand, if you see her stuck in pervasive depression, or anger, or withdrawal, or turning to antisocial behavior, including substance abuse, then you have cause for concern.

Fifteen and Up: Older Adolescents. By high school age, adolescents' view of death is increasingly like that of adults. Like us, they recognize the possibility of children's dying, and, like us, they recoil in shock and outrage at the unfairness of it. Their thinking tends still to be highly self-centered; they often find it hard to see beyond their own experience and their own pain.

Developmentally, older adolescents are focused on launching themselves into adult life. Their activity, in school and in their social life, aims at gaining the skills that they will need to function as adults. A sibling's death can be such a wrenching loss that it saps a young person's will to launch himself. A sophomore in college Reuben was busy with the work of getting his life started. His pain and outrage over his young brother's death were so intense that they derailed his efforts to get on with his life. He could not find a reason to go on in a universe that allowed his brother to die. He anesthetized himself with cocaine and stayed stuck until he could, with a friend's help, trust himself to grieve. Once he was able to grieve, he could get back to the job of beginning his life.

If you have an older adolescent, you already know that what you can do for him is increasingly limited; you can support his own efforts to grow and to grieve. Occasionally you can point the way or warn of pitfalls. You can be available when he decides to talk with you. Although this feels like precious little compared to all that you did for him when he was small, both your self-restraint and your availability can feel valuable indeed to him.

Reworking Their Understanding. Children's understanding of a sibling's death will change with time as surely as their size does. As they mature and the way they think is transformed, they will use their new capacities to transform their understanding of what has happened in their lives.

It is as if you had an immensely complicated set of mathematical equations to solve, and at the outset all you had was a pencil and all you knew was addition. You'd do what you could, but you couldn't get very far. As you learned new mathematical skills and acquired a calculator, then a computer, and then fancier software, you would bring each of your new gains to bear on your task. Each new gain in knowledge and equipment would enable you to make more headway: You would come to understand the equations in greater depth, and you would think about them in different ways.

Something like this process of continual reexamination and revision of understanding goes on for children as, over time, they develop a more sophisticated understanding of death. Two ages in childhood are marked by especially dramatic changes in children's thinking processes: five to seven and eleven to thirteen. If you have watched children move through either of these, you know how different their understanding is toward the far end of the age range, in contrast to the beginning.

When children who have worked out an understanding of a sibling's death enter a new developmental era, they will need to rework that understanding with their new intellectual tools. They are likely to bring up all sorts of questions—about what the sibling was like, and how they got along, about the dying and death and funeral arrangements, and about whatever religious explanations you have offered. For parents, this new round of questions can feel like something out of left field. It can stir up old pain. It may make you wonder whether the surviving children understood any of what you had worked so hard to explain.

The process can be uncomfortable, but it is cause for reassurance, not worry. You can take children's questions as evidence that they are growing, maturing intellectually. Their willingness to raise the questions with you offers further reassurance: It is evidence that you have created a safe climate, one in which they feel safe to reveal their concerns.

A Lifelong Task. When your child dies, nothing will ever be the same again in your children's lives. Their brother's or sister's death will cast a shadow across their lives as much as it does across yours. For the rest of their lives, your surviving children face an additional psychological task, of mourning their sibling, honoring him, and yet finding ways to move on with their own lives. Alan Wolfelt, director of the Center for Loss and Life Transition, puts it this way: "Young people do not get over their grief, they live with it."

To say that grieving is a lifelong task does not mean children will always be in mourning. The whole aim of grieving is to enable bereaved people to move on with their own lives. This is especially so for your other children, who have so much of their lives ahead of them. Yet children, like you, will need a good amount of time—more than our culture usually allots—to come to terms with a sibling's death. At the Dougy Center, children usually attend biweekly group meetings for about fifteen months. In an era of short-term treatment and shrinking resources, fifteen months is a long time. "To respect what we know about the process of grieving, we can't do it any other way," Schuurman says. "To make our groups time-limited would be contrary to our theoretical understanding of grief." For your children as for you, grieving takes as long as it takes.

In the wake of your child's death, as you make your explanations to surviving children and offer them comfort, you are wise to regard your efforts as a beginning, not an end. The younger your surviving children, the more they will need you to help them understand and grieve, and the longer they will need your help as, maturing, they rework their understanding. Helping children to make sense of what has happened to a sibling, and to all of the family, helping them to grieve, and helping them take the measure of their loss as their lives go forward—these are long-range tasks. The tasks will not always stand in the center of their lives, or yours, as they do now. But neither will their loss ever wholly recede from their awareness. As you and your children work on these issues, it will help you to know more about the significant differences between children and adults in how they experience their grief.

How Children Grieve Differently from Adults

"We talk with a lot of parents who are concerned that their children aren't feeling anything from a loss or aren't grieving," says the Dougy Center's Joan Hoff. "When we hear what the kids are doing, or we meet with them, it's clear that they are in great pain and are grieving. Too often parents expect a child to respond at the same time, with the same intensity, and in the same emotional style as the parents. Kids just don't work that way."

Robin, seven, watched cartoons the morning after her brother was killed on his bicycle. That afternoon she went to soccer practice. She returned to school the day after his funeral, and that weekend she went to a sleepover birthday party. "I watched her do this stuff, and first I thought, 'It doesn't matter to her. She must not care about her brother,'" says Dan, her father. "We were lucky we got some good advice from our pediatrician. He told us that kids feel just as bad, but they handle it differently. They need more breaks from their sadness."

Children do grieve differently, and the younger your children are, the more pronounced the differences will be. Here are some of the principal ways in which children grieve differently from adults and some recommendations about how you can help your children.

Children Are More Physical. Children tend to experience and express intense feeling in physical ways. Your children may need opportunities for active physical expression: playing sports, riding a bicycle, pounding nails into a board. You needn't prescribe the activity; children will know what they need and will find the outlets that work for them. The day his sister died after a long struggle with leukemia, Colin, fourteen, came home from the hospital, picked up his tennis racquet, and headed over to the courts at the high school. Three hours later his mother found him there, drenched in sweat, slamming balls into the backboard.

Physical symptoms are another form of expression. Your children may complain of headaches or stomachaches, may sleep much more or much less, or may show changes in appetite. Whatever your children's familiar patterns of physical response to stress, you are likely to see them now, in the face of this particularly severe stressor. If a sibling has died from an illness, one child may experience some of the same symptoms her sibling did. For parents, this can be especially disturbing. You should understand that the reproduction of her sibling's symptoms is not intentional or under her conscious control. Nonetheless, the symptoms need to be evaluated, so that both you and your child can be reassured about their nature and severity. Usually, when you can reassure your child that she does not have what killed her sibling and empathically appreciate her sadness, the symptoms will fade away within days.

Children Are Less Verbal. Even the most verbally competent child is likely to experience difficulty putting such intense and overwhelming feelings into words. The younger your children, the more this will be so. You can help your children by offering simple statements that name feelings: "You're feeling so sad about Jamie." "It just doesn't make any sense why Pete had to die, and it makes you furious."

Such statements leave children free to agree and say more, or deny it, or ignore it. Even if they seem to ignore what you say, you have done something important: You have let them know that you are aware of their pain and are offering a connection. They may not respond this time or the next, or the tenth time you say something. But you are establishing a climate of understanding that will make it more possible for them to talk when they feel ready.

Children's imaginative play offers another avenue through which they can deal with strong feelings. Charlie lost his sister to sudden infant death syndrome when he was five. Over the next year his play, both alone and with friends, revolved around rescues. He was the brave lifeguard who saved the drowning child, Superman who scooped a baby off the ledge of a building, Donatello the Ninja Turtle who thwarted a pack of villains and rescued a lost puppy. Once, watching him play, his mother said to him, "You sure are good at rescuing. I bet you wish you could have rescued baby Kate.

"Charlie said, 'Yeah' and kept on playing," Rebecca remembers. "It felt like I was talking to the garage door. But a few weeks after that, he started asking a lot of questions about why couldn't we save Kate. We told him about SIDS, in language he could understand. I think what helped the most was Rick and I talked about how helpless we felt, that we couldn't rescue her."

Children Express Their Anger Very Directly. Corey was five when her sister died of genetic anomalies within twenty-four hours after her birth. Her parents offered her clear explanations and helped her grieve appropriately. Yet when a pregnant friend came to pay a condolence call, she was "greeted at the front door by a wordless Corey, who took one look at her abdomen and punched it." Corey's parents talked to her about "hurt and angry feelings that were real and important but could not be expressed through violence. It got better. A few weeks later Corey and [her mother] saw a friend with a baby who had soft curly red hair [as Corey's sister had]. Corey turned away quickly, and Susan asked her how she felt. 'I feel jealous' was the reply. Words had replaced blows."[2]

Your children may have a period of more fighting, or quarreling, or simply being mad at everything and everybody. It will help them for you to make the distinction that Corey's parents did, that their feelings are important and expectable, but must not be expressed through violence.

Children Need Respites. Nina Gorbach runs a bereavement group for teenagers at the Hospice of the North Coast. She says, "The kids in my group tell me all the time, 'We can't grieve all the time. We need breaks. We need time to go be with our friends and do our stuff. We wish our parents could understand.' "

When a child watches cartoons and laughs, when he shoots baskets or goes to a party or sleeps over at a friend's, it doesn't mean he isn't grieving. It only means that children and adolescents cannot, do not, sustain the full-time focus on their loss that adults can and do. Just as you have found the situations and the people with whom you can grieve, you can trust that your children will find theirs. They will not necessarily be the same as yours, as their grieving styles will not be the same. When you visit the cemetery and feel your heart fill with sadness, they may be over at the fence, picking flowers or talking to a stray dog. Their times for grieving may be days or weeks apart. They may be able to follow your feelings, or they may need to flee from them. Like you, they will experience blindside reminders, those moments when a place, or a song, or a smell trigger a flood of memories that threaten to swamp them. You may hear about these times, or you may not.

Children Attune Themselves to Parents' Needs. More often than we realize, more extensively than we usually appreciate, our children read our moods and our feelings and accommodate them. When you are awash in your own grief, your surviving children may make a judgment about how much of their feelings you can tolerate. You will see then that much and no more. The downside risk about their effort to protect you is that although they may read you accurately, they also may not. On a particularly awful day, you may indeed be unable to tolerate your other children's sadness and may need to wall it out. But that may be true only that bad day or month. As your tolerance and staying power grow, the children may not revise their assessments. Children have a way of keeping the old, inaccurate pictures of parents in their heads for decades.

There is the risk that they may continue for years concealing their grief because they believe you cannot bear it.

If you suspect that this is going on with your children, you need to speak up. Without confronting them head-on (children have a horror of that kind of spotlight), you can let your children know that you are more available than they had thought. Something like "I know the last few weeks I've been pretty unavailable to you. I've been so sad about Timmy it was like I was the only person that existed. I just wanted to let you know that I'm in better shape now. I still feel terrible about him, but I also know you've been feeling terrible too, and I want to take care of you. When you're thinking about him, I can hold you, or we can talk. I might cry, but your sadness isn't going to hurt me."

Expect that your brief, carefully worded speech may be met with silence or grunted acknowledgment. That's okay. It doesn't mean you weren't heard or that what you said didn't matter. Children often need to absorb what their parents say and get back to it on their own time.

How You Can Help Your Child

"Children know what they need to do," says the Dougy Center's Hoff. "They just need some help from the adults around them so they can do it." The most important help you can offer your children is to make a climate in which they feel safe to grieve. Some of the specific steps you can take to create that climate are:

• Give your children clear and specific information about what has happened to their brother or sister. Answer their questions honestly and in plain language: "When your sister was born, some parts of her brain weren't made right, and her heart wasn't put together the way it needed to be to pump blood throughout her body. She lived for two weeks, but then her heart just stopped." "Donny was driving home from his game, and another car came up beside him, and one of the boys in that car opened the window and shot him. The car swerved into the guard rail and flipped, but the doctors think he died right when the bullet hit him." For the questions to which you do not know the answer, say that you do not know. Children can live with your honest admission far better than with an evasion or a lie.

• Reassure them that you will continue to protect them and take care of them. All of us deal with pain better when we know that the people who are important to us will stand by us. You can let them know that it will take a long time for all of you to deal with what has happened: "Maybe right now we're all so shocked it's hard to know what to say. But we're going to be living with what happened to Jody for a long time, and there will be times when you'll want to talk about her. I just want you to know I'm here for you when you want to."

• Keep your children with you, and include them in family and religious observances: viewings, funerals, burials, wakes, and the like. The question of at what age children should attend funerals comes up frequently. Talking with children, I hardly ever heard a child complain he was forced to attend a funeral against his will. Much more often, children complained that they had been sent away, excluded from this profoundly important event in their family's life.

Your child's funeral is indeed an event of terrible significance in the life of the family. With other family events, we find ways to include our children, even very young ones, in ways that respect their limitations yet enable them to participate. Young children should be offered the opportunity to join the family at all such services. If a child refuses, her refusal should be respected. She is likely to have reasons of her own, which she may or may not be able to explain.

You may need to have someone available to take care of your young child or to be with him if he cannot maintain the appropriate behavior. But the presumption that, as a member of the family, he will be included is in itself helpful and reassuring to a child.

• Include your surviving children in discussions about what to do with their brother or sister's clothes and possessions. They are likely to have strong feelings and wishes about specific items and about what to do with their sibling's space. As parents you will have the final say. But hearing out their wishes and honoring them when you can will do much to create the climate of respect for their feelings that will help them grieve.

• Include your children in all rituals and ceremonies, whether religiously prescribed or of your own devising. Your own rituals will probably come on anniversaries: your child's birthday, the day she died. They may be as simple as lighting a candle, visiting your child's grave, saying a prayer. Structured observances such as these give your other children a sense of order and comfort, reassuring them that the adults are taking care of things.

• Allow your children to see your grief. A stiff upper lip and an absence of feeling will leave them mystified and helpless. Seeing you cry, hearing you talk about their sibling will help them appreciate what you are going through. You can reminisce about your child in ways that invite his brother or sister to join you: "We're having macaroni and cheese tonight. . . . Remember how Timmy used to hate it, and he'd always sneak his to the dog?" None of this comes easily, especially in the early months. But remember that your grieving offers them a model they will draw on as they deal with their own feelings.

• The Dougy Center's principles are sound: grief is a natural and not a pathological state, and individuals do carry within them the capacity to heal. After the death of a child, most parents and siblings find a way to do the painful work that they need to do. But for about a third of those who lose a child, the path through the wilderness of their grief becomes too hard. Temporarily or permanently, they lose their way. They experience serious psychological difficulties and pathological distortions of the grieving process. In the next chapter we explore some of these difficulties and ways to resolve them.

· 9 ·

Suspended in Pain:
Barriers to Grieving
and Their Resolution

"My life stopped when Mark died."
—Richard

Your child's death plunges you into a wilderness of pain. No matter how much help and support you have, you must find your own way through your private wilderness. The path you make will have false starts and trails that lead nowhere. Months pass in which you feel utterly lost. For most parents, some combination of their own efforts and the passage of more time than they imagined enables them to build a path that leads toward a life they can live. As excruciating as your loss has been, as derailed as your life has felt, you find your way through. Grieving and healing are natural parts of the human endowment.

But about a third of parents lose their way. Temporarily or permanently, they get lost in their private wilderness. They despair of ever finding a path, or they cease to believe that there can be a life for them beyond their loss. Their lives narrow down to the compass of their loss. In many respects, their lives stop. This condition is called unresolved grief. For people stuck in unresolved grief, and for their partners and children who need them, it is as if when the child died, a great part of them died too.

Unresolved Grief

As you grieve for your child, you will find it helpful to know something of unresolved grief: what it looks and feels like, what kinds of life experiences and personality structures put people more at risk for it, and what you can do if you see signs of it in yourself or your partner.

Unresolved grief takes several recognizable forms: chronic grief, the inability to give up the child; delayed grief, in which life events claim a person's energy and attention and interfere with efforts to grieve; distorted grief, characterized by the person's focusing so intensely on anger or guilt that he or she cannot deal with other necessary aspects of grieving; and somatized grief, in which grief gets expressed chiefly through physical symptoms. Parents' stories illustrate each of these.

Chronic Grief. Richard is thirty-nine, stocky and intense. His face is drawn, and he speaks slowly, with effort. "My son Mark died four years ago. He fought a brain tumor for eighteen months. Mark and I were soul mates; there's no other way to put it. From the time he was born I've always felt a special bond with him, more than with my older boy. He thought like I did: very logically, and very good at mechanical stuff. We were working together rebuilding a '55 Chevy. It was going to be his when he was old enough to drive. I never saw a fifteen-year-old as good with a wrench as Mark was. Since he died I haven't even stepped into the shed where the car is.

"My wife had a pretty bad time with it too. In fact, if you looked at the two of us right after Mark died, she was the one falling apart. But she's got herself together pretty well by now. For me, some part of me died then, and nothing has been the same. I go to work, because I have to support my family, but I'm only half alive. Everything I do is just going through the motions.

"I stop at the cemetery every day on the way home. I sit by his grave and talk to him. I guess that sounds weird, but it's a kind of comfort for me. I tell him about my day, and I tell him how much I love him. I know he's not there, not the way he was when he was alive, but he's the one person who really saw things the way I did. I can't see any kind of life for myself since he died."

Richard says it very clearly: "My life stopped when Mark died." Every parent who has lost a child understands what he means. But Richard has been unable to start over, to find the pieces of his life and the people that are still there. For many parents locked in chronic grief, even their efforts to rebuild can feel like a betrayal of their child's memory.

Delayed Grief. At the time Ellen became pregnant, she was preoccupied with her mother's deterioration from early-onset Alzheimer's disease and her father's depression. "It was a nightmare," she recalls. "Mom was wandering away from home, Dad couldn't, or wouldn't, do anything except pour himself another Scotch. They lived up on the North Shore [of Chicago], and I was trying to manage their situation from the South Side, where we lived. It was all on me, because I'm their only child. Plus I had my job and Phillip, who was three, and Curtis, my husband. He held us all together.

"Sherry was a beautiful baby. I never had enough time to enjoy her because things were falling apart with my mother. She was only four months old when she rolled off the bed. Somehow her head got caught in the dresser drawer, and she stopped breathing. The paramedics got her started again and rushed her to the hospital. But she'd had serious brain damage. She only lived another forty-eight hours.

"My dad fell apart and started drinking all day. He got to be a bigger worry than my mother. I had to get him hospitalized and then get my mother placed in a nursing home with an Alzheimer's unit. The place we wanted for her didn't have an opening for two months, so she lived with us. Curt said we were running a one-patient hospital. I had to get her declared incompetent, and arrange a conservatorship, and figure out what to do with my dad, which eventually meant closing up their house and selling it, and finding a more supervised living arrangement for him.

"Mom went downhill pretty fast, and the worse she got, the sicker my dad got. He had a really major stroke, and then another one a month later, and never regained consciousness.

"In a year's time I lost my baby, and then my father, and my mother got so when I came to see her she didn't know that I was there.

"Somewhere in there I went onto automatic. Curt took over a lot of Phillip's care, and I mostly put out fires with my parents. Grieve? I didn't have time. Actually, I didn't dare. I was pretty sure that if I let myself start crying for Sherry I'd totally lose it.

"Months after I'd buried my father I started having these lurid dreams: babies coming out of their coffins, stuff like that. I was sure I was going crazy. I went to see a psychiatrist, and she told me I wasn't crazy, that I'd had to put my feelings about Sherry on hold and now they were coming up.

"It was strange, though, the way it worked out. I saw the doctor for a while, and we talked mostly about Dad. The way his drinking had affected me growing up, and how angry I was that he didn't help with Mom . . . or with anything, I guess.

"I couldn't even get into how I felt about Sherry until I worked out a lot of the stuff about Dad."

Grief delayed does not go away. It waits patiently until your life settles down. Then, in dreams or in flashbacks or by some abrupt reminder in your life, grief reasserts its claim. There will never be a time when it is easy or convenient to grieve. But it is unfinished business that you must take care of.

Distorted Grief. Sometimes parents' thoughts center on another person's negligence, or a doctor's treatment decisions, or some failure, real or imagined, on their own part that they feel contributed to the child's death. These concerns are real and painful, and must be addressed. Grief becomes distorted when guilt or anger becomes such a central preoccupation that it crowds out other aspects of a loss and interferes with healing.

The day after a drunken driver killed his son, Dave sat in the district attorney's office, demanding action. "I'm an attorney myself, and I knew the questions to ask and the buttons to push," Dave recalls. "Kyle was dead, and I was going to be sure his killer paid, big time. I made myself such a pain in the butt to the D.A. that prosecuting [the driver] was easier than listening to me. I followed every step in the trial, every continuance and delay; I didn't let up until he was behind bars with the maximum sentence.

"It took more than three years. That whole time, revenge and punishment was all I thought about. It was the only part of Kyle's death that I could deal with.

"When his killer was finally shipped off to prison, I thought I'd feel better. I didn't. I felt sick and empty. I'd dedicated three years of my life to revenge. I got it, but I still didn't have Kyle. As far as learning to live in a world that didn't have my son, I was in the same place I was the day he died."

Somatized Grief. When a person is unable to grieve or prevented from grieving, he or she may instead develop physical symptoms.

Theresa's husband and young son were killed when a car hit

the bicycle they were riding. When she was given the news, her family doctor administered an injection of Valium. At his advice, she continued to use high doses of the tranquilizing drug for more than a year. "I knew what had happened, but I was in such a chemical fog, I hardly felt it," she explains.

Her efforts to grieve were further hindered by her family's and her husband's family's stiff-upper-lip style and their refusal to discuss her loss. She accepted a job transfer to another part of the country, and in her new city she never discussed her former life.

Around the anniversary of her husband's and son's deaths, Theresa developed severe stomach pains. She spent months in exhaustive medical workups that found no physical basis for her pain. "My gastroenterologist told me he thought I needed to talk to a psychologist. I felt insulted, like he'd told me I was crazy. I guess I was scared I was. But I went, and my psychologist helped me see what happened. Between the Valium and my family's shutting down, and then the move, I'd never really faced what I'd lost. But my body knew. It was facing it whether I wanted to or not."

Interferences with Grieving

What factors influence our capacity to grieve and to heal? Why do some people experience more difficulty than others in dealing with grief? Which personality traits and life experiences combine to enable one person to grieve? Which other traits cause people to bog down? Psychological researchers have identified a number of factors that may interfere with grieving.

- A previous history of significant losses, especially losses in childhood
- Severe stressors in your current life

- Drug or alcohol abuse
- Negative or otherwise unsupportive responses to your loss from family and friends
- A stormy, highly ambivalent relationship with your child
- Personality traits that make it difficult for you to trust other people

The experiences of parents to be described illustrate how each of these factors can have a powerful impact on their efforts to grieve.

Previous Losses. Connie is the chief financial officer of a six-hundred-bed hospital in a large midwestern city. As she talks about the hospital's future and her current projects, she is poised, capable, articulate, the picture of a high-functioning executive. But that picture evaporates when she leaves her office. She lives alone, shunning all social invitations. Evenings and weekends she sits in her darkened apartment, remembering her daughter, who died of a brain tumor twelve years ago.

"I know I'm in chronic grief, but I just can't let go of her. I've lost so much in my life," she explains. "I grew up dirt poor, both my parents were alcoholics, and I was their only child. My father died of cirrhosis when I was eight, and four years later, my mother and stepfather and I were out on a lake in a boat. A storm came up and swamped us; neither of them could swim, and they both drowned. I got passed around among several relatives, none of whom wanted me. The only bright spot was my last two years of high school, with my aunt Betty, who treated me like a daughter and really helped me decide I was going to make a better life for myself. Aunt Betty died of a heart attack the summer after I graduated. I still miss her terribly."

When Connie's daughter's tumor was diagnosed, her husband started drinking heavily and eventually abandoned the family. "There I was, with three teenagers, one of them about to die, and no husband, no insurance, and no job. I caved in for about a week, but then I had to get going. I got a job as a ward clerk, and I did what I had to do. For a lot of years I couldn't slow down. Really, I guess since Aunt Betty, I haven't let myself feel very much. Now I just can't.

"When you've lost so much, you get brittle. I feel like an old rubber band that's been stretched too much, and there's no more stretch left in me. I've got enough for my job, and that's all."

People who lost a parent or a sibling in childhood and have been unable to grieve their earlier loss often feel fragile or depleted. Their new loss sets off resonances of the earlier pain, and they cannot bear to feel it all.

Severe Stressors. Ellen's experience with her mother's Alzheimer's disease and her father's depression and alcoholism is a good example of current stressors interfering with the capacity to grieve. As bad as they were, these stressors were time-limited: when her mother was safe in a care center and her father had died, Ellen's grief and her need to heal claimed their rightful priority.

Stressors that will not resolve with time (such as a disabling chronic illness, imprisonment in a concentration camp, living with a substance-abusing partner, living in a war zone) require so much energy just for survival that there may be not enough left over for grieving.

Substance Abuse. Use of drugs, including alcohol and some prescription medications, disables the brain. The work of grieving demands the full use of your thoughts and feelings. Grieving requires you to examine your life and the place your child occupied in it. Healing asks you to build a life that no longer holds your child. Even with a fully functioning brain, these are hard tasks. For a disabled brain, they are impossible. As long as you are using chemicals to anesthetize yourself, you are sentencing yourself to unresolved grief. If you want to heal from your loss, your first job must be to get clean and sober.

It will not be easy. As you stop using, your grief will flood you. The temptation to turn back to your old anesthesia will be intense. Living with your grief will be intertwined with the work of maintaining sobriety—two very demanding tasks.

Negative Response from Family and Friends. Theresa grew up in a family that dealt with all painful matters by ignoring them. After her husband and son were killed, her parents and brothers acted as if they had never existed. They did not speak of them, and when she tried to, they refused to listen. Her husband's family withdrew and would have nothing to do with her. "It was crazy," she reflects. "I could have my family or I could grieve. Either way I'd lose. At the time I was so shaky that I had to have my family. I buried my grief even deeper."

A painful loss leaves a person more needful of family and friends' support and more vulnerable to their disapproval. If the price of staying close is suppressing your grief, you may not be in a position to object.

Families who lose a child to murder, suicide, or AIDS are most likely to encounter negative responses: unspoken assumptions about the child's morality, lifestyle, and mental health, outright disapproval, withdrawal out of fear of contagion.

A Highly Ambivalent Relationship with Your Child. Not all children are easy to raise, and no parent-child relationship is without mixed feelings of love and anger, devotion and resentment. When the mix of feelings between you and your child has been particularly stormy and intense, you will experience more difficulty in your grieving. Grace remembers her daughter Iris: "She had never been an easy child, and by the time her father got sick, when she was eleven, she was already lying about where she'd go. The whole time he was going through chemotherapy, and getting worse, she was out smoking dope. I was furious with her, and frightened for her, and helpless.

"After her father died, it got worse and worse. I'd do so much to try and help her, and she'd lie and go do what she wanted. She was using more and more drugs, and sleeping around, and telling me the most outrageous lies. I'd drag her home and help her get straight, buy her new clothes. She'd thank me and swear she was going to change. Then, in a few months, it would start all over again. And there was her little sister, watching the whole thing.

"I began to feel used by her, and terribly bitter. When she was sixteen she ran away with her boyfriend, and I was almost relieved. The next few months were pretty peaceful. When the police found her in New York, she was already desperately sick with hepatitis, and [the boyfriend had] left her. I brought her home, and we had a week together before she died. We made peace then, as much as we could. But I still can't forgive her for what she put our family through, especially when her father was sick. I'm still angry and sad, and I still love her. I can't keep her and I can't let go of her."

Personality Traits That Interfere with Trust. Although each person grieves in his or her unique way, all of us share this human commonality: To heal and rebuild we need the help of other people. To bear the intense pain and disorientation of acute grief you need people to help you with the mechanics of your life, buffer you from the world, listen to your story, appreciate the depth of your pain, assure you that you are not going crazy. To rebuild your life you need people who understand the magnitude of your loss and the size of the job you face, who respect your journey, no matter how halting or detoured.

If you find yourself generally suspicious of other people's motives or feel that they are likely to rip you off, you know how difficult it can be for you to ask for help or to accept it. If much of your life you have been angry at others, wanting to punish them, this attitude can interfere with building the relationships you need to heal. If you always feel someone else is to blame when things go wrong, you risk staying stuck in blaming.

Dave talks about blaming: "Getting Kyle's killer put away was something I had to do. Too many drunks kill kids and walk away scot-free. I did it for Kyle and for every kid out there on the roads. But I know I also did it because I'm the kind of guy who always sees someone to blame. After the guy went to prison, I got very depressed. I started blaming my wife for my depression, and I guess for Kyle's death too. She wouldn't have any part of it; she told me to get help, that she just couldn't go on with me like this.

"Our rabbi is a guy I've known since college. We've played golf a lot and talked about our families some. Talking to him about Kyle was the hardest thing I've ever done. I kept telling him about the trial and about how my wife was too soft on Kyle. He just listened, then he asked me what I remembered about Kyle. I listened to myself sit there and blame Kyle for letting himself get killed. Everybody else was to blame.

"Making it everyone else's fault somehow made the world not such a crazy, dangerous place. But blaming everybody meant keeping them, especially my wife, at a distance. And I'd never really grieved. I'd been too busy looking for revenge.

"I talk about this like these realizations just dropped into my lap. They didn't. It was months of work, and I'm still not done. I'd talk to our rabbi, go home and think for a few weeks, talk again. It scared the socks off me. If I quit blaming, I'd be so weak and vulnerable. I hated feeling like that. I still do. But I had to change, or I'd have spent my whole life angry."

The Replacement Child

Another kind of interference with grieving that some parents experience is the phenomenon of the replacement child. This situation comes about when, after the loss of a child, for whatever reasons one parent or both cannot adequately grieve. Instead, they unconsciously designate another child as the dead child's replacement. The replacement child may be a living sibling, usually of the same sex, or it can be a baby conceived and born, or adopted, soon after the loss.

The psychological hazards are considerable, both to the replacement child and the parents. The child is assigned a task he cannot possibly perform: He must replace the dead child and make up that loss to his parents. His task is further complicated by the fact that nothing of this expectation is stated explicitly. All that the child knows is that whatever he is, whatever he does, it is not what his parents want. Worse, his parents do not seem to see or value what he himself is—his particular looks and tastes and abilities. They may even resent the ways in which he is himself, because those ways remind them that he is not his dead sibling.

One well-known replacement child has documented his experience. J. M. Barrie, the English playwright who wrote *Peter Pan*, was six when his brother David, thirteen and his mother's favorite, died in a skating accident. His mother stayed in her darkened bedroom, clutching David's christening robe, refusing food or company. Young James was sent by his oldest sister to console their mother.

> [My sister] told me not to sulk when my mother lay thinking of him, but to try instead to get her to talk about him. . . . At first I was often jealous, stopping her fond memories with the cry, "Do you mind nothing about me?" but that did not last; its place was taken by an intense

desire to become so like him that even my mother should not see the difference, and many and artful were the questions I put to that end. . . . He had a cheery way of whistling, she had told me; it always brightened her at her work to hear him whistling, and when he whistled he stood with his legs apart, and his hands in the pockets of his knickerbockers. I decided to trust to this, so one day . . . I secretly put on a suit of his clothes, and thus disguised, I slipped, unknown to others, into my mother's room. Quaking, yet so pleased, I stood still until she saw me, and then—how it must have hurt her! "Listen!" I cried in a glow of triumph, and I stretched my legs wide apart and plunged my hands into the pockets of my knickerbockers, and began to whistle.[1]

Here the child himself has taken on the task of replacing his dead sibling. What evolved was an intensely close attachment, in which, for both mother and son, the boundaries between the dead boy and the living one blurred. Barrie attributed the growth of his imaginative capacity to this unusual relationship with his mother. For that, generations of fans of *Peter Pan* must be grateful. But Barrie's personal life was plagued by significant difficulty in forming any other close attachments, especially with women. The task of standing in for his lost brother left him forever a Lost Boy.

A replacement child is a strategy of desperation. Not only does the strategy fail, but parents who create a replacement child compound their loss. In addition to their loss of the original child, they deprive themselves of their other child, whose unique qualities they cannot enjoy.

As a parent you should be aware that your other children may very consciously and actively try, as young James Barrie did, to fill the place of the sibling they have lost. The impulse is a normal one arising from their awareness of your suffering and their wish to offer themselves as consolation. A sibling may take on characteristics of the child that you especially valued: for example, interest in a particular sport or academic subject, religious commitment, politeness.

You can recognize with your child her effort to console you, and appreciate it. You can also reassure her that you love and value her for herself. Usually the child is relieved to know that you understand what she has been doing, and is also enormously reassured in knowing that you do not need this sacrifice from her.

Indicators of Unresolved Grief

Over the last fifty years a number of researchers, including Eric Lindemann, Aaron Lazaare, and William Worden, have identified and listed symptoms and indicators of unresolved grief. Although their lists can be helpful, they should be used cautiously, with considerable respect for the particular person's timing, personal style, and situation. It is too easy to look at a person in the throes of acute grief and say that he or she is not functioning well. Not functioning well is a hallmark of acute grief. We have seen that during this phase people experience major disruptions of their usual mental processes; major lapses in thought processes, extremes of denial, even hallucinations are more often the rule than the exception. And given the extreme stress of losing a child, acute grief may last for many months.

Timing, then, is a critical part of assessing whether you or someone you love is experiencing unresolved grief. You should be very sure that acute grief, with its hellish unpredictabilities of feeling, has begun to subside, that what you are looking at are recurrent, pervasive states. Personal style will determine how you look at symptoms: What is extreme and uncharacteristic behavior for one person can be well within the limits of normalcy for another. Social and cultural context—how people of your ethnic and religious background generally react—also shapes our determinations of normal and appropriate behavior. With these caveats in mind, we can look at behaviors that may be indicative of unresolved grief.

• Wooden and formal behavior that masks intense feelings of anger
• Development of physical symptoms that your child experienced in illness
• Furious hostility toward specific persons connected with your child's death
• Chronic guilt and lowered self-esteem
• A feeling that the loss took place yesterday, even though it occurred months or years ago
• Loss of patterns of social interaction, interruption of friendships and formerly valued social activities
• Searching that continues over time, with a great deal of apparently purposeless behavior, restlessness, moving around
• Panic attacks, physical expressions of fear—such as shortness of breath and choking sensations
• Avoidance of customary mourning rituals (funerals, visits to the grave, etc.)
• A relatively minor event triggering a major grief reaction
• Self-destructive and self-punishing behavior
• Radical changes in lifestyle

As we noted, many of these symptoms occur during the phase of acute grief. If one or more persist for more than six months past acute grief, with no signs of change or improvement, then you may be looking at unresolved grief. The "signs of change or improvement" is an important part of your assessment. People heal in their own ways, on their own timetables. The rate of change is not so important; you can be moving very slowly, but as long as you see indicators that you are moving, then you can trust your own process. When you see *no* movement—when, as Richard described, your life has stopped—then you have cause for concern.

A Word About Time. Time enjoys a reputation for being a great healer. There is the temptation, when you are stuck in your grief, to tell yourself and the people who love you that you simply need more time. Time is certainly a great ally in healing. But there is no magic in tearing pages off the calendar; the simple passage of time itself heals nothing. If you cannot get yourself unstuck, time alone will not heal you.

Getting Help for Unresolved Grief

When you have decided that you have a problem with your grief, you have taken an essential first step in resolving it. No matter what anyone else thinks or says, nothing changes until you decide for yourself that something must be done.

What must be done? You need to talk with a mental health professional. If that idea sets your teeth on edge, or insults you, or scares you, please read on. Consulting with a psychotherapist does not mean you're crazy or seriously disturbed. You're probably not. It means that a normal process, grieving, has gotten derailed, and you need some help getting back on track.

Most of the time your heart functions normally. But if it doesn't get enough oxygen, or if it stops beating or beats too fast, you don't try to fix it yourself. You go get some expert help from people who have studied how hearts work. Trying to fix unresolved grief without help is as sensible, and about as effective, as trying to treat your own heart attack by yourself. There are some kinds of problems that you simply cannot solve without the help of other people.

How Does Psychotherapy Help? Although therapeutic approaches will vary, any effective psychotherapy for unresolved grief will offer a therapeutic relationship, identification of barriers to grieving, support as you move through the grief process, and help in reconnecting with family. Let's look at each in turn.

Your relationship with your therapist offers you an arena in which you feel safe and empathically understood. Although an empathic hearing doesn't fix everything, without it, not much gets done.

It's important to identify the barriers to grieving, those elements in your own life history and personality that are working against your being able to grieve. As you look for these barriers with your psychotherapist, you are likely to learn a great deal about yourself and your family. As you come to understand what has interfered with your grieving, your therapist will help you find ways to move beyond the interference.

Dave, whose son Kyle was killed by a drunken driver, says "My rabbi asked me about deaths in my family growing up. My grandmother, my dad's mother, died when I was five. I remembered my dad getting so angry, threatening to sue the hospital. He said the surgeons killed her. He stayed angry all his life. I don't think he ever grieved for his mother. I hadn't thought of that stuff in years. But it began to make sense, the way I was behaving. I had to ask myself, did I want to end up like my dad?"

The therapist offers support and reassurance as you move through the work of grieving. Once the interferences are dealt with, your grief wells up by itself, and grieving takes its natural course.

He or she also helps you reconnect with the rest of your family. If your partner and other children have dealt with their own feelings, your being stuck in your grief has opened up a chasm between you and them. As Ellen says: "Phillip had kind of given up on me, and he looked to Curtis [my husband] for everything. It was a lot of change for all three of us, to get used to me being Phillip's mom again. The grieving I did with just my doctor, but when I started to get back into the family, Curt and I met with her together to work out some of that." You may work with your therapist by yourself, or with your partner, or with all the family, depending on your situation and what you and your therapist feel will be most effective.

Dr. Elliott Rosen is a psychologist and family psychotherapist with the Family Institute of Westchester in Mount Vernon, New York, who has written extensively on helping families grieve. Explaining the importance of exploring the bereaved parent's own family history, especially the family's losses and how they dealt with them, he says, "People are cut off from any awareness that [how a family deals with] loss is patterned from generation to generation. Getting that history, and showing it to them in a genogram [a diagram that shows marriages, divorces, births, and deaths over several generations] can be a terrific tool to help people understand what has happened."

Rosen stresses the importance of the last step, reconnection with family. "There is a powerful intrapsychic dimension to grief. I'd be the last to say that what goes on inside a person isn't important. But you don't resolve grief only from within, particularly with the loss of a child. A child doesn't die in a vacuum. He has all those connections with extended family, and school, and the community. As a person becomes able to grieve within, he needs to reconnect to his family, and the world that knew the child. Helping rebuild those connections is an essential part of the therapeutic process."

Psychological help for grieving works like a catalyst in a chemical reaction. Without a catalyst, certain reactions simply will not start. Other reactions may start but will proceed very slowly. A catalyst enables a reaction to start and helps reactions keep going at a faster rate than they would without it. If you or someone you love has been stuck in unresolved, interminable grief for a child, you should consider a psychological catalyst.

What About Medication? Dr. Sidney Zisook is professor of psychiatry at the University of California San Diego School of Medicine and a nationally known researcher in psychopharmacology. About the use of antidepressants to treat unresolved grief, he observes, "As recently as ten years ago, there existed a mythology about grieving, that pain was somehow good for you, that if you were depressed you were grieving hard. There is simply no empirical support for that notion. Rather than depression being necessary to get over grief, most of us in the field feel that depression impedes the work of grieving. Depression is an illness to be treated, and antidepressant medication is often a useful part of that treatment.

"Antidepressants don't treat grief," he adds. "The role of antidepressant medications is to treat depression that is associated with grief." Part of your psychotherapist's task is to assess with you whether you are experiencing depression, and if you are, to assess the severity of your depression and to work out a plan to treat it. That plan may include a trial of antidepressant medication.

"More often than not, when you see persistent, unresolved grief, you'll also see a significant depression," Dr. Rosen says. "We used to believe that antidepressants would interfere with the grieving process. The thinking on that has changed. For many people, antidepressant medication enables them to keep going in their life while they do their grieving." The appropriate antidepressant in the correct dosage is likely to lessen symptoms of fatigue, give people more energy, allow them to sleep better, improve their ability to concentrate, and reduce their sense of emotional vulnerability. People suffering from depression usually welcome these changes.

What to Look for in a Psychotherapist. Whole books have been written on choosing a psychotherapist, but it boils down to two factors: competence and a good fit. In treatment for unresolved grief over a child, competence is especially important. If you are considering a therapist, ask about his or her training and experience with grieving parents. Grief for a child is a unique grief, and its course is different from that of other griefs. You need to be sure that your therapist is knowledgeable in this area.

A good fit means that you feel comfortable with the therapist: that you feel he or she is respectful, attuned to your feelings, and equipped to understand your situation. The things you will be talking about are not easy. Comfortable doesn't mean no discomfort; on the contrary, it implies that this is someone you can trust when the going gets painful. It is an intuitive judgment; only you can decide whether you can work with this person. It may take more than one session to arrive at your judgment, but by the end of two or three sessions you should know whether this will work or not. If you feel it will not, cut your losses and look for someone else.

How Long Will It Take? Length of treatment is difficult to predict. Two of the factors we have discussed are the most important influences on how long therapy will take and what the outcome will be: life events and family patterns that interfere with grieving, and your own motivation and staying power. "Once we've identified the patterns and the person starts to grieve, we usually see real change in three to four months," Dr. Rosen says. Your experience may be longer or shorter, depending on what work you have to do. A shorter treatment course does not imply greater psychological health, nor does a longer course imply more problems. As we have said of so many aspects of grief, each person's experience is unique. You must respect your own timetable.

If you are mired in grief that you cannot resolve, you have a choice to make. You can stay where you are, with its known pain and familiar constrictions. Or you can seek help for yourself, with the uncertainty that change inevitably brings. If you seek to change, you cannot predict where your life will go. The only certainty you can count on is that if you do not look for help, you will continue to feel the way you do now.

Part Three

~

Families Speak

T here is no easy way for a child to die, no circumstances of death that diminish the pain the parents and siblings feel. Each child's death is unique, an incalculable loss to the family. Each family's efforts to heal are theirs alone.

How your child died will shape the way you experience your loss. If you received a diagnosis of a life-threatening condition or a terminal illness, perhaps that was the worst moment. You had some time to prepare yourselves: weeks or months, perhaps years. You learned to live on hope. You learned to value each day with your child. Perhaps you thought about what mattered most in your lives. You probably shifted your priorities. You watched as the disease stalked your child, spread its reach across his life. You saw it claim his strength, trample his future. You saw your hopes soar, then stumble, then die.

If your child died by stillbirth or sudden infant death syndrome or drowning or a car accident or a fall, then you know too much of surprise. You carried your baby, or put her to bed, or spoke to her with the confident, normal expectation that you would see her soon. Now you live with plans that can never unfold, words that cannot be taken back, and a huge section of your future canceled. You had no time to get used to it, no time to say good-bye. Unexpected deaths, with their flattening shock and total helplessness, bring another layer of complexity to your grieving.

If your child died by violence—murder, suicide, abuse—you live

153

with your private horrors of imagination and memory: picturing what he went through, seeing him die alone, perhaps in terrible pain. These pictures will not die, and they interfere with your efforts to grieve. Your rage and fear and wish for revenge haunt you.

Each death carries with it unique problems for the family whose members must go on. Yet all families face similar concerns, as well as face the continuing question central to all grieving: What can you keep of your child in memory and what must you let go? In the chapters that follow, parents and siblings who have lost a child speak about important aspects of their experience: first responses, concerns specific to the way the child died, what helped and what did not, and barriers to resolving their grief.

Survivors also speak about where they are now in their lives. Some of their resolutions are remarkable, reflecting inner sources of resiliency that leave us awed. Some are clearly less than optimal, testimony to the ravages of their loss. All reflect the best that that person could do.

· 10 ·

The Loss of Possibility: Stillbirths and Infant Deaths

*"I want people to understand
that even though she only lived
two months, she was a real person."*
—Anna

First Responses

"Everything was going great. I was in my eighth month, I was doing everything I should, I felt good. A Sunday night a week before my due date, I went into labor. It kind of came and went for two hours, then it stopped." Corinne pauses. "I think that's when the baby died.

"She'd been kicking a lot, and after that I didn't feel anything. On Tuesday I called my doctor. They gave me an appointment for the next day. That night my labor started again." She begins to cry.

Corinne is twenty-seven, a legal secretary. Her husband, Larry, is ten years her senior and a junior high school guidance counselor. This was their first pregnancy.

"When I went in on Wednesday, it felt really different from all my other visits, where he'd find the heartbeat really quick, and he's say, 'Oh, you're fine.' He had his stethoscope, and he kept searching. He was very quiet. He just kept listening. His face was so serious.

155

"Then he tried the Doppler and couldn't get anything. Then he did an ultrasound. It went on a long time. He looked up at me, and his face was very sad. He said, 'Corinne, I'm so sorry. Your baby has died.' He held my hand."

Corinne leans back on the couch, and her eyes drift toward the ceiling. "I guess I knew when I went into his office. But when he said that, I couldn't pretend to myself any longer.

"Except I did." She sits up straight again and fixes her enormous green eyes on me. "I went back and forth. When I called Larry, I told him what happened. He came and got me at the doctor's office, and we just held each other.

"Then when I called my mom, and Larry's mom, I said, 'They think something's wrong with the baby.' I really believed that when I said it, that maybe there was just something a little bit wrong.

"We went to the hospital, and they did another ultrasound. I told the nurse to be extra careful, in case the doctor had missed something.

"When Dr. Keyes was inducing me, I asked him was he prepared in case he'd been wrong and the baby was alive. It's like I knew and I didn't know. Or wouldn't let myself know. In some way I think I'd known since Sunday night. But it was so unbearable I couldn't let myself know all the time.

"I delivered about eight that night. The nurses washed Emily and measured her, and wrapped her in a blanket and handed her to me, and then they left Larry and me alone with her."

Corinne's arms come together as if she were holding a newborn. "She was such a beautiful little girl. Everything about her was perfect. Her fingers and toes were long, just like Larry's, and her hair was black like his.

"The next day we had a lot of visitors, people from our church that we've been close with. I was glad they came, but it was pretty tiring. That night, after everyone was gone, it all came over me. I cried and cried. That's when I felt my faith really sustained me. I didn't worry about letting go, because I knew that God would hold me up.

"I cried for Emily. I kept saying 'I want my baby.' That was the most terrible pain. I cried for close to three hours, but even when it was happening I felt at peace. That feeling came back to me, through the worst of my grieving: of being at peace and knowing God was in control. It helped me grieve."

Scott, whose son died at two months of sudden infant death syndrome, remembers how hard it was to let himself know what happened. "The next few days I'd walk past his room, and find myself thinking, 'Oh, he'll be up from his nap soon,' or I'd wonder if it was time for Hallie to nurse him. Once I even started to say something to Hallie. She didn't say anything, but I remember the look on her face. By the third day, I wasn't doing it anymore. The thoughts had kind of faded. But they helped me get through those first days."

Corinne and Scott each responded to the terrible news of their children's deaths with a measure of denial. As we saw in chapter 5, denial is an emergency measure, a way of protecting the self from too much pain. For each of these parents it served that function well, allowing them a few hours in which to gather their internal strength and connect with the people close to them. Denial tends to subside, as Scott put it, in the face of its flagrant contradiction of the facts.

As denial subsides, parents are left with their loss. Throughout the pregnancy their child has grown not only in utero, but in their minds. Long before they see or hold their baby, she has taken on a life composed of their hopes and longings for themselves. They must grieve not only for the baby who has died but for their hopes, that piece of themselves that died with her.

Specific Concerns

How Others Respond. Corinne and Larry remember the days and weeks after Emily died with a kind of wonderment. "It was horrible, in one way. I've never hurt so much in my life," Larry says. "But the way people came through for us was amazing. People in our church organized a dinner detail. Every night for a month—a whole month—someone showed up at our house with dinner. They didn't stay long, or talk a whole lot, but there they'd be with dinner. It was great, because we were both such wrecks I don't know how we could have cooked or shopped."

A week after Corinne delivered, she and Larry held a memorial service for Emily at their church. It is a small church, with only eighty members. To their surprise, 250 people showed up. A friend sang, and three members of the congregation played hymns on flute and guitar. Their minister had himself lost a child by stillbirth. He spoke about his sadness for Corinne and Larry and of his own experience; then he said that everyone has had stillbirths in their lives, of children and of relationships and hopes. He invited others to come to the microphone and speak. "So many people came up and spoke, about their feelings for us, and about the losses in their own lives. We felt so held and part of a community."

At Larry's school, students planted a tree in Emily's memory. Two friends he played volleyball with, younger, single men, each visited Larry at home and said, "I'm so sorry. I can't imagine what this is like for you. But I want you to know I'm thinking of you, and if you want to talk, I'm here." For some time Corinne had been part of a prayer group with three other women, and the four of them had come to rely on one another. They were her chief support over the next year as she grieved.

"The help we had from our families and our friends was pretty amazing. We're learning that this is the kind of loss that you never get completely over," Corinne muses. "But I think that knowing how much people cared about us and understood how we were hurting helped us put our lives back together."

Corinne is right. The outpouring of support that she and Larry received *is* indeed amazing, and sadly, it is far from typical. Contrast their experience to that of Jack and Maria, who also lost a child, their son Luke, by stillbirth. "I have a lot of family around here, and most of them didn't come to the funeral," Maria says. She is a short, intense woman, whose mobile face reflects her pain at her family's withdrawal.

"That made me feel so terrible. The cousins I grew up with didn't call or come around, or anything. It's like it never happened.

"My mother couldn't stand to see me cry. Every time she saw me looking sad she say, 'Oh, you must be tired. Why don't you go take a nap.' " Maria shakes her head slowly, in bewilderment. She takes me to a wall in her modest living room and points to two framed pieces of embroidery. The names of her older son, born before Luke, and of her daughter, born since, are worked in exquisite stitchery among flowers and baby animals. "My mother does one of these for each of her grandchildren. But she wouldn't do one for Luke. All she'd say was 'You need to forget him.' That really hurt.

"Later I found out from my aunt that my grandmother, my mother's mother, lost a baby when he was six months old. That was in Mexico, before they moved up to Oakland. She never mourned him, and nobody in my mother's family ever talked about it. So my mother was just doing the way she'd been raised.

"Jack's Anglo, and his family was even worse. They wouldn't talk about it; it's like it never happened. Jack didn't cry, and he hated it when I did. He'd come in and see me crying, and he'd say, 'What are you crying for?' like he didn't know. He made me feel so hurt and alone. Luke was his baby too.

"Then he started staying away a lot, and money was coming up missing. I asked him, and at first he denied anything, but I kept on asking and finally he admitted he was doing coke. I was totally flattened. First Luke, and then this. I took Rodrigo and left. We stayed at my sister's. After a week Jack came around to see me, was real nice, brought me flowers. He wanted me to come back. It took a long time before we got back together. I told him I couldn't handle his doing dope again, ever. And we'd have to get counseling. It's been really hard, but we've been back together now for three years.

"What got me through it was Empty Cradle. It's an organization in San Diego started by women who've lost babies themselves. It's really families helping families. The first time I went there I felt like I was the only one in the world who had ever lost a baby. It was a big room, and people kept coming in. By the time the meeting started there must have been forty people there, and I realized that every one of them had lost a baby. People talked about their feelings, and they were having the kinds of feelings I was. I started to feel like maybe I wasn't so weird."

For parents, a child who is stillborn or who dies within days is a distinct and special person. Corinne remembers the vigor of Emily's kicks, her long fingers and dark hair like her father's. She shows me a photograph of Emily, and her footprints, taken at the hospital, now framed and hanging in their bedroom. Corinne is pregnant again. "When this child is born," she says, "I'll tell him that he has an older sister, who's in heaven. Emily was part of our lives, and she'll always be a part of our family."

All the parents I've talked to voice the same feelings. They keep photographs and videotapes, hospital ID bracelets, blankets, tiny T-shirts: the mementos of their children's too-brief lives. No matter how short their lives, or how little chance their parents had to know them, the children were real and intensely important. Try to imagine parents' hurt when the people closest to them treat those children, and their loss, as unimportant.

In the name of consolation, relatives and friends tell parents, "It's a blessing she died when she did." "It was for the best." And endlessly, "You're young; you can have other children." To a grieving parent, these assurances dismiss their child, because he was so young, as having had no value. Jack's frustration boils up: "When people said we could have other children, I wanted to grab them and say, 'What do you think Luke was, some kind of toy that we lost, that we can just go get another?' " He adds, "If you do nothing else for parents who have lost a baby, just spare them that phrase."

Parents are very clear about what helps: "You don't have to make a whole speech. 'I'm so terribly sorry about your baby' says it all." And, "Don't stay away. We need you with us. At the funeral, sure, but also the next month and six months after that. Losing a baby isn't like having the flu; you don't get over it in two weeks."

Causes of Death. Stillbirths and genetic problems tend to come as a shock. Buoyed by the apparatus of hope, young families move through a pregnancy expecting the best, awaiting the child of their imaginings. Prenatal checkups assure them that the baby is developing well, and ultrasound and amniocentesis rule out problems. Brothers and sisters feel the baby in Mommy's tummy and look forward to the day they can hold it. Death comes unexpectedly.

The lively kicking stills. The heartbeat, so loud and fast in every previous examination, now cannot be found.

Or labor proceeds, and the baby who comes is not the child

the parents imagined. His color is poor and does not improve. Parts of him do not look right. The delivery room staff are quiet, and their faces are grave.

Sudden infant death syndrome robs families with no warning. The baby they kissed and put to sleep in good health is still and cold in the morning. There was no sound, nor were there any signs of distress.

Explanations are often incomplete, sometimes painfully slow in coming. Jerry and Cynthia, whose first child was born with serious cardiac malformations and retardation, learned within a week that Jerry carried a rare chromosomal abnormality, poorly understood and entirely unsuspected. Their daughter Jill died fifteen days later. It took eight months to get the autopsy report.

Families who lose a child to sudden infant death syndrome face the double blows of unexpected loss and medical ignorance. Doctors can tell them that it strikes infants chiefly between four and nine months, that it occurs most frequently between October and May, and that something mysteriously goes amiss with the tiny center in the brain that regulates breathing. They cannot tell them what causes it or how to prevent it.

In such infant deaths there is no one to blame, nor is there anything that parents should have done differently. No amount of information will change the outcome. But parents need all the information, and the clearest explanation of it, as promptly as physicians and hospital staff can supply it. The combination of loss and mystification makes a fertile breeding ground for self-blame. Knowing what there is to know and understanding its implications are the most potent antidotes. Knowing reduces fears, for parents and for young brothers and sisters.

Helping Children Understand. For young children, a sibling's death is especially shocking. As we saw in chapter 2, the illusions that make childhood a safe place include the belief that people only die when they're old. When a baby brother or sister dies without warning, perhaps even before a child has seen him or her, that child sees the world become a frightening and unpredictable place. After her sister died of sudden infant death syndrome, Amanda feared going to sleep because she knew Kelly died in her sleep. When her mother understood Amanda's fears, she could tell her daughter what she needed to know: that only little babies died from it and big girls of four never did. With more information and her mother's help, Amanda calmed; bedtime struggles subsided.

Drs. Susan Scrimshaw and Daniel March write with great sensitivity about their daughter who died of genetic anomalies within twenty-four hours of her birth, and of their five-year-old daughter Corey's efforts to understand. When Corey first saw her sister Elisabeth in the isolette, taped with tubes and monitor wires, she said she looked like E.T. before he died, and she wondered if her sister would die too. On a second visit she noticed her cleft palate and reacted in typical five-year-old fashion: "Oh, gross." Then she stroked her sister's skin and marveled at its softness. She touched her curly red-gold hair and thrilled when Elisabeth responded to the sound of her voice. After Elisabeth died, Corey said, "I want to see her dead." Although her request surprised Corey's father and left him unsure how to proceed, the charge nurse arranged for them to see Elisabeth.

> Corey was sad and fascinated at once. She reviewed the physical deformities apparent to her, and reminded herself that Elisabeth had other problems she couldn't see and that couldn't be fixed. She touched Elisabeth several times, repeating that she would never be forgotten, that it was very sad that she had died, and how much she loved her. After several minutes we left the room, thanked the nurse, and went home.[1]

When a baby has died stillborn or soon after birth, young siblings should be told as soon as possible what has happened with as much detail as their age permits them to understand. Erna Furman, a child psychoanalyst in Cleveland, is a leading researcher on how children deal with death. She states, "In all bereavement, it is extraordinarily important that all of the realities of the death be known and appreciated by the survivor, particularly the cause of the death."[2]

Brothers and sisters should be offered the chance to see the baby and hold him if they wish. If they decline, they should not be forced. However, most children will probably want to see and perhaps even touch the baby. No matter how young they are, they feel their parents' misery and understand that something sad and terrible has touched their family.

When they do not see the baby, children have a much harder time coming to terms with the finality of the death. Despite their parents' best efforts and carefully constructed explanations, younger children especially will have misunderstandings and misconceptions. A three-year-old whose brother died of sudden infant death syndrome firmly believed that the doctors brought him back to life at the hospital and gave him to another family. Another preschooler listened to all the explanations of his mother's stillbirth, but continued to believe the baby he never saw now came to visit him as a ghost.

Nothing prevents these distortions more effectively than a chance to see the baby for themselves. Alicia Acosta is a social worker for the neonatal intensive care unit at Children's Hospital in San Diego. She describes the unit's approach to families when their baby is dying. "We explain very clearly what's going on with the baby, and we let parents know what their choices are, as far as being with the baby when he dies. We encourage them to be there, and we're glad to have brothers and sisters there too. There's a small room next to the unit where they can take the baby; I've been in there when there've been seven or eight family members, including toddlers. The toddler might not know exactly what's going on, but they're curious. They want to touch the baby. We've found it really helps the whole family with their grieving to be there."

Children remember the child who died and continue to think about her. As they grow older and their capacity to think about death changes, they will raise new questions. The most significant changes in children's thinking processes occur between ages five to seven and again at eleven to thirteen. Josh was three when his sister died of sudden infant death syndrome, and his parents explained the death in words that he could understand. Toward the end of kindergarten he began peppering his parents with questions: Where was Amy now? Where was heaven? Was it near Hartford, where Grandma lived? Sometimes he had pinched Amy; was that why she died? When he grew up, if he had a baby would it die like Amy? Josh's questions puzzled his parents and troubled them; they had tried so hard when Amy died to explain things to him. Had they muffed the job? Their doctor reminded them that with his newly gained abilities to understand time, the finality of death, and his responsibility for his own actions, Josh had to rethink what he had been told.

Guidelines for Helping Children. Here are several guidelines for helping your children through a stillbirth or an infant's death.

- Give children clear and accurate information about what happened to the baby, in language suited to their ages.
- Avoid such phrases as "went to sleep," "went away," or "passed on." They confuse children and may leave them wondering whether what happened to the baby could happen to them, or to you.
- If there are facts or causes you do not know, tell your

children that. "Sometimes a baby's brain just forgets to tell it to breathe. Nobody knows why that happens."

• Allow your children to see the baby while he is still alive. If the baby has already died, and your children wish to see him, do your best to arrange that. Hospital staff and funeral directors are usually cooperative.

• Expect that your children's grieving, and their efforts to make sense of what has happened, will go on for a long time, even when they don't speak of it.

• Expect that as your children's thinking processes mature, they will have to rework their understanding of the sibling's death.

What Helps

When parents talk about what helped them after their baby died, several kinds of answers come up: a hospital staff's respect for their grief, responses that confirmed their baby as a real person, responses that helped them stay connected with other people, and any act that shored up their own coping mechanisms.

Respect for Their Grief. Corinne shows me a postcard-sized photograph of a leaf floating in water. A haunting image—all its tones are dark—it conveys a feeling of emptiness and endings. "At the hospital, they put this on my door even before I delivered. I was there for two nights, and you know how in hospitals there's always somebody coming in, to take your blood pressure or empty the trash. It told anyone who was about to walk into my room what had happened. I didn't have people bouncing in and congratulating me on my baby."

Alison, a young single mother whose baby was born eleven weeks premature, his lungs perilously underdeveloped, remembers his last day in the ICU. "We knew by then that Ben wasn't going to make it. They said that it was up to me when to disconnect him. After we did, they took him out of his isolette and handed him to me. We stayed in this little room, away from all the monitors and noise, and I held him and rocked him, and his heart slowed down and then stopped. They said, 'Stay as long as you need to with him.' I stayed another couple of hours, crying and singing to him. Nobody bothered me. They made sure my family knew, so I didn't have to go home alone." She shows me the strands of Ben's hair a nurse clipped for her, his footprints on paper, and a card signed by all the staff who cared for Ben.

Their Baby Was a Real Person. "I really appreciated it when people used Luke's name," Maria says. "That made me know he was real to them too. My sister was wonderful. She'd look at his picture from the hospital, and she'd talk with me about what I thought he'd be like, or how big he'd be by now."

A baby who dies stillborn or after a brief life has too little chance to become known. She provides her parents painfully few materials with which to envision her in their minds. Other people's appreciation for how much she mattered helps parents nourish their own attachment to their baby. This can be as simple as using the child's name, asking whom she looked like, or what a parent remembers about her. Jack: "A woman I've known for years at work has a son the age Luke would be. He started kindergarten this fall, and she talked a lot about it. One day she stopped by my area and said, 'Luke would have started this year too. I've thought about him.' That meant a lot to me, that she remembered."

Connecting with Other People. Parents say again and again how isolating their baby's death was. They felt utterly alone, the only people ever to have lost a child. Every contact that makes them feel cared about, that makes them feel their pain is understood, rebuilds their connection to the human community. Psychiatrist Judith Herman, writing about trauma and isolation, says, "Sharing the traumatic experience with others is a precondition for the restitution of a sense of a meaningful world. . . . The response of the community has a powerful influence on the resolution of the trauma."[3]

Corinne and Larry confirm Herman's observation. "All those people showing up for Emily's memorial service made us feel very cared about. Emily's death is the worst thing that's ever happened to either of us, but the way our friends stood by us has been really important. We didn't feel so alone."

Bereavement groups help so well because they offer parents that connection. A month after Jill died, at the urging of the hospice nurse who had followed her, Cynthia and Jerry joined a group for parents who had lost a child. "I can't say enough good about that group," Jerry reflects. "Everybody there knew just what we were going through, because they'd been there too. I'm the kind of guy who keeps things to myself, and I'd have probably gone off the deep end if I hadn't had the group pushing me to open up. That was the only place where I really felt I could."

Empty Cradle and Compassionate Friends speak to the same need: connecting with people who have been there. "It's the one place I never have to explain myself," says a mother whose child died of sudden infant death syndrome. "People there know why you need to talk about your baby." As the worst of their pain recedes, many parents stay with the group to offer their help to others. Maria continues to work with Empty Cradle as a parent facilitator, talking by phone with newly bereaved parents. She also speaks to hospital staff, especially obstetric and delivery teams, sensitizing them to parents' concerns. "It helps me, knowing I can make things a little better for some other mom," she explains.

Reclaiming Their Own Ways of Coping. It is a truism of grieving that each person grieves in his own way. A person's way of grieving arises out of his particular set of coping mechanisms: the unique and personal ways he has evolved to deal with stresses and challenges in his life. The overwhelming shock of the death, and the emergency mechanisms characteristic of the early stage of acute grief initially tend to override a person's own style; in acute grief we are all more alike than different. One of the important shifts in grieving occurs as a person reclaims his own particular coping style.

Whatever you do that you have always done, whatever structures your life and helps you feel good, helps you make sense of what happens to you: these are the ways that you cope. Every reclaiming helps, large or small. If you usually run and have not been, starting to run again is regaining ground. Getting back to routines is painful and awkward at first, but each return is ground regained. "The first time in the supermarket I thought I'd fall apart," Corinne says. "But we couldn't eat other people's cooking the rest of our lives. The first night I fixed ribs, which we both love. When we sat down to eat, at first we felt horrible, pigging out on ribs when our baby had died, but then Larry said, 'What are we supposed to do, live on gruel?' and we actually laughed."

Maria: "I went every day to the cemetery for a whole year. I brought Luke balloons, and little toy trucks, and once a teddy bear, all the things I wanted so much to give him and never could. I knew he was dead, but I couldn't give him up yet. I'd get Rodrigo off to preschool, and then I'd go and spend the morning there. My mom was sure I was crazy. She was really worried and she told everyone in the family she wanted to get me committed."

Her yearlong vigil reflected Maria's particular style and the situation she found herself in. "The more my mother and Jack told me to put it behind me, the more I knew I had to listen to my own heart. I didn't understand it then. But I look back and I see that I *had* to make it clear how important he was to me. Maybe if they'd been able to grieve with me, I wouldn't have had to do what I did. Doing what I did made me trust myself more. I came out of that year much stronger."

After Kelly died, Donald and Jane were crushed with guilt and self-doubt. "It wasn't real reasonable, I guess," Donald remembers. "But we both felt like what kind of parents were we, that we couldn't even keep our baby alive. We went different ways with it. Jane had her hands full with Amanda, who was four, and scared she was going to die."

Jane adds, "In a way, that was a blessing. She was scared, and couldn't sleep, and I realized I was still every bit as much her mother. I started reading everything I could find about children and death. I talked to a child psychotherapist a few times about her. He said he didn't need to see her, that we would talk together, and I could be the one to help her. That was a real vote of confidence: he still believed I was a good mother. Being a good mother has always been really important to me. Finding I could help Amanda with Kelly's death was the thing that helped me feel better about myself."

"For months after Kelly I never picked up my flute except for gigs," Donald says. "I'm a real expressive player, and the one thing I didn't want to do was feel anything. The guy I respect most in the band finally told me that my playing stank. I was mad, but he was right. I started practicing one day, and I damn near fell apart. I didn't go near it again for another month. When I did I'd be playing and crying—a real mess. I blubbered and practiced all summer, and somehow got it sorted out. It still hurt, sometimes beyond what I thought I could bear. But somewhere in there I got the idea of writing a piece myself and having a concert for Kelly.

"Jane says she could tell right away when I started playing

again that I was going to make it. She says I use my playing to work things out. I suppose she's right."

Barriers to Resolving Grief

Parents who have lost a baby have told us what helped them and their children in their efforts to heal. They've also charted the roadblocks they encountered that were specific to losing a baby. What gave parents the most difficulty after a baby died were too-constant reminders, anxiety about their living children, and the idea of a replacement child.

Too-Constant Reminders. As the searing preoccupation of acute grief subsides, your grieving develops its own rhythms. A song, a baby the age yours would be—memories surge unbidden. You are awash again, aching, unable to move or speak. Then, slowly, like waves from the shore, the pain recedes.

The calm times start to last longer. You read a page and remember what you've read. A new movie sounds interesting, and when you go, you can follow the plot. Having lunch with friends, you taste your food, hear what they say, even ask about their children.

A walk, a visit to your baby's grave, time by yourself in the early morning before anyone else wakes up: you learn to make your own times for thinking about your baby. Slowly your heart accepts the arrangement. You will make these times as often as you need them, and, in return, your grief will not surge into your throat as you sit at a stoplight or midway through a committee meeting. Living with your loss, you come to set your own pace. There must be time to grieve, and there must be time to be away from grieving.

A situation that thrusts your loss too constantly in your face will interfere with your healing. Before Jill was born, Cynthia was the manager at a downtown delicatessen. "We were right in Center City, and we did a huge lunch trade. Everybody knew I was pregnant. When I got back, everyone who came in asked about the baby, and I'd have to say that she'd had serious problems and she'd died. It never let up; it was so awful I finally quit. They all meant well, but all the questions made it so I could never get away. Home is where I thought about Jill; I needed work to be a place where I could get away."

Anxiety About Other Children. A baby's dying leaves parents feeling like failures. They could not produce a healthy child. They could not keep their child alive. These self-indictments are not reasonable, but they come with a terrible force. The helplessness you feel may make you want to redouble your efforts to keep your other children safe.

"Losing Luke made me realize how fragile life is," Maria says. "After he died, I got really protective of Rodrigo, my older boy. I couldn't stand it when he was over playing at a friend's, and I wouldn't let him go on field trips with his preschool unless I drove. After a while Rodrigo got so he didn't want to leave me; he'd cry and get real scared. He got so he wouldn't go to school. I knew I'd done this to him. I felt terrible." Maria and Jack took Rodrigo to a psychologist, who saw them all together. As Rodrigo's parents began to talk about how helpless they felt about Luke and how much they needed Rodrigo to be safe, they were able to relax their vigilance, and Rodrigo's fears ebbed away.

Anna is an attractive woman of fifty, a partner in her accounting firm and a mother of two young teenagers. As we sit on the deck near the pool, watching her children cavort in the water, she looks the picture of serene self-possession. Fifteen years ago her daughter, her first child, died of sudden infant death syndrome. "To this day, it takes a conscious, continuing effort not to smother them with caution. My husband and I help each other with it, and the kids know it. They know about their sister, but at their age they can't understand why it's so hard for us. But they're good about it. They say, 'Mom and Dad are whiteknuckling again.' I don't think the anxiety ever goes away. The best I can do is try to mute it, for their sake as well as mine."

Anna is right. A baby's dying makes such a tear in the canopy that nothing can make it whole again. Yet, for children, part of feeling safe must be the sense that their parents are able to protect them. Although that sense is part illusion, it is a useful one. Parents' efforts to mute anxiety help their children, and, as Anna recognizes, help parents as well.

A Replacement Child. Parents who lose a baby are usually of an age to have another, and often they do. A child born after a baby who died is potentially at psychological risk. If she comes into the world too soon after the child who died, when her parents have not adequately mourned the child who died, she may carry the complex burden of being a replacement child.

The replacement child phenomenon occurs when parents cannot deal with their grief over the baby who died. Mourning is such painful work that the temptation to sidestep it is great. Rather than face the painful emptiness, parents may simply attempt to fill it. Irving Leon, a psychiatrist in Birmingham, Michigan, writes perceptively about what may happen:

> The attachment to the deceased child is not relinquished, but transferred onto the replacement child, who may then become the focus of anxiety (should the loss be repeated), devotion (in part from the original attachment) and hate (over not actually being that lost child). Even when parents do not purposely regard or plan another child as a replacement for the loss, it has been found that the process of forming a new attachment may impede the mourning process, making pregnancy itself a barrier to resolving

grief. . . . While actively seeking to become quickly pregnant after perinatal death may indicate a refusal to mourn
that loss, the act of becoming pregnant or forming a new
attachment may in itself inhibit mourning.[4]

When parents make their new baby a replacement for the one
who died, they saddle her with an assignment no adult could
master: to make up to the parents for the loss of a brother or
sister she never knew. The child seems to absorb the assignment as she grows up and, with it, a conviction that she will
never be seen wholly as herself or valued for who she is.

Most parents are attuned to these possibilities and sensitive
to the complexities of their feelings about a child born after
their loss. Cynthia: "After Jill died, we knew we wanted another baby. But we didn't get pregnant again for about a year
and a half. We weren't using anything, but I'm really glad it
didn't happen. Neither of us would have been ready for it."
Jack: "When I found out Maria was pregnant, I wanted to have
another son; I was thinking of names that would give him the
same initials as Luke. It's probably really good that Elena was a
girl. It forced me to see her for herself. If it had been a boy, I'd
have probably still tried to make him into Luke."

Despite the barriers they encounter and the tears in their
canopy that they cannot mend, after the death of a baby,
parents and their other children move toward healing. Waiting
for their second child to be born, Jerry says what many families
feel. "Since Jill came into our lives, I think about a lot of things
I never used to. I just want someone to tell me that my child's
going to live to be an adult."

· 11 ·

The End of Hope:
Terminal Illness and AIDS

*"After Ben got sick, the future terrified me.
The future held his death.
I shut out the future.
All that mattered to me was today."*

—Derek

First Responses

The worst moment is the diagnosis. There were symptoms that puzzled you, that rest and fluids and aspirin could not resolve. There were tests, too many of them; repeated finger pokes and blood draws; hours in impersonal waiting rooms; X rays and CAT scans; too many unfamiliar doctors, some kind, some brusque and mechanical. Then the appointment with the specialist, from whom you hoped to hear that it's all been a mistake. You and your child can go home now. Instead there are the words that blind, pierce, sear.

"We saw the oncologist first thing in the morning, and it took all day for what he said to sink in," a mother recalls. "I heard 'leukemia,' and after that I didn't hear another thing. The rest of the day other pieces of what he said sort of came back to me. And it was days before I could get my mind around what it meant for Lindy. For us all."

175

Most parents agree that learning of their child's diagnosis is the worst moment. The doctor's words come with the force of a death notice. The shock and disbelief that follow are much the same as that which other parents experience when they are told their child has died. Parents speak of hours and days of simply being unable to take it in, unable to comprehend fully what the diagnosis implies.

Anger wells up quickly. It is outrageous and unfair for a child to die, and parents feel their rage. Because our culture allows men more latitude in expressing anger, fathers speak up more often, rage at doctors, drive too fast or drink too much. "I was furious," a father remembers learning about his son's lymphoma. "It didn't matter that there wasn't anybody to be angry *at.* I felt so cheated, for him and for myself."

Mothers' fury burns just as intensely but is more likely to turn inward, into self-blame: "Why didn't I notice that cough sooner?" "I should have watched his diet more closely." Parents have voiced appreciation for doctors and other medical personnel who reassured them that nothing they did or failed to do was responsible for their child's illness.

Scaldingly vivid in memory, these first responses give way very quickly to determination. By the time doctors talk with parents, usually during a second visit, about survival percentages and treatment plans, parents' moods have shifted from despair and anger to a decision to fight. The stakes are nothing less than their child's life. For their child's life, they will make the fight of their life.

Changes for the Whole Family

The shift toward fighting the illness brings about striking changes in the lives of everyone: parents, the diagnosed child, and siblings. The family's focus shifts from the future to the present. As your child's illness becomes a central concern, your family's priorities must change. If the illness carries a stigma, as AIDS does, you may face another layer of pain and loss in other people's response to your child. Your other children struggle with their feelings about their sibling's illness, and they must also adapt to the family's new priorities. Your child's place in the family changes. He needs you in different ways now, and over time you need him and may look to him in ways you previously did not. Treatment may bring a remission and a glorious reprieve.

When a relapse comes, the crash, the end of hope, it can be the worst time of all. Because no two people come to the end of hope at the same time, you find yourself frequently out of step with your partner and with your child. You face the task of and the opportunity for anticipatory grieving. Finally you must find a way to let go of your child and help her to die. In the changes described here, you are likely to recognize yourself and your family.

Focus on the Present. The most dramatic change is the one Derek describes at the opening of this chapter: the shift in focus from the future to the present. Raising children is a future-oriented enterprise. The values we teach them, the expectations we hold them to, the plans we make, the money we save, even the foods we give them all reflect our commitment to their future. And our pleasure in our own future is intimately bound up with theirs. A terminal diagnosis slashes through the tapestry of our future, tears out the warp where their design was to emerge.

Ben knew the design of his future. This year, eighth grade, he would be the starting center on the basketball team. Looking at the tapestry of his future, Derek hoped this would be the year his bright, awkward son could begin to pull it together: make his height and his intelligence work for him, begin to fulfill the promise that had been muffled in the four years since Ben's mother had died. Both of them wished that the headaches that plagued Ben would lessen. Instead they got worse. On a bright October morning, Ben woke up and yelled to his father that he couldn't see.

The next afternoon they sat across the desk from a neurologist who had studied Ben's CAT scan. A tumor was growing in Ben's brain, he explained. As it grew, it pressed against the optic nerve. Now the size of peach pit, it was pressing hard enough to darken his sight. They could slow its growth with radiation and drugs, but they could not stop it. They could buy him some time: a year, two at the most.

"He said they could start radiation the day after next. By the time we got there for Ben's first treatment, I'd rethought my whole life, all my priorities. The future didn't matter anymore. Really, there wasn't a future; it terrified me. All that mattered was what I could have with Ben today.

"I think that the change in me was the biggest shock to Ben. Bigger even than his diagnosis. You must understand that all his life, and his sister's, I've been the world's worst workaholic. I own an art gallery, and I write for two art publications. There's never a moment I'm not working. Since my wife died, my mother has lived with us, and she's really done most of the raising of them. I was too busy. For me to take the day off to take him to the doctor, well, that told Ben that things were really serious.

"I took him to all his radiation appointments. That got to be an important time together for us. His sight recovered well enough that he could read large print. He lost all his hair, but it didn't seem to bother him that much. It bothered me a lot more. We had a lot of good days that year. I can't explain how important each day became. I cherish every one of them.

"Ben wanted so much to go to New York. I go there a lot on business, and he'd always wanted to come. The next spring he was pretty weak, but we decided we'd go at spring break. We all went, my mother and Candace, my daughter, and I. We did all the things Ben wanted to do: saw a couple of Broadway shows, went to the Statue of Liberty and the UN, checked out the scene in the Village and SoHo. I'm so glad we took that trip. He talked about it to everyone. The day before he died he said, 'I'm glad I saw New York' and he smiled."

Changes in Your Priorities. Focusing on the present, newly precious because you know how finite it is, you come to value your child more deeply. All your interactions with her take on a new significance. "This can be hard to explain if you haven't been there," says Myra. "When Rachel was two we learned she had Tay-Sachs disease. It's a genetic disease that's always fatal. We knew she probably wouldn't live to start kindergarten. Her time with us was so limited that we appreciated every good minute we had with her."

Gloria buried her daughter, who died of AIDS, and raised her grandson Timmy until his death, also from AIDS, contracted in utero from his mother. Her losses have etched deep lines in her face, and she speaks slowly: "Timmy's illness made me look at my own health in a completely different way. After we got his diagnosis, I wanted to die. I couldn't bury my own grandchild. Then he had his first bad spell, and I saw how much he needed me. I thought, 'My God, I can't let anything happen to me. I'm all he's got.' I started taking vitamins, I got a flu shot, I even started an exercise class." She smiles, remembering. "I got so I was real careful when I crossed the street."

If you are a mother, you were probably the person most involved in your child's care. You committed the most time, your life was most transformed by her illness. What you could not have seen, should not have seen at the time is that those changes in your life were themselves time-limited. They would last only as long as your child lived. When she died, in addition to all the rest that you had to contend with, you had to reconstruct your life, find a new center and a purpose for your days.

Including Your Other Children. As his illness gains ground, your child and his needs become the center of your family's concern. His bedroom becomes the literal and emotional center of your house. Radiation treatments, visits to the doctor, medication routines claim first priority. The changes can be particularly hard for siblings, who see their needs put on hold. Mark, Rachel's brother, remembers: "Sometimes we couldn't go to the park, because the nurse was coming to see Rachel. I knew she was sick and it wasn't her fault, but I hated it. They always had to do everything for her."

In *Living with Death and Dying,* her book for parents of dying children, Elisabeth Kübler-Ross writes with great sensitivity about brothers and sister of the dying child. Siblings should take part in the child's care, she assures parents, in whatever ways they are comfortable with: reading to her, making pictures or scrapbooks, bringing the family dog into the room for her to stroke. Children who become valued contributors to the dying child's care feel more a part of the family. The knowledge that they are helping counterbalances their resentment for the inevitable deprivations. Although Mark envied his sister's central place in the family, he also volunteered to read to her and insisted that he be the one to cover her with her special blanket each night at bedtime.

"Whatever we did with Ben, Candace was a part of," Derek remembers. "That was a decision we all came to, right up front. After we got his diagnosis, we sat down, all of us, and talked about what Ben's illness might mean, how things would change. Candace was starting her junior year, and a lot of her life already went on away from the family. But she said that she wanted to help Ben every way she could, and she wanted Gram and me to ask her to do things. The times she got the angriest were when we didn't ask her to help or didn't talk to her about what was going on."

AIDS and Other People's Responses. The oldest parents I spoke with, Janet and Guy, nursed their thirty-seven-year-old son Tony through his final months as he died of AIDS. "Don't think for a minute losing an adult child is any easier," Janet says. "In a lot of ways it's harder. The older they are, the more you've grown accustomed to the idea that they're in the world permanently."

Since Tony died, she and Guy have involved themselves in a support group for parents of AIDS patients. "One of the worst things that happens after your child gets a diagnosis of AIDS is the way your friends and the whole community react. People you thought were your friends just disappear. Mothers won't let their children play with your child. You hear about real horror stories, people's houses burned or the child turned away from school. It's awful enough to see your child dying, but when your neighbors turn on you, it's beyond what anyone should have to endure."

Gloria agrees. "Timmy loved school, and he was such a friendly little boy. He'd make a friend, they'd play together, then that mom would find out who he was, and the child would say, 'I can't play with you anymore.' The last time it happened, it was a boy on our street that Timmy really liked. When he told him, Timmy came home and he was very quiet. After that I think he just gave up. He came down with a cold after that, and two weeks later he died."

Guy feels that the answer is much more public education. "People need to know you don't get this disease from drinking fountains or borrowing a pencil. They need to know it's safe to be in the same room with an AIDS patient." He speaks with particular concern about the tendency to classify AIDS patients as victims or sinners. "It really doesn't matter whether you got it from a transfusion or homosexual relations or a dirty needle. You're just as sick, and you and your family need other people's support just as much."

Janet is less patient. "I don't have time for that [classifying patients by the origin of their illness]. That's other people's problem. Having AIDS doesn't make you a saint or a sinner. Being healthy doesn't make you a good person."

Losing Ground. The hardest change for parents to watch is the disease gaining ground. "Every time Ben had to quit doing something he loved, it was hell—for him, and for us to have to watch. After the first radiation treatments, his oncologist said he couldn't play any sports for a year. Until then he'd held out the hope that he could play basketball. He sulked for a few days, but then he went to the coach and offered to be the team statistician. The coach and the other boys were all for it, and it worked until about midseason. Then his vision completely went out. That was a very hard time.

"He hated having to ask for so much help and having to be read to, but he put up with it, because he wanted to keep up. He despised using a white cane. He'd say, 'People will see me and think there's something wrong.' Every time he lost ground, I'd try to cheer him up; I felt that was part of my job. But then I'd go to the gallery and sob and kick the walls."

Your Child's Maturation. Knowledge of their illness affects children deeply. Although they maintain hope and denial, at some level most children recognize that they will die. Usually they know it and face it long before their parents do. Your child may begin to show a degree of maturity, of understanding that far exceeds his chronological age. Gloria remembers Timmy's calm acknowledgment of his situation. "He sat in a roomful of adults, he was six then, and they were making a video about

AIDS. He said, 'I've got AIDS, and I'm going to die before anyone in this room. I wish my mom and dad had said no to drugs.' "

You may have observed your own attitude toward your child changing as he became more mature. Your child's new maturity may have helped you face your own pain. Mike speaks about changes he saw in his son Alec, who had bone cancer. "He was ten when he got sick, just a regular ten-year-old boy, into sports, crazy about hockey. At first he hated all the hospital stuff, especially the shots and the bone-marrow samples. He cried and kicked up a fuss. All along, though, he knew just how he was doing, better than we did, even better than his doctor. He had a good remission, ten months, and I was sure we were home free. He was the one who knew different. Probably a month before anything showed up on tests, he started getting quieter, spending more time by himself. He would walk over and hug me, and tell me what a good father I was.

"I found myself talking more with him, about his mother and his little brother. He seemed so wise. It was like talking with an adult. Once he said he was worried for Damon, his brother, because Nan and I had to spend so much time with him, Alec. He told me I should take Damon to a Rangers game. He was too weak to go, but he'd watch it on TV, and he'd look for us. There was that selflessness and generosity that wasn't there before. I admired him so, and I felt so close to him."

Remissions. The life expectancies for many illnesses have lengthened significantly. New drugs and aggressive treatments bring remissions, buy precious months, even years. "A remission is like the sun coming out," Gloria says. "All you want to do is enjoy the sunshine. You forget there ever were clouds. You don't want to get near the doctors. You just want to hold on to what you have."

Your child gets stronger, plays harder, perhaps goes back to school. Your hopes surge. Perhaps this is a cure. You don't want to know the odds; you've beat them. If your euphoria looks like denial to some people, that's their problem. All you know is that your child feels good. It is all you should know for now. There is nothing to be gained by peering around the corner. Your pleasure in this time with your child strengthens you, sustains you for the times to come.

Relapses. "That was the worst part, a lot worse than when he actually died," Mike remembers. "Alec had ten months. That's long enough to believe in a miracle. He got back to school and finished sixth grade with his class. When he walked across the stage on his crutches to shake the principal's hand, the whole audience stood up and cheered him. We went to the doctor in July, and that's when they found the new growth in his shoulder. I just caved in. We'd run out of treatments and we were running out of time. That's when I knew he was going to die.

"It was awful. Nan, my wife, was still hoping. I couldn't talk to her. She didn't want to hear. Alec withdrew; he didn't talk about it. I think he was protecting us. He knew, but he wasn't sure we could handle it.

"I can't begin to describe the agony I felt. I don't know how long it went on. It felt like a year, but it was probably a couple of weeks. Then I began to pull back a little. I could see Alec pulling back too. He was starting to have a lot of pain, and for the first time it crossed my mind that, for him, maybe dying would be a relief. He'd lost so much already, his leg, any prospects for keeping up with his class. He hurt so much, and he was so tired, he couldn't do any of the things he liked. What kind of life is that?

"I felt like a monster, thinking this stuff. For months everything we'd done had been aimed at helping him keep going. But one day I looked at him, and I realized he'd already begun to let go."

A relapse forces you to look at the future you dread. The talk shifts to bringing your child home, helping her be as comfortable as possible. It is the end of hope and the beginning of grieving.

Anticipatory Grieving. When hope has run out, when you know it is no longer if, but when, you can begin to grieve. "It helped," Mike remembers. "Somehow, now that I knew what would happen, I felt steadier. You can't imagine what it's like, living with that much uncertainty for that long. It felt better to know where I stood.

"I cried, and I felt like hell, but you know, I could do what I had to do. I talked to our priest and made arrangements for burial. Alec never talked about what was happening, but I could see him getting weaker and more distant."

Parents who saw the end before it happened say that that time to grieve in advance was helpful to them. When their child actually died, they had already faced the worst. They were more able to help their child let go.

Nan: "Mike and I were always in a different place. I was still looking for one more treatment, one more hope. But I could see the change in Alec too. I couldn't face it until the last weeks. The day he died, I was home with him alone. In the morning he said, 'I'm so tired.' I said, 'I know you are. You don't have to fight anymore. It's okay with me.' He held my hand and shut his eyes and smiled.

"I came back in his room a little later, and I swear I could feel him slipping away. I told him how much we all loved him and that if he needed to go, he could go. He squeezed my hand and then he was gone."

What Helps

Parents who nursed a child through a terminal illness are very clear about what helped them. They speak of friends who saw them through, medical personnel who treated them as partners, hospice care that enabled their child to stay at home, and support groups where they could connect with other parents. Mothers whose lives had been centered on their child's care offer some thoughtful advice for the months after your child dies.

Family, Friends, and Community. Parents marvel at the depth and the breadth of support they found. They found it only when they could ask for it. "It got down to where Brendan needed a bone-marrow transplant if he was going to live. The odds for finding a donor that matches are twenty thousand to one. I'm a very private person, and I'm no good at organizing," says Rob, his father. "I told our priest about it, and the next Sunday he announced it from the pulpit. After services people I barely knew came up to me. One woman said she'd like to get a campaign started. I only knew her to say hello to. People started raising money, and someone got it on the radio. We got 1,300 people to come get tested. I was amazed."

Quieter efforts matter just as much: the neighbor who picks your other child up for soccer practice, your sister who calls to ask how it's going and offers to spell you for a while.

Friends help too simply by listening. The strains of caring wear so hard on you and your partner that, much as you would wish, often you cannot be there for each other. Again and again, parents say that it was friends they turned to for support.

Medical Personnel. A nurse who explains the procedure and tells you what you can expect; a doctor who treats you like an intelligent equal, who takes the time to explain and to answer your questions—these are the people whom parents appreciate. They value the people who saw their children as individuals, not just small bodies with a disease.

"They're all just doing their jobs," Nan reflects. "But the ones that helped the most were the ones that seemed to understand how frightening a hospital can be and how helpless parents feel."

Hospice Care. Hospice care, which enables terminally ill people to be cared for at home in the final stages of their illness, is relatively new. Ann Armstrong Dailey, director of Children's Hospice International, lists fifteen programs in the United States and Canada that offer comprehensive home care exclusively for children. The National Hospice Organization states that 1,000 of its 1,800 member hospices care for or will consider caring for a child.

Parents whose children used hospice care have high praise for the arrangement and for the caregivers. "We live thirty-five miles from the hospital, and Timmy was in there three different times. I stayed with him, and my husband came every day, but it was a strain," Gloria says. "To have Timmy at home, in his own room, with his toys and his dog, and everything familiar, was so much easier. It made a bad situation a lot easier to handle.

"Pam, the hospice nurse, came to see him twice a week, and more at the end. She stayed in close touch with his doctor. Any time she saw a change, she'd call her. I'd hear her telling Dr. Slater what she was seeing, and then she'd suggest a change in his dosage, or a different medication, and Dr. Slater would okay it. That worked a lot faster than my always having to get Timmy in there for a visit, and it was a lot easier on Timmy.

"Whenever Timmy started a new medicine or a treatment, [Pam would] work with me until I understood what to do. She taught me so much about how to care for him, and she always had ideas about how to make him more comfortable. She was there when he died, and I think by that time she cared as much as we did. We couldn't have kept him at home without her."

Support Groups. Many parents call support groups their life-line. Myra: "When your child gets sick, you feel totally alone. You don't know what to expect, or how you're going to get through it. When the hospital social worker told me about the Tay-Sachs group, I wasn't sure I wanted to do it. I didn't want to be with a whole bunch of depressed people. Stan went by himself the first time because I wouldn't go. He came home and he said I had to come. Well, I think that group got us through it. They all knew exactly what we were dealing with, and they really cared. Every one of those people was there at Rachel's funeral, and we're still very close with a couple we met in the group."

Support groups offer a place where you can bring your questions and your fears. No matter what you're feeling, no explanations are necessary; everyone has been there. Kathleen Carroll is a social worker who organized parent support groups for the American Leukemia Society in New York and has written extensively about her experience. She observes, "When parents have a child with a life-threatening disease, they feel so helpless, and impotent. In a support group, they find that they can genuinely help each other, sometimes by what they know about the illness, but mostly by listening, and caring. They come away knowing that they've helped, and they feel more capable and hopeful. That's powerful stuff."

Janet: "For families with AIDS patients, they're just critical. The people in your group know what you're going through. They're there for you, all from the first day your child tells you, right through the funeral, and afterward too. There are times when nobody around you knows what you're going through, and you can't talk to your partner. But you learn you can always talk to the people in your group."

The Hole in Your Days. That is what Nan called the feeling during the months after Alec died. "Ever since he got sick, taking care of him had been my first priority. I cut back my hours at my job, and then when he got worse, I quit altogether. I used to do a lot of other things: my softball team, Damon's Cub Scout troop, projects with my church. All of it fell by the wayside. I like to do needlepoint, but I couldn't concentrate anymore. Those last months, when I look back, all I did was take care of him, and sit and wait.

"After Alec died, my life was completely empty. I don't just mean my grief. I didn't have anything I had to do. Taking care of him was all I'd done for so long. I remember about a week after the funeral, Mike went back to work, Damon went to school. I sat at the kitchen table and thought, 'There is nothing for me.' I drifted in and out of Alec's room about ten times that morning. Even his room was strange. The hospital bed was gone, and his dresser, which used to be covered with all his medications and supplies, was bare. I felt disoriented. I didn't know where I belonged.

"I went back to my old job right away. That was a mistake, because I wasn't ready to be there. It took me a lot of time—months—to figure out that whatever I used to do, it wouldn't work the same anymore. Nothing in my life was the same anymore."

Seven months after her son Phillip died, Gillian says, "I don't yet know what I'm going to do. I feel useless. I feel like I'm having a midlife crisis five years too soon." She adds that she had been asked to serve as a patient advocate at the hospital where Phillip was treated. She was pleased to be asked but felt she wasn't ready yet to see that much of other children's suffering. Although she is uncomfortable in her present state, she feels certain that, with time, she will move toward new solutions.

Other mothers who had cared for their children say much the same, and they offer this advice: Take it slow. Take care of your own needs for a while. You probably have forgotten what they are, have been too absorbed in sustaining your child to know what you want for yourself. It will take you a while to remember. Nothing in your life, as Nan observes, is the same anymore. What you want now and what you value are likely to be different.

Be willing to experiment, these mothers say, because you may not find your balance on the first try. Whatever shape your life takes from now on, you are still the mother of your child. The solutions you fashion that work for you will somehow incorporate the memory of her: in the work you do, in how you value the people in your life, in whatever memorials you make.

· 12 ·

Sudden Deaths

"Jess never had a chance."
—Burt

First Reactions

"Mom, it's me. We went to the movies, and then we went out for pizza. We were laughing so hard that the Coke came out my nose! We're going to leave in a little while, and I'll be home by twelve-thirty. Do you still want to go running tomorrow?"

Carol said good-bye, hung up the phone, and turned out the light. She'd wake up when Maryann came in.

"I woke up and heard a car in the driveway, but it didn't sound like Maryann's. Someone was pounding on the door. Joe was at his parents', up in Michigan, and I was alone with the girls. I looked at the clock. It was two-seventeen.

"Our bedroom is at the end of the hall, and as I walked to the front door I looked out the windows. From each window I saw pieces of a picture: the trunk of a car, then the front of the car, and then a man at the door.

"He showed me his badge through the window, and he said he was a sheriff's department detective, so I let him in. He was wearing khakis and a flannel shirt and New Balance running shoes. I can remember the plaid of his shirt. I can tell you the color of the logo on his shoes.

"He said, 'There's been a serious motor vehicle accident on I-65. Your daughter Maryann was killed.'

"I screamed. I covered my ears and said, 'No. Don't talk to me. You're a liar. She's upstairs in her bed.'

"I rushed at him and pounded on his chest with my fists. He didn't try to stop me. I only stopped pounding because I couldn't breathe. My throat had closed up. I was gasping for air. I ran out of the room, and ran into Susan's room and woke her up. 'There's a man in the living room and he's telling lies about Maryann. He's got to stop it.'

"Susan came out and talked to the detective, and he took something off his clipboard and handed it to her. I thought it was his business card. Then Susan handed it to me. It was Maryann's driver's license.

"I could feel all the emotion drain out of me. I was frozen inside a large block of ice. I sat down beside Susan on the couch, and the detective told us what had happened.

"After he left, I couldn't move. I just sat on the couch and waited for it to get light. Susan was sobbing, and I held her, but I didn't move off the couch for four hours. I stayed inside the block of ice."

Although eleven years have passed since that spring night, Carol remembers the events with photographic precision: the changing views of car and officer from the hall windows, the plaid of his shirt, her desperate insistence that Maryann was upstairs in bed. Most parents whose child died suddenly have memories like this: vivid, intensely painful, threaded through with irrelevant details. The scene of the telling stays with them, the beginning of their ordeal.

What followed for Carol is familiar, an expectable response. When a person is confronted with something so overwhelming and so painful, the mind acts to reduce the flood of stimuli. Denial is the first line of defense. *Ward off the news.* When some irrefutable fact punctures the denial, then shock sets in. Shock is the mind's emergency shutdown, a blunting of all response until the person can regroup her resources. You will see it in survivors of an earthquake, a violent crime, or any other event that has left a person helpless and flooded with more than she can handle. *Go numb.* These responses are involuntary, beyond the person's control. Carol's image of a block of ice describes her experience of shock with painful eloquence. She knew that her daughter was dead, but she was immobilized, physically and psychologically: unable to move, numb to her own grief.

No Time to Say Good-bye

A child's sudden death adds more tasks to the complex work of grieving. There is the brutal shock of learning the news. There are the emergency measures of denial and shock, and the searing pain as the shock response ebbs and the terrible reality comes home. With the reality comes the painful knowledge that there have been no good-byes. No chance to sum up love or remember old pleasures. No chance to apologize for mistakes and insensitivities. No chance to hold her, tell her all that she has been to you.

Sudden death freezes the relationship in time. All that was left undone, unsaid, now stays with the living, unwanted mementos. Brothers competed and fought; now the one who survives cannot resolve the tension with his brother, or confirm his underlying love. A mother who envied her daughter's youth and agility could not tell her how proud she was of her dancing. Now she carries the burden of her unspoken praise.

Burt lives with the endless ache of efforts beginning to bear fruit and then being stunted. He remembers his son Jess: "It had been a godawful time for Jess. He had learning disabilities, and he'd been ditching school all through junior high. His freshman year, he went to the alternative school, but things didn't get any better. He was hanging out with some pretty wild guys. There was beer, and I expect there were drugs. I was working over in Brattleboro, better than an hour's drive from home. Summer before his sophomore year, I worked out an interdistrict transfer and told him that he'd be going to the regional high school there. He complained and threatened to run away, but come the first day of school, he was sitting in the truck. We had that hour together, twice a day. We probably talked more those eight months than in five years before that.

"I could see him changing. He was taking wood shop, and the way he talked about his teacher, and the project he was working on, I couldn't believe it. This is a kid who had never stuck to anything in his life. He worked on a box, one box, for three solid months. About ten blocks south of the high school there was a cabinetmaker's shop. Jess found this guy, talked him into a job sweeping up his shop and doing odds and ends. I began to hear a lot about Leo and the shop. Jess started talking about apprenticing with Leo, becoming a cabinetmaker. Mostly now I just listened.

"I knew I was preparing to let go of my son, to see him go into the world. Things were starting to work out for him.

"And then that asshole came around the curve, too drunk to steer. Jess never had a chance."

Burt was also critically injured in the accident that killed Jess. He spent twenty days in the regional trauma center, most of it in a coma. He remembers drifting in and out of consciousness, dimly aware that something bad had happened. He was still unconscious when his son was buried. Deprived of the chance to see his son, or even see him buried, Burt could not take in the reality of Jess's death. "I kept thinking he was away, visiting, and that he'd be home some time soon. I'd even get mad at him for being gone so long. It was months before I could really hold on to the fact that he was gone for good." Not seeing Jess dead made the painful reality even harder to grasp.

Making It Real: The Child's Body

Sudden deaths are usually violent: car accidents, shootings, stabbings. Families face not only the death, but the mutilation of their child's body. All too soon after they have learned of the death, usually when they are still in shock, they are asked to come to the hospital, sometimes to the morgue, to identify the body. Martha looks back at her experience the night her son died.

"When we got there, even before anyone talked to us, we saw how the nurses looked at us, and we knew it was bad. A doctor took us into a small room and said, 'Your son will never go riding in the car with his friends again.' He explained that Ira had very severe head injuries and hadn't regained consciousness. My husband had the sense to ask if there were facial injuries. The doctor said yes, he was pretty messed up, and he'd lost an ear.

"That brought it home to me, how much he had suffered in the accident. I couldn't bear to go in and look at him. I just didn't want to see my son slashed and torn up. My husband went in. He said Ira looked pretty awful. He died about an hour later.

"Now I wish I'd gone in to see him, no matter how awful it was. Even after all this time, it's hard for me to accept that he's dead. I still see him everywhere. I'll see a boy who looks like him from the back, and I'm startled, my heart starts pounding, and I think, 'Could he still be here?'

"That's something I'd tell any parent. No matter what condition your child is in, go and see him. If you have other children, and they want to see him, let them. It makes it more real."

Most parents who have had a child die suddenly would agree with Martha. Carol refused to go to the morgue to identify Maryann until her husband got back to town and could come with her. "Partly I didn't want to do it alone, but partly I knew that, no matter how bad it was, Larry needed to see her too."

At the morgue, Maryann's parents were given her purse, her watch, her rings, and her shoes, but not the clothes she had been wearing. Her clothes were so soaked with blood, they were told, that they had been destroyed. Carol still speaks angrily about that decision. "Those were her clothes. No matter what condition they were in, they should have been returned to us." Even the bloody evidence of her child's suffering was important to her; it would have helped her in her struggle to make the death real.

The task of making the death real persists for all families who lose a child, no matter what the circumstances of the death. Parents and siblings say it takes a year or more to get it firmly fixed in their understanding that their child will never be with them again. But the sudden, blindsiding experience of unexpected death complicates the task. Seeing the child, seeing the scene of the death, reclaiming his effects—all help the family know what has happened.

Helplessness and Responses

The two most painful conditions that all human beings must bear are loss and helplessness. Your child's death floods your family with both in overwhelming doses. The abruptness of the separation when a death is sudden particularly increases your sense of helplessness. *He is dead. We could not protect him.* Much of what survivors do in the weeks and months after a child's death can be understood as efforts to ward off the painful fact of their own helplessness. Family members may say and do things that feel peculiar, abrasive, self-defeating, even to themselves. If you understand your words and actions as efforts to help yourself feel less helpless, they make more sense. Your actions and responses include the if-onlys, blaming yourself, the search for facts, the search for understanding, and taking action.

The If-Onlys. Every parent I've talked with speaks of their if-only thoughts, the intensely painful, obsessive ruminations about the death that preoccupy and torment them. If only I hadn't let him go to that party. If we'd just been able to get closer to shore before the fog came in. If he'd only come back for his backpack. "If I had talked longer on the phone with her that night," Carol muses, "*even thirty seconds longer,* she'd have come into the intersection later. That driver would have already been gone." To someone listening, these thoughts might sound like futile ruminations. But for parents, whose lifelong commitment has been to protect their child, such thoughts reveal both their keen awareness of how helpless they are and their wish to make things come out differently. If only x, he'd be alive and well and here today. If-only is a fantasy about control, a fantasy that offers temporary respite from the loss and from the awful helplessness.

Parents tell us that if-onlys are the worst in the early weeks and months. Over time, as they find other ways of dealing with their helplessness, the ruminations subside. The if-onlys never quite go away. Chuck's two-year-old daughter drowned fourteen years ago, in a pond on his land. When he goes to work the fields on that part of the family farm, he must drive past the pond. "After fourteen years, the if-onlys aren't a daily thing anymore. But if I'm real tired, or something's going bad for me, they're back."

I'm to Blame. Related to if-only, only more corrosive, is self-blame. In *When Bad Things Happen to Good People,* Rabbi Harold Kushner tells of a couple in his congregation whose son died suddenly in a car accident. When he came to call on them, they blurted, "We didn't go to temple on Yom Kippur, and this is our punishment." As irrational as it looks to others, claiming responsibility serves an important purpose for parents. If their actions caused their child's death, then the world is an orderly and predictable place—a harsh place, with cruel laws of causality and retribution, but predictable. Some parents may find it easier to bear the notion that their angry words or neglected observance caused their child's death than that the world is randomly cruel. If the world is predictable, they are less helpless.

Self-blame is another fantasy about control, one that exacts a terrible price for its illusory comfort. The price is this: If you believe you caused your child's death, then you must punish yourself endlessly. Self-blame is a life sentence, with no expiation. Tethered to your sin like an ox to a yoke, you tread your guilt in an endless circle. You get nowhere, resolve nothing, only deepen your track. The way out requires that you find a way to bear the helplessness that comes with being human. Contradictory as it sounds, frightening as it feels, we can move forward from our losses only when we can live with our helplessness.

Surviving children are vulnerable to another variety of self-blame. Children of five or younger tend to see their world in highly egocentric terms. That is, all events revolve around them, and they are the cause of all things. This way of experiencing events arises both from the immaturity of their thought processes and from their extremely limited life experience. At five, the ability to reality-test—to check assumptions against the observable facts—is not yet firmly established. Preschoolers will remember their thoughtless remarks about their brother or sister ("I wish she'd never come back"), and assume that they caused the sibling's death. Their self-blame will be silent, and unless an adult intervenes, it can stay with them indefinitely.

Although as they grow older, children have more experience with cause-and-effect relationships and greater ability to reality-test their assumptions, they are still likely to believe their thoughts or words caused a sibling's death. Their own guilt and confusion and their awareness of their parents' pain may combine to silence them, preventing their beliefs from ever being aired. Children need help from their parents in sorting out their beliefs about a sibling's death. Without help, they are likely to impose needless guilt and pain on themselves. Chapter 8 offers more explanation about how children grieve, and what they need from their parents.

What Happened? The Search for Facts. Two days after Ira died, his father and sister rode with an Illinois state trooper to the crash site. They followed the dark smears of skid marks across the blacktop. They scrambled down the embankment and through the flattened blackberry brambles to the oak tree that stopped the car. Paul, Ira's father, photographed the splintered trunk and listened intently as the trooper talked about momentum and energy absorption. His daughter, Judy, walked around, kicking up dead leaves, finding bits of glass and metal and, then, Ira's ear.

"I saw her reach down for something. Then she dropped it and started retching. I ran over and held her, and the trooper had some kind of bag he put it in. It was awful, but I'm glad she found it," Paul says. "I went back to the place a couple more times. I also got the state police report on the accident and the autopsy report. I sometimes wonder what I thought I'd learn. All I know is that I needed to find out everything I could about what happened to Ira. Finding out what happened doesn't bring my son back. But in some way it helped."

The work of finding out what happened, and every detail of how, helps families feel less impotent. It is something to do, a task and a purpose at a time when all purpose has drained from their lives. There are emergency medical technicians and hospital staff and medical examiners and police to talk with. Talking with them fills time, which now stretches in aching, empty vastness. After her six-year-old daughter was killed in a traffic accident, Melanie could not stay in her apartment. "I'd come home from work, and I couldn't breathe in that place. I'd take Kenny and we'd go over to the street where it happened. I'd stop people and ask them if they'd been there that day, and what they'd seen. I had to get out of my house and I had to know more." These recollections from strangers provided Melanie with a connection to her daughter, mental snapshots of her last moments.

The search for facts is in part a search for your child as he was and will never be again. At once a holding on and a letting go, the search reflects the enormous resiliency of human beings: Searching for facts may be the first step toward building a new reality, toward learning how to live a life without your child.

Martha, Ira's mother, did not go to the crash site. "Paul and I divorced when the children were small, but we've stayed on good terms. He followed all the hearings, the trial and the sentencing, and he kept me informed. Finding out all that stuff was what he needed to do. But it didn't do anything for me." Martha read the autopsy report and questioned a nurse friend about the terms she didn't understand. But for the most part, she dealt with her helplessness in another way. She searched for understanding.

Why Has This Happened? The Search for Understanding. In the high-ceilinged living room in a suburb north of Chicago, pale winter sunlight pours through the windows. Although two feet of snow sits on the ground outside, this room is a sheltered garden. Three large fig trees flank the south-facing windows. Daffodils and freesias spill out of pots, perfuming the air. Books on perennials, on bulbs, on succulents, on a dozen kinds of specialized gardens crowd the bookshelves and sit stacked on tables. The couch is bright with pillows in floral prints, and behind it, on a narrow table, yellow tulips bloom in a cachepot. Beside the cachepot, photographs in silver frames show a girl in the first flush of adolescence and a full-faced, smiling young man.

Martha talks about the time after Ira died. "The next six months, I just took care of myself and Judy. Gardening saved my sanity. I worked in my yard every day, until I was so tired I couldn't move. A friend said to me, 'If you'd been hurt this badly physically, you'd be in intensive care.' I guess the garden was my intensive care unit.

"Judy and I talked a lot about Ira. She was angrier about it than I was. We'd go to the cemetery and she'd say, 'Ira, how could you go and leave me here like this?' I couldn't answer. She stayed home from school a lot that spring. She'd sit on her bed and play his tapes and cry."

Five months after the accident that claimed her brother's life, Judy was killed by a drunken driver.

"She was starting to feel better. She was going to a back-to-school party. She was wearing an outfit that she'd designed and I'd sewed for her. When I dropped her off at the party it was dusk; the light was fading. There were all these fourteen-year-old girls frolicking on the lawn, near the road. There's no sidewalk out there, and not much shoulder. I drove away [then] came back and hailed her and her friends over to the car. I told them to be careful and stay out of the road, that drivers wouldn't see them.

"I'd been home maybe twenty minutes when the phone rang. It was one of the girls at the party. She said Judy had been hit by a car.

"The driver was drunk. He was speeding, and he didn't have his lights on. He saw the girls and hit the brakes. The brakes locked, and he skidded. Six girls were standing at the edge of the lawn. They all ran, but Judy was the one closest to the road, and he skidded and ran into her. She died the next day.

"After she died, the house was so still. I missed her desperately. While she was alive, we were still a family. Now what was I?" She pauses. "Our language has no word for a mother who has lost her children.

"I knew I had to understand why this happened. But I couldn't do anything then. I couldn't read, or concentrate, or think. It hurt to breathe, it hurt to move, I was sure that my heart would stop any minute. I went back to my ICU. I worked outside until the snow was too deep.

"When I could read again, I got hold of everything I could find about death, and near-death experiences, and life after death, and reincarnation." She gestures to a tall bookcase in the hall. "That's just a part of it. I read in every major religion, their ideas about heaven and hell and afterlife. And a lot of minor ones too. I read philosophy and theology and anthropology and mysticism; I covered a lot of territory.

"The next five years I worked, I gardened, and I read about death. That was all I could do." She speaks softly. "Grieving takes a lot of energy.

"I can't say that I found any one idea that changed my thinking, but all my reading forced me to think harder about what I believe. I've come to believe that my children are with me still in many ways. There are times when I feel their presences, and I think that they are trying to help me understand that there is a design and a purpose to all of this. There's a reason that they're gone and I'm still here, and my job is to figure out my purpose here."

For Martha, the search for understanding has begun to bear fruit. "It's seven years now. Just the last year I feel like I've started to figure it out. That's a long time, but I don't know any way I could have shortened it. I thought of all the things I did for my children, that I couldn't do for them anymore. But I realized that I could still do things and help other people. I helped organize Plants and People. We work out of a storefront

on the South Side, teaching people how to grow things, helping them make gardens. I believe in gardens. I think they can
save your life." She pauses and looks thoughtful. "You know,
I've gained an awful lot, and I want to be able to use it."

Taking Action. Three days after she buried Maryann, Carol
drove to the office of the local Mothers Against Drunk Driving
chapter. With MADD's help she learned how drunken driving
charges were handled in her county and how she could deal
with the district attorney's office to insist that it prosecute the
man who killed her daughter. She followed the case through
inquest, hearing, indictment, continuances, jury selection,
trial, appeal, multiple continuances, a second appeal, and sentencing. Seven years after Maryann died, the driver went to
prison.

Carol gained a brutal education in the realities of the legal
system. She is glad she did it. "For those first two years it was
all I could focus on. If I hadn't had the court stuff to pour all my
rage into, I hate to think what I would have done." Over time
she found that her interest shifted toward prevention. These
days she speaks for MADD two to three times a month at high
schools. An intense, passionate speaker, she tells her young
listeners about Maryann, and shows them her daughter's picture and pictures of other teenagers killed by drunken drivers.
"I couldn't save Maryann, but I truly believe that my work and
our chapter's work have saved a lot of other kids' lives. The
police and our district attorney go after DWIs a lot more ag-
gressively these days. The kids I talk to come up to me afterward, and you can see I've gotten to them."

Parents whose son collapsed and died at football practice
start a scholarship fund in his name. Three siblings plant a
memorial grove in the park where their sister was murdered. A
father whose son drowned in a canoeing accident lobbies his
state legislature for stricter water safety laws. A couple launches

a campaign to redesign a "killer highway," a stretch of road with blind curves and a high accident rate, on which their daughter died. A concert violinist gives a free concert each year in memory of her infant son, killed in a car accident. These parents explain that such activities come out of their need to do something about what happened to their child. One parent's greatest need may be to assure himself that others will remember the child who has been such an important part of his own life. For another, what matters most may be to change the conditions that led to her child's death.

When your child's death has resulted from someone else's negligence or drug or alcohol use, your need to act is compounded by outrage. Honoring your child's memory may not feel like enough. You want punishment, even vengeance for her death. You may wrestle with your wishes. Carol: "That was the hardest thing, especially the first year, when I was blind with pain. Every time his lawyer got a continuance, I felt that driver was sidestepping his punishment. I wanted to go strangle him personally. Some time in the second year, I began to see that my anger was getting in the way of remembering Maryann. I thought, 'That's crazy, that's letting him hurt me even more.' After that I forced myself to let go of it. Some days my anger just surges. It shakes me all over. But I work at it, because I can't let it get between me and Maryann."

Burt is a large man with a physically imposing presence. "The guy who killed Jess got off with six months in a work-release center. If I had a nickel for every hour I've spent thinking what I want to do to him, I could retire. He lives about five miles away, and a few times I've had a real strong urge to hunt him down and kill him. I'd work it all out in my mind, and be getting up to walk out the door, and something in me would say 'Don't do it.' I haven't, yet." Burt knows that his anger contributes to his chronic depression and creates severe strains in his marriage. "I'd let it go if I could, but I'm scared that as bad as it is, it also keeps me together." His anger has become a suspended action, a defense against helplessness that at once sustains him and interferes with his finding any solace.

Resolutions: What Hinders, What Helps

The suddenness of your child's death enormously complicates the work of grieving for you and your family. When death and the news of it come suddenly, families must integrate the awful knowledge of their child's suffering, even mutilation. A painful new awareness now burdens your child's legacy. *She lay bleeding in the cold. That driver jumped the divider and came at him head on. He died in the emergency room, alone. She never saw them coming.* Vivid details and horrible imaginings flood your thoughts, increasing pain, delaying resolution.

Hospitals, police, attorneys, and news media demand parents' involvement at a time when you are depleted and vulnerable. Involvement with these agencies is unavoidable. At best, they may be of real help to you. But each of these groups has its own agenda. Their efforts may even work against your own need to come to terms with your loss. Arthur's son died from bacterial contamination of a hamburger he ate at a fast-food restaurant. Arthur reflects on the wrongful death lawsuit he is pursuing against the meat processor: "It's a double-edged sword. Bernie died because of their negligence, and they have to be held to account. I really believe that. But there are days when I just want to tell my attorneys to forget the whole thing. I'm trying to make some peace with my life and figure out how I'm going to live without Bernie. It seems like every time I'm getting somewhere with that, the phone rings and it's my attorney with something about the case and all the pain gets stirred up again."

There is not a single right way to handle the additional

206 · THE WORST LOSS

complications that a child's sudden death brings. Carol and Paul each needed to find all the facts and follow the legal proceedings against their child's killer. Martha retreated from facts and, for a while, from people. "If I could have, I'd have just left town for a year," she remembers. Despite his second thoughts, Arthur finds some consolation in the lawsuit that he sees as holding the responsible parties to account. Burt fantasizes a rawer vengeance and finds no peace.

Parents who have come to a resolution they can live with speak of the importance of allowing their feelings to emerge. Martha: "I didn't know anything about grieving. But I knew the only way I'd survive was if I let myself feel. Whatever it was, I'd allow myself to feel it. That was the only way I could see to get through this." Paul: "I'd get so involved in the legal stuff, and I'd have to grab myself by the shirt and sit down and figure out what I was feeling. It always felt like it would kill me, but afterward I'd feel a lot better. I think grief must kill the people who don't feel it."

For many parents the most helpful resolution has been finding another way to use their capacities for parenting. Hank is a sheriff's deputy whose youngest child died at age eight when he fell from a tree. "I was cheated out of raising Colin," he says. "Everything I was doing got cut off midstream." A year after Colin died, Hank volunteered to work as a drug education officer. "I'd chased criminals for twelve years. It was time to do something different. I go to grade schools and junior highs, a lot of them in some pretty bad areas. The kids I see really need what I'm telling them. I'm giving them a better shot at growing up, and that helps me heal. It's as close as I'll get to raising Colin."

· 13 ·

Murders

"At first I blamed myself and I blamed God.
I figured between us we should have kept her safe."
—Father of a murdered girl

We sit at Sylvia's kitchen table—the place in her house, she explains, where the serious talking gets done. She is a tall, solidly built woman, the daughter of Czech immigrants, who has raised five children. As she waits for her coffee to cool, she recounts in a flat voice how she learned that her youngest daughter had been murdered. "I was driving home from the grocery store, and on the radio it said a Jane Doe had been found in Liberty Park. That's the county park outside of town. The description was brown hair, brown eyes, five feet five. That could be a lot of girls. But right away I knew it was Leslie.

"You don't know what that's like. Your own child, that you've raised and you've always done your best to protect, a Jane Doe. Calling the medical examiner, having to identify her. They showed us pictures; we identified her from the pictures. They advised us against seeing her. They said she was pretty badly beaten up. We had a closed casket at the funeral."

News of a child's murder comes suddenly. It is never news you expect. *He was coming home from practice. She broke up with him three months ago. He was just waiting for the light to change.* Like all sudden deaths, the news brings shock, disbelief, denial.

But even before the first protective reactions fade, your child's murder also brings a set of unique complications.

Special Complications

Sylvia sums up the distinctive problems that face a parent whose child has been murdered. "You're victimized three times: by your child's death, by the criminal justice system, and by society."

Parents mention other aspects of their child's murder that gave them particular pain. Specific to murder is intentionality. The murderer hurt your child, on purpose. Murders are seldom easy deaths; you imagine your child terrified, in horrible pain, unprotected. Rage and desire for revenge surge through you, undermine your judgment, lunge against your self-control. Primitive fear stalks you. You may develop post-traumatic stress disorder (PTSD), the syndrome in which images or feelings about the traumatic event continue to overwhelm you. Guilt becomes your constant companion. Police and court proceedings intrude on your grief, demand your compliance yet ignore your need to know. Other people respond as if your child was at fault. We can look at how each of these issues affects families who lose a child to murder.

Intentionality. Although other deaths, including many accidents, can be violent, a murder is unique because it is intentional. The murderer intended to do harm to your child. The idea is itself painful, hard to imagine. "Sean was a good kid, friendly to everyone," his father says. "How could anyone want to hurt him? That's where I get stuck."

An intentional act also feels like a preventable one. Somebody, somehow, could have prevented it. It is the if-onlys again, even more fiercely when your loss has been by murder. If the police had patrolled more often, if you had watched her more closely, if you hadn't insisted that he get that after-school job, if you'd home-schooled him instead of sending him to the junior high . . . If, if, if—when your child has been murdered, you are painfully vulnerable to these thoughts. They are not rational, you would tell another parent. You did all that you could, you would assure them. You cannot keep a child in a Styrofoam box. But when the child is yours, the if-onlys haunt you.

Violence and Pain. You were not there when your child died. To your desperate questions "Did she suffer?" "Did he live long in pain?" there are no answers. You grasp for scraps, secondhand information. Often the impersonal language of a coroner's report is all you have. Still you reconstruct the scene, play it over and over in your mind.

"The medical examiner's report said Leslie was hit with a rifle butt and a hammer. She died from a series of hard blows at the base of her skull. They could tell how long her body lay there before she was found by the growth of the maggots." Sylvia's face sags, ages perceptibly. She stares out the window for a long time. When she speaks, her voice is weary with pain.

"Think about that. Picture it. I did, every day, all the time, for months. I'd wake up in the night, seeing her. I was sure I was going crazy."

What was your child thinking before he died? Did he know he was going to die? Was he scared? Did he know how much you loved him, how you wanted to protect him? Parents said that this uncertainty, not knowing their child's emotional state, was one of the most painful and persistent aspects of their grief. What you do not know you cannot lay to rest.

Rage and the Desire for Revenge. The killer has taken away your most precious possession. Rage sweeps over you like a fire out of control. Geoff, a pacifist all his adult life and an ordained minister, talks about his son's murder. "The day after Sean was stabbed, I sat all day in my study planning how I would kill the kid who did it. It's a good thing that it took them a few days to find him. If he'd been in police custody the next day, I truly believe I would have killed him. I got past that, mainly by thinking about what it would do to my wife and the other children. They'd been through enough. They couldn't take me being jailed too. But the rage stayed, for months. I'd think about what happened, and it seared through me. It was like being stabbed myself. I'd never known rage was such a physical experience."

Your rage is so intense that it may scare the people around you. Charlotte Hullinger, who founded Parents of Murdered Children after her daughter Lisa was killed, put it this way: "The anger felt by the parent of a murdered child is too threatening to many people, and so they try to calm us down and discourage us from fully experiencing the intensity of our emotions. And yet if healing is to take place, it must be by expressing and working through our feelings, no matter how negative or destructive they may seem to others, rather than by denying and repressing them."[1] Hullinger's message is clear: the only way out of your pain and your rage lies straight through it.

Fear. Close to rage lies fear. When someone you love is killed, your own canopy of safety is punctured. When your child is the victim, the whole canopy is ripped away. You are exposed, unprotected. Geoff: "Even when I was planning to kill that kid, I was scared he was coming to kill me. So was my wife and our other boy. Even after he was locked up. For a long time, we didn't feel safe in our own house. That's a terrible feeling. Sean's murder robbed me of my own sense of safety." Other parents agreed with Geoff. Over time, they said, their fear subsided. Some sense of safety returned slowly.

For children whose brother or sister is murdered, fear persists much longer. Geoff: "Lenore, my daughter, was ten when Sean was killed. She had nightmares for months and had to have a light on in her room to go to sleep. The nightmares are gone, but at fourteen she still has a night-light. Every night when I walk up the stairs, the light from her night-light reminds me of what that killer did to my family."

Post-traumatic Stress Disorder. This piece of psychiatric terminology came into use to describe the persistent reactions of some Vietnam veterans. As researchers and clinicians learned more about the syndrome, they recognized that it may result from many other traumatic stressors, such as natural disasters (earthquakes, hurricanes), rapes, and certainly the murder of a family member. You do not have to have witnessed your child's murder to experience a post-traumatic stress disorder.

PTSD symptoms include:

- persistent reexperiencing of the event by intrusive, involuntary recollections (flashbacks), nightmares, or a sense that you are reliving it in the present;
- a tendency to avoid any reminders of the event, by avoiding thoughts and feelings about it; inability to recall part or all of it; avoidance of people, activities, or places that evoke memories of it;
- generalized numbing of feelings, a sense of detachment or estrangement from other people, restriction of range of feeling;
- a conviction that your own future will be cut off;
- difficulty falling asleep or staying asleep;
- difficulty concentrating; and
- extreme alertness, vigilance, inability to relax, even in safe and familiar surroundings.

Any of these symptoms is expectable in the first days and weeks after your child has been killed. Your other children are equally vulnerable, equally likely to experience symptoms. If they do not recede, or if you see them interfering with your ability to get on with your life, you should seek psychological evaluation. PTSD usually responds well to treatment; untreated, the symptoms do not resolve.

The Reverend Wanda Henry-Jenkins lost her mother to murder and, years later, her brother-in-law. Her recent book *Just Us* is an eloquent description of the special difficulties families face when one member has been murdered. Discussing the effects of fear on homicide survivors, she coins the term homicide stress syndrome: "I call the post-traumatic stress associated with murder *homicide stress syndrome* because the reaction is directly related to the homicidal death of your family member. . . . Murder is a brutal, traumatic loss which produces emotional scarring. . . . Homicidal loss produces scars that time alone will not eliminate."[2] Henry-Jenkins also advocates professional treatment and involving yourself with a support group for homicide survivors.

Police and Courts. Many families level their harshest criticism at the police and the courts, the institutions that they had believed were there to help them. "You learn pretty quickly," Sylvia says, "that a murder is between the state and the defendant. You don't count. A lot of the people you talk to, detectives, people from the D.A.'s office—to them, the victim's family is a nuisance. You take up their time, you want to know what's going on, little things like that."

Leslie, Sylvia's daughter, started using drugs in high school and became increasingly involved with dealers. "The people she hung around with were scum. There's no other word for them. Leslie wasn't scum. She made a lot of mistakes, and I can't say a lot for her judgment. But she was still a good person.

When a young girl gets killed and there are drugs involved, the police see it only one way. They talked about Leslie like she deserved what happened to her. Nobody deserves what he did to her.

"When your child has been killed, that's a very vulnerable time for the family. The police say things without thinking. What they say stays in your mind forever.

"My husband and I went to see the district attorney. By that time I'd talked with Parents of Murdered Children, and I knew what to expect. We dressed very well; we wanted him to know he couldn't roll over us. If you're poor, or you don't know your way around the system, they'll roll right over you. Ignore you, not return your phone calls, tell you nothing. They're so busy, you're in their way.

"He wanted a plea bargain [an agreement with the defendant by which he admits to, or agrees to be tried for a lesser charge: second-degree murder, or manslaughter, or involuntary manslaughter, all of which carry shorter sentences and prospects for quicker parole]. We said nothing below second-degree murder. Anything less would be a joke."

Sylvia's experience is fairly typical. Police departments and criminal courts tend to be overworked and understaffed, conditions that do nothing to promote sensitivity to the needs and feelings of victims' families. Parents learn very quickly about the readiness of defense lawyers to smear their child's reputation for the sake of their client and about the realities of plea bargains.

Mel and Harriet's son was shot by a storekeeper who mistook him for the man who had robbed him a week earlier. They talked with a lawyer about bringing suit for wrongful death. "He asked us all about Mike. Mike was unemployed when he was shot. We knew that he smoked a little pot. The lawyer warned us that a defense attorney would find these things out, and maybe other things we didn't know. He could blow those things into a full-scale character assassination. He told us we might or might not win the suit, but either way, he could guarantee it would get ugly in court. We decided we'd gone through enough. We didn't need that."

Especially disturbing to parents are the lengths of sentences meted out and the actual time served by their child's killer. Because of stringent requirements for evidence in federal and most state courts, it is extremely difficult to secure a conviction for first-degree murder. Prosecutors often seek a plea bargain. Parents are shocked to find that their child's killer may actually serve as little as four years.

The man who beat Leslie to death served six years. "In the eyes of the state, that's all my daughter's life was worth. Six years," Sylvia observes grimly.

When justice is not done, when your child's killer is not caught or his sentence was disproportionately light, you will encounter more difficulty in grieving. Many parents say that they could not allow themselves to experience the full range of their grief until the murderer had been sentenced. "I couldn't let down until the D.A. told me [the killer] was on his way to the penitentiary," says Mel. "Until then I was in some kind of awful suspended state." Bitterness with the system's treatment of your child's death may delay or interfere with your grieving.

Other People's Responses. Friends and co-workers may pull away, just when you most need support. "Murder is so awful it scares people," Mel speculates. "It's like they're scared it might be catching." Too often, parents have felt from their friends the same implied judgments that police might have made, that somehow their child had brought the murder on herself or was somehow responsible. At a time when they most need their friends' support, many parents have found that it isn't there.

Sylvia reflects on her experience with friends. "It was tough. We knew a lot of couples socially, and I had some girlfriends.

But there wasn't anybody I felt that close to anyway. My family's mostly in Chicago. How much can you talk to people when they don't really understand what you're going through? Nobody else does, unless they've lost a child themselves. I was brought up always to keep family business in the family, and going to Parents of Murdered Children was hard. I did it because I thought if anybody knew, they'd know."

A Load of Guilt. No matter how a child dies, parents end up feeling guilty, a failure because they could not protect him. When your child is murdered, your guilt multiplies a thousandfold. The if-onlys appear again in the form of guilt and self-blame. They can come to dominate your thinking, corrode your self-confidence, and undermine your ability to function in every aspect of your life. Over time they are likely to subside, but not before they have exacted a heavy psychological cost.

Alicia liked her sister-in-law and was glad to leave her two-month-old son in her care. She went back to her job as a secretary, comfortable that Dominic was in good hands, cared for by someone she knew. She was shocked to get a call at work from an emergency room physician, requesting permission to treat Dominic. Her sister-in-law had brought him there, unconscious. He stayed for several days in the pediatric ICU, never regaining consciousness, then died. Doctors told Alicia and her husband about the shaken baby syndrome. When an infant is shaken severely, the brain is jarred against the skull so hard that it bruises and swells. If the swelling cannot be reduced, pressure on the brain causes damage, even death.

The sister-in-law confessed that she had shaken Dominic when he wouldn't stop crying. She was tried for manslaughter. "It was horrible," Alicia says. "My husband's sister. It tore us apart. The guilt tore us apart. Dominic was a baby. He depended on us to make the right decisions. He couldn't even speak. For a long time I blamed myself. Sometimes I still do."

In his excellent study of bereaved parents, *Beyond Endurance,* sociologist Ronald Knapp offers a useful observation about guilt. He found that the parents who, after their child's murder, received the most information about what happened were best able to work through their guilt.[3] Like all parents who lose a child, these parents felt guilty because of their inability to protect their child. But having reliable information enabled them to place events in a more realistic perspective more quickly. Knapp's findings underscore Erna Furman's statement that after a death, everyone copes better when given accurate information.

Interferences with Grieving

In order to grieve and to look toward the rest of your life, you must be able to bring some sense of closure to your loss. Closure does not mean forgetting or dismissing. Rather, it means recognizing that you have done one piece of painful work and now can turn to the next task. Of all the ways in which a parent loses a child, murder may be the most difficult to bring some closure to. Anger, fear, disillusionment with the criminal justice system all serve to keep your wounds open. Two other factors specific to murder may also interfere with your efforts to grieve: insufficient information and the desire for revenge.

Lack of Closure. If many of the facts of your child's death are unknown, or if your child's killer is not found, you will rightly feel that justice has not been served; nothing feels finished. Too many children disappear; they run away or are kidnapped, and are simply never seen or found. Their pictures haunt us from milk cartons and posters. The not knowing throws a long shadow across their parents' lives. This kind of loss and not knowing may be the most painful of all to bear.

Parents of soldiers missing in action, mostly in Vietnam,

know too much of this uncertainty. Miles and Sharon are in their seventies. In 1968 their son, Miles, Jr., was declared missing in action in Vietnam. "We heard nothing for twenty-one years," Sharon says. "We cried, we felt torn apart, and yet we could never wholly let go. It's your child. You *can't* let go. When they finally found some proof, it was pretty grisly, but convincing. They found part of a jawbone that they could match with his dental records. It was a relief. It was really over. The part of each of us that had held our breath for twenty-one years could now let go."

When your child has disappeared or his murder remains unsolved, he stays planted in the center of your mind. You cannot make room for anything else in your life. When events offer you no closure, you must make it for yourself. After Jamaal was shot, police could find no clue, no suspect. Ted stayed angry and fearful for months. Then he immersed himself in work, hoping to find relief. "Nothing worked for me until I let myself grieve," Ted says. "Somewhere in all that pain, I realized that it was up to me to write my own ending. I could spend my life blaming the cops, or I could decide that I was going to let it go. Not stop caring, but put my heart toward something I could make happen. I needed to take care of myself and Susan, and I needed to find a way to honor Jamaal."

If you live with not knowing what happened to your child, you know the price it exacts from your days. Like Ted, you may want to find a way to write your own closure, to decide how much, and for how long, you will let your not knowing stand in the way of your living.

Revenge. If your child has been murdered, you think about revenge. Geoff speaks with the authority of a man who has been there: "I decided not to act, for my family's sake, but I'd be lying if I told you I don't still think about it sometimes. People around here know what happened to Sean, and sometimes I'll

get a phone call, usually at night, usually from a father who
wants to talk about revenge. I tell these guys you need to think
about what you want the rest of your life to be about. The
people I've known who organized their lives around revenge
have been shriveled up, empty. Revenge sucks you dry, gives
you nothing back.

"I believe this," Geoff adds. "But I also know how much hard
work, continuing work, it takes [not to focus on revenge]. A lot
of people preach against hate, but most of them haven't had
their child killed."

What Helps

Parents who feel they regained their balance after the murder
of their child speak about their private decisions, about connecting with other parents, about their continuing sense of
connection with their child, and about memorials.

Private Decisions. A crisis is, as the word's origin reminds
us, a crossroad; in a time of crisis, you must decide which road
you will travel. Somewhere in the blur of time and pain after
Leslie was found, Sylvia remembers thinking that the killer had
gotten Leslie, "but he wasn't going to get me." She means that
no matter how much pain and anger her daughter's death
brought, she would not allow herself to be destroyed by it.
Haunted by visions of revenge, of killing his son's killer, Geoff
also came to a decision, that taking revenge would bring him
nothing he wanted and much pain. You cannot control fate,
cannot prevent your child's death. You can control what you
make of the rest of your life.

Parents of Murdered Children (POMC). Founded in 1978
by Charlotte and Robert Hullinger, whose daughter Lisa was

killed by a former boyfriend, this organization has made a significant difference for many parents. It now numbers one hundred chapters and another two hundred contact persons around the country. Through its chapters' self-help groups and its national hot line, it offers emotional support to families who have lost a child. It also offers information and guidance in negotiating the criminal justice system.

Webb went to a POMC meeting a year after his son was killed in a convenience store robbery. "Calvin's dying was totally senseless. He'd just gone in there for a Coke. I was so angry for so long, I pretty much drove all my friends away. The people at POMC were the ones that would still listen a year later when I still needed to talk about it. They'd been there themselves." When the chapter asked for volunteer speakers, Webb surprised himself by stepping forward. He is a reserved man more at home with his hunting dogs and the quiet of the backcountry than at public forums on criminal justice. He explains, "The chapter had done a lot for me. I wanted to give something back." He has become an articulate speaker and a forceful advocate for other parents in their dealings with the courts.

"It's been four years now," Webb reflects. "If I hadn't found POMC, I don't know what shape I'd be in. They say I've done a lot for the chapter, but I've gotten more than I've given." Webb plans to taper off his speaking and advocacy work this year in order to spend more time with his new grandson.

Parents may be as active as they wish, in support groups and advocacy work, or they may choose only to get the organization's mailings. Because your child's murder is such an overwhelming and isolating event, you may find it particularly helpful to talk with other parents who have survived the murder of their child.

Parents of Murdered Children can be reached at their national headquarters:

Parents of Murdered Children, Inc.
100 East 8th Street, Room B-41
Cincinnati, OH 45202
(513) 721-5683
Fax (513) 345-4489

Staying Connected with Your Child. Murder tears your child from you so unexpectedly, shatters your life so violently, that all the work of grieving lasts longer and goes harder than with other deaths. As you struggle to sort out what you have lost, it is vital also to find what you can keep. Parents who have lost a child by murder often report dreams and a strong conviction that their child is still with them. Your dreams of your child may at first be frightening, painful: visions of his dying, reminders of your helplessness. Over time they may change.

For months after Leslie was killed, Sylvia's dreams were filled with bloody images. "I finally had to ask her not to come to me like that. It hurt too much," Sylvia says. "I didn't have any dreams of her for several years. Then, on her birthday, she appeared in a dream, very serious-looking. She came up to me and hugged me. That hug was so real I woke up. I could see her there, in the bedroom, for several seconds."

Sylvia speculates that Leslie knew she was feeling bad and came to reassure her. "I felt better after that. Calmer. My heart didn't beat so hard anymore. She hasn't come back since then, but it's okay. That hug will last me the rest of my life."

Mel feels his son's presence when he is fishing. "I'm in the middle of a lake, usually early in the morning, with the mist rising from the water. It's very quiet, and I just know he's there with me." Mel chuckles. "It's funny he comes then, because he used to bitch and moan about getting up early. When it happens, I feel like he's with me again. He helps me keep going."

Mel's and Sylvia's experiences are not uncommon. Neither

can present any scientific explanation, but both are sure that their children have sought them out, offered them comfort. That is what matters. If your child finds you in a dream or sends a messenger, simply accept your gift.

Memorials. Whether your child was a newborn when he was killed or an adult with a family of his own, he lived his life, and he mattered to other people. There is far more to his life than his murder. At some point in your healing, as you put your life back together, you may find that a memorial to your child will help you hold on to the best parts of him. Wanda Henry-Jenkins writes eloquently about memorials: "Most of our holidays and holy days celebrate the transforming good works of persons whose acts of courage have advanced humanity. These celebrations allow public and private groups an opportunity to remember and testify about the nature of someone's contributions. . . . I believe an important sign that your grief has been resolved is your ability to set aside specific times during the year when you choose to commemorate and celebrate the transforming good works of your deceased loved one's life."[4]

How you commemorate your child's life will be up to you. You may want to talk about your ideas with other members of your family, your child's friends, and people whose lives she touched. Memorials can be ceremonies, such as an annual candlelight service or a silent gathering in tribute to your child. They may be public, inviting and involving anyone who wants to come. Mel and Harriet organized a high school basketball tournament. You may decide to plant a garden at the playground where your child was killed, or raise money to endow a scholarship at her school.

You will have private memorials as well. Perhaps a flowering tree you plant in your yard will mark her place in your life. You might contribute to a cause that had meaning for her, hang an ornament on your Christmas tree that uniquely reflects your child. Webb calls his work with POMC his continuing memorial to Calvin. The common thread that runs through each of these memorials is parents' decision that their child's life will be remembered and celebrated.

· 14 ·

Suicides

"The worst part is that I couldn't keep my own child alive."
—Anita

*I*n her carefully furnished living room, Dr. Fen Hwang sits across from me and stares at her hands. She is dressed entirely in black. She speaks in a flat tone, barely above a whisper. Her words are slow, heavy with grief. Christian, her eighteen-year-old son, killed himself in the summer, a month before he was to start his freshman year at Cornell.

"He gave us no sign. We had no idea he was thinking about killing himself. He was out with his friends that night and came home late, but it was summer, and he often stayed out. In the morning he didn't get up, and finally I went up to wake him. He was so still. When I touched him, I knew something was wrong. His body was cool. I called 911, and the paramedics came. I'd already tried to find a pulse, and there wasn't any. I knew, but still I begged them to do something. They worked on him for a while, I think just to let me know they cared, but it was too late.

"We found the bottles of medicine in his bathroom. One was for lowering blood pressure and the other was for reducing heart rate. The prescriptions were in my name. He had taken my prescription pad and written prescriptions, and gotten them filled in another part of town. The pharmacist remembered him: 'A nice, polite young man. He said he was getting his grandfather's medication.'

"He didn't leave a note. We don't know what he was thinking. We'll never know.

"Now I worry so much about Lily, my daughter. What will she do? Could she do the same? And for my husband. He hurts as much as I do, I know, but he won't talk about it."

Unique Problems

The fact that your child died by his own hand compounds your loss immeasurably. Beyond all the grief and helplessness that other parents feel, your child's suicide confronts you with particular problems, complications of your grief that are unique to survivors of a suicide. You feel a profound sense of failure, that you could not prevent his death. Closely tied to your sense of failure is the implied rebuke: You could not make his life worth living, you could not offer him enough of . . . of whatever he needed so that he would want to live. You feel a terribly personal abandonment, that he preferred to die rather than be alive with you. You also feel the pervasive stigma that surrounds suicides, the assumption by other people that something was wrong with your child and, by extension, wrong with you. Taking one's own life, once unthinkable, has now become painfully real, frighteningly close. You fear for your other children, for your partner, perhaps for yourself.

Each of these issues affects your efforts to grieve. In the pages that follow, we will consider each of them through the eyes and experiences of other parents whose children have committed suicide.

The Worst Failure. As parents, you have been committed to protecting your child, teaching her how to live in the world, instilling in her the values and the personal resources to handle whatever life deals her. When she cannot or will not cope, and chooses instead to die, your loss cannot help but feel like your personal failure. Fen goes over the months and days before Christian's death, combing her recollections for threads of enlightenment. "He must have needed something from me," she insists. "He must have been asking for something. I couldn't give it to him. I am foul, unworthy. Often now I want to die too."

Victor agonizes over his failure to help his son Douglas, who overdosed on cocaine. "The last year of Doug's life he was living on the street, just existing from score to score. He'd come by the house when he was sick or totally broke. Do you know what it does to you, to see your son like that? We'd tried so many things, for so many years, by then we were numb."

Although he left no note, Douglas's family feels certain that his overdose was intentional. "He was streetwise. He knew his tolerances. Once, months before it happened, he told me he knew how much it would take to kill himself, and that's what he'd do if things got bad. He didn't let us know how bad he was feeling. But that night I should have known; I should have done something for him. . . . I feel abominable," Victor continues. "My own son, and I couldn't make him want to live. There must be something wrong with me."

The responsibility we feel as parents to take care of our children is so strong that, when we cannot, no matter the circumstances, we feel profoundly that we have failed. When a child takes his own life, the whole family is left feeling that they did not do enough for him. Although undeserved, each person's sense of failure and unworthiness is pervasive, and slow to alter.

A Personal Rejection. My child preferred death to being alive with me. Parents say that this is what they felt, whether it made sense or not. Victor: "That whole last year, after he left home, I couldn't make any sense of it. Why he'd want to sleep in alleys and rummage in dumpsters instead of living with the people who loved him. Then when he died, it was ten times worse. It's like nothing about us, his own family, is worth staying alive for. I can't tell you how much it affected every one of us. If he'd thrown a hand grenade onto the table in the middle of dinner, it wouldn't have caused as much damage."

Doug's brothers—Greg, twelve, and Nils, fifteen—echo their father's feelings. "I wanted him to get back to how he used to be," Greg mourns. "When he killed himself I felt like he did it because he didn't want to see me anymore." Nils blames himself: "The last time I saw him I told him he stank, because he did. For a long time I believed he killed himself because of what I said."

The Hwangs left Taiwan when Christian was a baby in order to make a better life for him. They endured the disruptions and strangeness of a new culture and a new language so that he could have a better chance. "So much we went through for Christian, and then for Lily too. Then he didn't want what we did for him, not even enough to stay alive. What we did—it was all wasted," Wu-Hung, his father, cries. "His family worked for him, and he abandoned us."

Parents speak of their child's suicide as a repudiation of their values, a slap in the face, a desertion. They feel utterly devalued, rejected, unwanted. Many speak of feeling contaminated, that there must be something terribly wrong with them that would make their child want to die. They worried that their child was dangerous, that he would be destructive to their other children. Feelings of worthlessness, incompetence, inadequacy were universal. Fen's specialty is emergency medicine. After Christian's suicide, she took a leave of absence. She explains,

"In the ER I see two, three suicide attempts every week. My job is to keep them alive. After what Christian did, I lost all confidence in myself. If I can't keep my own son alive, how can I help anyone else?"

Stigma. Every parent speaks of the stigma attached to suicide, the cloud of fear and disapproval and humiliation that surrounds a child's taking her life. Distracted with pain and grief, parents still find themselves agonizing about what people will think of their child and of them. The Hwangs tried to prevent the facts of Christian's death from being known. "It was crazy," Lily, seventeen, remembers. "[The family] told me not to tell anyone. Like healthy eighteen-year-olds just die in their sleep. I told them everybody knew what happened, but for a long time they wouldn't say anything to anybody. I was really torn between respecting them and needing to talk to my friends."

Hoping to avoid more exposure of their pain, Victor and Megan arranged for a private funeral service. "It was the saddest, loneliest funeral I've ever done," their minister reflects. "The four of them huddled together, listening to me. They didn't need a minister then. They needed their friends around them. I tried to talk to them about having an open service, but they said they couldn't face people." Looking back, Megan agrees that having a private service was a mistake. "We cut ourselves off from support when we needed it most."

You will find that suicide frightens people, makes them uncomfortable. Friends may avoid you, or avoid the subject, or offer perfunctory, painfully brief condolences. As you talk with people, you may have to pave the way for them with a statement such as "John died last month. He took his own life." As painful as your news is to tell, most people are likely to be relieved that you can speak of it. Your willingness to speak gives them permission to speak and a model for directness. When you speak, you lift the stigma and allow them to offer you their concern and support.

Resolutions: What Helps

Parents remember what was helpful to them in the days and months that followed their child's suicide. They speak of prompt involvement of caregivers, their need to talk about what had happened, encouraging all family members to talk openly, examining their guilt and reappraising their own responsibility, reaching out to others, marking anniversaries, and, as we have heard from so many parents, respecting their own timetable for healing.

Iris Bolton, a trained grief counselor in Atlanta, lost her twenty-year-old son to suicide. Writing about the days immediately after her son's death, she recalls that

> Literally, I can still remember the exact words that introduced me to postvention therapy, and made my recovery possible. "You will survive," the man said. His gaze locked my eyes to his. I sensed his sincerity and his determination that I should share his vision. The man was Dr. Leonard T. Maholick, an Atlanta psychiatrist and an old friend. "You will survive," he repeated firmly, "if you choose to." It was a beginning.[1]

Other parents echo Bolton's experience that, in their first days of confusion and despair, they truly did not know whether they could survive. They wanted desperately to talk about their experience and found that a professional, outside the family and therefore not personally affected by their child's death, was often the most helpful person to talk with. When they were offered reassurance that they had the strength to survive, they found they were better able to draw on that strength.

Dr. Edwin Schneidman is a psychologist and Professor of Thanatology Emeritus at the UCLA School of Medicine. He has spent a professional lifetime studying suicide. In his article "Postvention: The Care of the Bereaved," Schneidman defines postvention as therapeutic "activities that serve to reduce the aftereffects of a traumatic event in the lives of survivors." Its aim is "to help survivors live longer, more productively, and less stressfully than they are likely to do otherwise."[2] Schneidman advises professionals to begin working with surviving family members as quickly as possible. Similar advice comes from Dr. Mary Giffin, former director of the Irene Josselyn Clinic on Chicago's North Shore and co-author of *A Cry for Help*, a book about teenage suicide. "Every family of a suicide must be viewed as 'at high risk.' Such a family is one which, without help, will likely become non-functional, unable to care for itself as a family and as individuals, except in the most marginal way."[3] Giffin adds that not every family needs psychiatric treatment. For many, the support of family, neighbors, clergy, and support groups will enable them to take care of themselves. But her message is clear: The death of a child by suicide is potentially devastating to the whole family. No family should face such a loss without help.

The day after she found her son, Fen talked with a psychologist, whom she continued to see weekly for several months. "It really helped me through it," she remembers. "She helped me think about how to help Lily and when to leave her alone. We all hurt so much that we couldn't help each other for a long time. I needed someone who wasn't in pain, who could listen to me."

Talking with Each Other. Your child's death deals a massive blow to the whole family. Everyone is injured; no one is spared. Every one of you—parents, brothers, sisters—feels responsible for the death, feels guilty, feels a failure. You all face the task of making sense of your loss, understanding what happened, finding a way to go on. You have the capacity to help each other. But to help, you must hear each other's pain and share your own. Some families have always done this. For others, the talking and listening may be difficult, unfamiliar work.

After Doug's funeral, Victor and Megan decided that continuing to keep silent could destroy their family. Hard as it was, they had to talk with people, starting with their boys. "It wasn't easy," Victor remembers. "The first thing we got was a load of anger from Nils, for not having Doug's friends there. We were ready to quit talking then. We kept on, though, because we couldn't see how else we could survive as a family if we didn't work together." Nils and Greg talked about the pain they had felt for years, watching their adored older brother leave school, start using drugs, drift away from the family. They hated that he stole their things when he came home, hated their parents for throwing him out, and felt guilty for their own relief when he left. Each of them blamed himself for Doug's overdose.

"This stuff came out over months. Sometimes I dreaded when we'd talk about Doug because I knew I'd hear more about what the other boys had gone through, and I'd end up feeling worse for not having known. Things changed, though. Gradually we all got a clearer picture of Doug as very depressed, feeling hopeless for himself, but warding off every help that anyone offered.

"One night Greg and I had gone out for a hamburger. Driving home, out of the blue he said, 'You know, in some ways, Doug was a real jerk.' I said, 'Yeah, sometimes he was.' That was all. It was a kind of pivotal moment. After Greg said that, all of us seemed to get a better understanding that what Doug did was about himself, and not an indictment of us."

Megan adds, "After we could say that he was a jerk, we could all say more about what we loved and missed about him. We'll none of us ever stop hurting for what he did, but we feel closer to each other now. How strange that was his final gift to us."

Are You Responsible for Your Child's Death? After your child kills herself, this is the most painful question you face, and often the hardest to resolve. We have seen that, no matter how a child dies, no matter what she did or did not do, parents feel responsible. It comes with the territory of parenthood, the charge and its awful corollary: It is your job to keep your child safe; if she dies, you must have failed.

Did your child make requests for help, direct or muted, that you missed? If she had a psychiatric illness, did you pursue treatment and support it? Were you psychologically available to your child? These are complex questions, easy to pose, much harder to answer. There is no pattern of answers or profile of parenting that guarantees detection of every suicidal impulse.

Pediatrician and child psychoanalyst D. W. Winnicott speaks of "the good-enough" mother. He means that no mother, no parent, can be one hundred percent attuned to her child one hundred percent of the time. Nor does a child require that. The work of parenting is much more of a percentage game. We do our best, and then we have to trust that our percentage is good enough. When a child kills herself, your first assumption is that you were not a good enough parent and, therefore, are responsible. But you need to look further.

Psychiatric clinics and suicide prevention services use the term "psychological autopsy" to describe their review of all the facts they can gather about a suicide and their efforts to put together a picture of the suicide victim's psychological state. You have probably conducted your own psychological autopsy, talking with other people who knew your child, going over your own interactions with her, reading whichever papers and notes she left, doing all that you can to understand what led to her decision. Sometimes the picture you can put together is clear; sometimes nothing explains what she did.

Reid is a high school teacher whose younger son Ethan shot himself at age nineteen. Reid talks about his efforts to understand his son's action and about his own responsibility. "Ethan had intellectual difficulties and psychological problems since he was five. He also had serious learning disabilities and real problems relating to other people. He just couldn't warm up to anyone, including his family. In his whole life he only had one friend. He was in psychotherapy for years, he took medication, he was hospitalized twice, there were endless tutors and special help. I don't know of any reasonable avenue that we hadn't tried for him, at least twice. The older he got, the more I feared for his future. I didn't see how he'd be able to support himself. He could see the discrepancy between how his brothers and sisters were functioning and how he was, and that was terribly painful to him.

"He was nineteen, and he'd had seven jobs since he quit school. He'd been fired from his job at a fast-food place, for absenteeism. He bought a rifle, went to his apartment, and put a bullet through the roof of his mouth.

"He didn't leave a note, but as his mother and I have remembered things he'd said over the previous year, I believe he was feeling that his life was nothing but failure and disappointments, it always had been, and he couldn't see any change. I think he saw what he did as less painful than going on. I miss him terribly. This sounds awful, I guess, but I also feel relieved."

Despite their best efforts at a psychological autopsy, Fen and Wu-Hung have no good answers for why Christian killed himself. Lacking answers, they tended to hold themselves responsible. The less you understand about your child's action, the more vulnerable you are to feeling that, by acts of omission or commission, you are responsible. Fen: "Slowly I am beginning to think that if we did our best job, that is all we could do."

Iris Bolton speaks of grandiosity, the conviction that you are powerful enough to prevent someone from killing himself if he is indeed determined. Some of that grandiosity lies within all of us. After a suicide, it must be brought to light, examined carefully. If your child was truly intent on killing himself, he would have found a way despite your best efforts.

Your sense of responsibility is not a fixed and final thing. As you live with your loss, you will think again and again of what happened. Perhaps in time you can recognize that if your aims and intent were good, and you did all that you could do, you cannot ask more of yourself. Perhaps in time you can let yourself let go of the awful, self-imposed responsibility.

Reach Out to Other People. "Things got better when we started talking to our friends," Megan remembers. "I began to feel I might survive this. I'd say that to anyone whose child suicides. Talk to your friends. Talk to your family. Find a group for relatives and survivors of suicide. Not everybody will be wonderful; after a tragedy you find out who your friends really are. Other people are your safety net. If you don't look for them, you'll just keep on falling."

Other parents agree with her. They also remember how hard it was at first to look for support. Your child's suicide fills you with so much pain, so much shame and helplessness, that you want to withdraw. Yet everything we know about how people heal tells us that it is exactly when we feel most alienated from the human community that we most need to reconnect. At a time when you feel so bad, the effort to get to a group, even to pick up the phone, seems staggering. Yet to survive your loss, that is what you must do.

Other people can hear your pain. They can remind you that you are still a decent, competent, worthwhile person. In groups such as the one that Sharing and Healing sponsors, you can see that people *do* rebuild their lives. At a time when you cannot believe in a future, other people can show you, by their own lives, that a future is possible.

234 · THE WORST LOSS

Mark the Anniversary. Some part of your memory keeps remarkably accurate time. It recalls when a painful event oc-curred, and when that month and week come around again each year, you will feel the grief and the rage and the helpless-ness come flooding back. This phenomenon is called anniver-sary reaction; it seems to be universal, part of our human endowment. If you have allowed yourself to grieve, over time the intensity of your anniversary reaction will diminish. But for the first few years, you are likely to feel your loss again with great force. You will be wise to mark your calendar, expect an upsurge of feeling, and set aside time for remembering.

Doug killed himself in late September. Each year his parents and brothers mark the last Saturday in September as Doug's day. They spend the day together, at home or on a hike. They talk about Doug, especially the good memories. Last year Nils said he wanted something around the house that he could look at, to remember his brother. After some discussion, the family decided to plant a tree. Together they drove to a nursery, chose a flowering dogwood, and planted it. "It's helped us all," Megan says. "Every time I look at it, I think of Doug, and I think of what we still have."

Resolutions: What Hinders

Ambiguity. If you cannot be sure whether your child in-tended to kill herself, you may have particular difficulty in coming to a livable resolution of your grief. As child psycho-analyst Erna Furman reminds us, all people, children and adults, deal better with loss when they know the facts. "In all bereave-ment, it is extraordinarily important that all of the realities of the death be known and appreciated by the survivor, particu-larly the cause of death."[4] Young people die in one-vehicle accidents, and falls, and overdoses in which the cause of death is clear, but the victim's intentions are not. In the aftermath you may be prey to corrosive uncertainties: How could she let it happen? What was she thinking? What did she want to have happen?

Facing questions like these, you may at some time in your grieving simply decide that you cannot know. If the questions have caused you only pain and stirred up self-accusations, then you may ask yourself what you gain by holding on to them. Letting go is not easy, nor is it quickly accomplished. But as you relax your grip on the unknowns about your child's death, you may find new strength to take hold of the rest of your life.

Silence. Throughout this book, parents speak about the healing value for them of being listened to and of listening. If you do not talk to the other people who loved your child, you invite chronic depression, isolation, and a slow death of your spirit. Your silence also inflicts damage far beyond yourself. Too many suicides by young people have at their root an unmourned, undealt-with suicide in the previous generation. If you are reluctant to talk, ask yourself how many lives you want your child's suicide to claim.

Good Outcomes

Your child's suicide will be with you all your life. That you cannot change. But other parents have said that the pain gradually decreases and their hope for their lives returns.

Fen and Wu-Hung drove Lily to college this fall. After they left her, they drove across New York state to Ithaca and walked around the Cornell campus. "It is a very beautiful place," says Wu-Hung. "We talked about Christian, and how he would have loved it, and what he might have studied. Then we went

236 · THE WORST LOSS

to dinner, and we started planning a trip to Taiwan, just the two of us."

Three years after Douglas overdosed, Megan looks at the dogwood tree, its leaves burning scarlet in the afternoon sun. Her eyes fill as she reflects. "Not a day goes by that I don't think of Doug and miss him. The way the rest of us decided to handle his death, by taking care of each other, has made us all stronger and closer. I called it Doug's gift to us, but it's really been our decision that out of our terrible loss we would make something good. I guess that's our gift to ourselves."

In the next section, parents and families talk about the first year after their child's death and about the rest of their lives: what sustains them, how they go on.

Part Four

~

The Rest of Your Life

Your child's death leaves you with the terrible question: How will you go on with your life? The tapestry of your future has been torn apart; you cannot recognize it as yours. So many of the assumptions that organized your life have now collapsed. Nothing will ever be the same again. Grief-stricken, disoriented, you cannot see from the beginning of the day to the end. How will you manage a future when you are not even sure you want one?

Other parents have asked themselves these questions. Painfully, gradually, they have tried out answers, rejected some, kept the ones that worked for them. In this last section, we look at the ways parents and families managed in the first, critical year, and then for the rest of their lives.

Even as each person's grief is unique, so is each person's resolution. Some of the ways that other people have coped may seem foreign, or idiosyncratic, useful for them but not likely to be a good fit with your own life. Yet as you read, you will find that some of what these others have learned and practiced will be familiar because you have found a similar solution. Some of their approaches will be new to you, perhaps something you'll want to try.

No matter the age of their child or the nature of his death, parents who felt they were healing focused on three principles: allow yourself to feel what you feel, trust your own timetable for healing, and connect with other people. As you read about their experiences, you will find that these principles can guide you in your own healing.

237

· 15 ·

Getting Through It:
The First Year

---

*"I wanted to be told that I had some
awful disease that would kill me. Soon."*
—Dave

*T*he funeral lies behind you. All the food that friends have
brought has been eaten. Their dishes sit stacked on the counter,
waiting to be returned. The refrigerator is empty. Your house,
which rang with children's laughter, is silent. You do not know
how you will get through the next hour. A whole day is a
trackless swamp. A year of living without your child is beyond
imagining.

Other parents have felt the ache of grief enclose their heart
as you do now, have stood where you now stand. They offer you
their conviction that you *can* get through it. That you will not
always be as awash in pain as you now are. In this chapter
parents who have lost a child talk about what helped them get
through that awful first year. As you read their recommendations and reassurances you may find some thoughts that will
help you through yours.

Believe That You Will Not Always Feel Like This. Your
pain is so intense, so overwhelming, that it becomes impossible

to believe that you could ever feel any other way. "Maryann was killed on Friday night, and on Monday morning I was sitting in the office of Mothers Against Drunk Driving," Carol remembers. "Their chapter president talked to me. She'd lost her son in an accident two years before. We talked for a long time, and I don't remember a word she said. All I remember is that her hair was combed, and she had on makeup, her clothes looked nice. I thought, 'She lost her child, and she could get dressed and drive to the office. Maybe it's possible.'

"That's part of why I decided to work with MADD. The other parents there were like constant reassurances to me that people could lose a child and hurt the way I was hurting, and still go on."

Each person's pain takes its own course. But when yours feels endless, and more than you can bear, it may help to remind yourself that there will be a time when you will not feel the way you do now.

Connect with Other People. Parents emphasize the need to connect with other people. Losing a child is too much to face alone. Much of your grieving may be silent, inward, solitary; you will contend with many aspects of your loss alone. But the strength to keep going, to believe that keeping going is worth it, comes from your connections with other people. Other people's taking care of you, their understanding of your pain, and their belief that you can rebuild are the crossbeams that bear you up.

The people you need may be in your immediate family. It may be an old friend who comes through as she always has, or it may be someone you've hardly known who now comes forward. "When you lose a child, you find out who your friends are. You get some surprises," Lenore observes. "A woman I knew at work just to say hi to went out of her way to talk with me. She told me about Compassionate Friends, and she kept at me, badgered me, really, until I said I'd go to a meeting with her. I'm so grateful to her; the group has been my best support. And she and I have become friends."

Many parents say that other parents who had lost a child were their greatest help. They understood as no one else could. Because they knew what that first year was like, they could help parents anticipate feelings and reactions. Ted: "You can live with some pretty awful stuff if you've got someone telling you 'Yeah, that happens, but you get through it.' " Parent support groups such as Compassionate Friends and Survivors of Suicide are the surest places to find other parents.

Assume That You Will Have to Educate Other People. You have learned by now how uncomfortable your loss makes other people. Some will stumble through the clichés of sympathy; some are so uncomfortable they avoid you altogether. Fran, whose young son died in a skateboard accident, remembers: "I was walking down my own street, and a woman from my church, someone I've known for years, saw me coming and crossed to the other side. I wanted to shout, 'It's okay, Millie, I'm not contagious.' " In the same way that the loss and the pain are yours, so too, you will find, is the first move. You will need to speak of your loss, to let others know that they can speak of it with you. You will need to tell people who knew your child that you still want to talk about her, that you welcome their talking about her too. If you want your child's friends to come by, you will need to invite them. If your family deals with loss by clamming up, you will have to tell them that you need to talk, need them to listen and to talk as well.

It isn't fair. You have work enough holding yourself together. You shouldn't have to coach other people. But there it is. For every friend and relative who can move to your side gracefully, there are two more who will reach out to you only if you reach out first.

Keep the Lines of Communication Open with Your Partner and Other Children. As we saw in chapter 7, you and your partner may be able to help each other, or you may not. Especially if you cannot help as much as you would wish, it is important to keep talking and keep listening to each other. The lines you keep open, even when you cannot help each other, become the lines along which you rebuild your relationship. If you withdraw from each other in your pain, it will be harder to find each other in your healing.

"We kind of stumbled into that idea," Allie says. "After Gene started seeing a therapist, he did most of his grieving with her. I did a lot of talking at Compassionate Friends. For a while we didn't talk with each other much. That started to feel too isolating. One night at a Compassionate Friends meeting I did a whole lot of crying and remembering. When I came home, I said to Gene, 'Listen, I need to tell you what came up for me tonight. I don't want you to feel you have to fix it, or comfort me, or anything. I just want you to know where I am.' Later he told me that helped: just knowing what I was doing, without anything expected of him. We got in the habit of giving each other updates. 'Dispatches from the front,' Gene called them. We didn't do it all that often. Sometimes a month would go by. But it helped us stay in touch."

Your children especially need the lines open with you. With a younger child you are likely to be more active in helping her grieve: maintaining a receptiveness so that she feels it is safe to speak, answering questions and clarifying what happened. With your adolescent, you may have the opposite and equally difficult assignment of tactfully backing away as he works on his grief less obviously, or with someone else, or, for long stretches, not at all.

Like your relationship with your partner, your relationships with your children have been altered by their sibling's death. Open lines give children the feeling that they can speak and be heard respectfully, or not speak and have their need for silence honored. When you offer children this respectful openness, you enable them to use you as they need to.

Allow All Your Feelings to Emerge. "*Allow* my feelings to emerge?" you may say. "I can't shut them up." Of course your sadness and sense of loss and your outrage are there in full force. But a loss of this magnitude cuts so wide and deep across your life that it evokes a whole kaleidoscope of feelings, some of them much harder to acknowledge.

You miss your daughter so much; if you took a few extra sleeping pills, you could stop hurting and be with her. . . . His sister has been a disappointment, a heartbreak ever since junior high; how could she survive the crash and not he? . . . She should have broken it off with her boyfriend a long time ago; if she had, she'd probably be alive now. . . . Your husband should never have bought him that skateboard. . . . You can't stand to see your neighbor's son on his swing, still alive when your boy is dead. . . . How could she leave you alone when she knew she was your only confidante? . . .

Envy, anger, thoughts of suicide, of revenge: some of these less comfortable feelings will likely be part of your grief. They also need to be heard and accepted. When you push them out of your thoughts, they do not go away. Left in the dark, these feelings fester and grow stronger. Paradoxically, if you allow yourself to feel them and voice them to an accepting listener, they tend to lose their awful power. They shrink down to manageable, forgivable size, and they come less often.

"For months after Linda was killed, I thought about killing myself," Karen says. "It scared me a lot, because I've never thought like that before. But it was there, in the back of my mind every day: If I were dead, I wouldn't have to hurt like this. I got so scared I told Wayne, my husband. He said he'd been thinking about it too. It was funny; once we'd told each other, I didn't feel so worried about doing it. He said he didn't either."

Realize That You Cannot Always Help Your Partner or Your Children. Your pain is so intense in these first months that it disables you. Many days it will be all you can do to get dressed and go through the motions of your day. As much as you love your other children and your partner, as much as you want to help them, there will be times when you simply have nothing to give.

Gillian and Steve lost their youngest child to a rare form of leukemia after a yearlong fight. Eight months later they talk about what their lives have been like since Phillip died. "We take each day as it comes," Steve says. "If it's a bad day, we don't try to pretend it's a good one." Gillian agrees: "You can just take a look at the other and know what kind of day they're having. If it's a bad one, you back off.

"Early on we said, 'Let's not shut each other out.' We've pretty much stayed with that. But we've also learned that you can't always be there for the other. It takes a lot of trust, and a lot of patience."

Steve: "A couple of months after Phillip died, some good friends of ours were having a birthday party for their son. Our other children wanted to go. Gillian took them. I stayed home. That was one I couldn't do."

When you cannot function at the level you usually expect of yourself, it hurts. It is easy to fall into scolding yourself, feeling inadequate. The fact is that for now you *are* inadequate. You may need to remind yourself, as Martha's friend reminded her, that if you'd suffered a physical injury as severe as your emotional wound, you'd be in the ICU. You wouldn't expect a person in intensive care to be fully herself or particularly available to the rest of her family. You expect an ICU patient to accept her limitations, not push herself, give her body a chance to heal. Your injury is severe and pervasive. You will need to lower your expectations of yourself. You must give your heart time and opportunity to heal.

Expect an Emotional Roller Coaster. Grieving your loss, you will see your feelings swing widely. One moment you are composed and objective; the next, you are helplessly awash. Worse, you cannot see it coming. Memories blindside you. This unpredictability of your feelings is for most people one of the most painful aspects of grieving. It makes you feel unreliable to yourself, even crazy. "I stayed at home for months," a mother remembers, "because when I was out with people I could any second get so flooded with grief that I'd start crying. It happened when I was alone at home too. But at least I didn't look so weird in front of other people."

All bets are off. All your former assumptions about your life and your future are now up for reevaluation. You feel as if you can't count on anything and you can't count on yourself. We do not appreciate how much stability our assumptions provide us—I'll go back to work when the kids are all in school, we'll buy a bigger house in a few years, we'll stay in this neighborhood because the boys have so many kids to play with—until they get knocked out from under us.

You will build new plans for your life and a new set of assumptions. Your feelings will recover their stability. The blindsides will come less often. But for now, the roller-coaster swings and plunges will be part of your life.

Take Care of Yourself Physically. "After Kyle died, I started having a lot of physical pain," Dave remembers. "Chest pains, really sharp. Back pains. Stomachaches. I went and had a complete physical. When the doctor told me I was in great shape I was disappointed. I wanted to hear I had some awful condition that was going to kill me. Soon."

Dave's experience is not unusual. Most people feel the pain of their loss not only in their heart and mind but throughout their body. Nearly three centuries ago, reflecting on the relationship between mind and body, Dr. Samuel Johnson wrote, "Sorrow that hath no vent in tears maketh the organs of the body weep."

A growing body of research now documents the ways in which stress, particularly loss, depletes the immune system. In a remarkable paper entitled "Immune Variables, Depression, and Plasma Cortisol over Time in Suddenly Bereaved Parents," physiologists Mary Spratt and Douglas Denney describe their research on the immune systems of parents who had lost a child unexpectedly. They found that three weeks after their loss, the parents showed significant alteration of three biochemically measurable components of the immune system. Eight months later, all three measures remained abnormally altered.[1] Neurobiological research confirms what Dr. Johnson knew.

You are fragile now and more vulnerable to illness and accidents. Aching from your loss, you need to be kind to your body. Nothing fancy—just the basics of good care. Get enough sleep. Allow yourself to take naps. In the first months, a day is an awfully long stretch of time to get through without a break. Eat enough, and eat healthful foods. You may not feel much like eating, and even less like shopping and cooking. Do it anyway. Getting back to your familiar routines will bring comfort and a measure of predictability that you sorely need.

Exercise. Again, nothing fancy. If you've played a sport, get back to it. Take walks. Physical activity gets you out of the house, gets you thinking different thoughts, moves you, however briefly, beyond the compass of your loss. At first it will be hard. Much of what we do to care for ourselves does not come easily. For now, nothing you do will come easily. Do it anyway. Go through the motions. In time your activity will give you release, even pleasure.

Set Aside Time Each Day to Remember Your Child. Setting aside time to remember your child may sound unnecessary, when your mind is flooded with his memory. Gene explains what he did. "My therapist taught me this. She told me to set aside a piece of time every day, fifteen or twenty minutes where I could be by myself, uninterrupted. This was my time to think about Will. Whatever came up or wherever my thoughts went was fine. At first it felt unnecessary, because I was thinking about him all the time. It was like fencing off a space in the middle of an endless prairie; there was no difference between what was inside the fence and what was outside. But after a while there began to be a difference. The time I set aside to think got much more focused. Most of the important work I had to do about Will got started in those times.

"Of course I thought about him the rest of the day. But as I got back to work, and all the demands on me, that reserved time did something else. It was like a deal I had with myself. When I'd get overwhelmed with memories, I could remind myself that I had this time, like an appointment, that was just for this stuff. Little by little I got to where I could keep stuff inside the fence. Think about it then and have more of the rest of the day for other thoughts. It was a relief to get some time where I wasn't always thinking about him."

Parents who learn this technique usually find it helpful. As with all the recommendations that other parents offer, only you can judge whether it works for you.

Feel Free to Get a Mental Health Checkup. Grieving, as we have said throughout this book, is a normal process—disorienting, excruciatingly painful, more protracted than people expect, but normal. But because grief is so all-consuming and so disruptive of their usual thought processes, many people believe that they are going crazy. Talking over your reactions with a

mental health professional may provide you the reassurance
that you are well within normal limits.

Months after Jamaal died, Susan continued to have memory
lapses. "I'd have a conversation, and ten minutes later I
couldn't remember what I'd said, or what the other person had
said. If I didn't make lists I couldn't get through the day. It
really worried me. I've always steered clear of psychological
stuff, but I decided that if I was losing my mind I'd better know
about it." When she talked with a psychologist who specialized
in grief-related problems, she learned that memory loss is a very
common symptom for parents who have lost a child.

"The bad news is that it can go on for years." Susan grimaces.
"But the good news is he told me it's very common and not a
sign that I'm losing it. So I make more lists and take notes. I
only went once, but it helped."

Offer Yourself Some Pleasures. Your child's death destroys
so much of your life that the idea of pleasure is, for some time,
simply beyond imagining. You cannot understand how people
smile, go to the movies, take vacations. Yet there comes a point
when you want and need some relief from your pain. Grieving
is such hard work that you must have some time off.

The first time you go back to anything that once gave you
pleasure, you may feel unsure or disloyal. Eating chocolate,
going swimming, visiting with friends, watching a movie, making love—whatever you do feels different now. You will need to
give your pleasures, and yourself, more than one chance.

For Emily, swimming was exercise and pleasure. In the
months after Pete was killed, she let it go. "There was the shock
of his death, and after that, all I wanted was to crawl under the
covers and stay there. Plus, my whole chest hurt. It hurt to
breathe. Then one of the women I swim with called me. She
said everybody missed me, and when was I coming back. I told
her I didn't know. But I thought about it all that week.

"The first time I went back was awful. I'd gained weight and I hated how I looked in my suit. I was out of shape and out of breath. Nobody knew what to say to me. I don't know why I even went back a second time. The second time was still awful. It was a couple of weeks before it started to feel good again. The water felt so good, and my whole body felt good. I realized nothing in my life, nothing, had felt good since Pete died."

Parents sometimes feel that when their child has died, having fun would be an act of disloyalty. It would somehow negate his importance. "For months I didn't feel right going anywhere or seeing friends," Kate says. "Rick finally said to me, 'Do you think if you deny yourself she's going to rise from her grave?' That shocked me. But it made me realize that that's sort of what I was doing." Remember that when you carry such a heavy load you must rest from time to time. If you do not insist on some pleasures for yourself, you will not be able to carry your load.

Seek Spiritual Support. Whether you actively practice your faith or have had nothing to do with it since childhood, you may turn to it now. Remembering her son who died of heart disease, Fran says, "Nothing has ever tested my faith so severely [as his death], and nothing helped me through [his death] as much as my faith. I will never understand why he had to die. But if I trusted in God, I had to trust that He would see me through this. Faith didn't make the pain less, but it provided me a keel through the worst storms."

Even if you do not experience faith as strongly as Fran did, you may find comfort now in whatever you believe. Betty Spangler is a nurse who leads a group for bereaved parents at Children's Hospital in San Diego. Talking about the first year after a child dies, she observes, "The parents I see who come through it the best are often the ones with some kind of spiritual connection. It could be they haven't been near a church since they were [children]. But you'd be amazed at what people remember."

For some parents, the idea of a God who permits children to die raises more questions than faith can answer. You must decide for yourself whether a spiritual connection will help you in your grieving.

Expect Setbacks and Detours. The path through your grief will be anything but straight. That is not a reflection on your capacities; it is simply the nature of human grieving. It tends to take its own time, always longer than we expect. It sets its own course, filled with switchbacks and loops.

Too often the metaphors for grieving sound like a kind of psychological trash collection: You are told to "get it all out," as if your heart were a grocery sack you could turn upside down and empty. It's probably closer to how our feelings work to liken our grieving to tracing out the roots of a large tree: You follow one root as far as it can take you; then you must find your way to another root and follow that one wherever it goes.

As you come toward the end of a root or a piece of remembering, you will feel a sense of peace, some lessening of the chronic ache. Then comes the first Christmas without her, or Mother's Day, or simply a song she liked on the radio, and you feel again the way you felt in the first weeks. All the ground you've gained, the composure you've painfully constructed are washed away in the painful swell of memory.

In fact, you do not lose the ground. The progress you have made is still there, hidden for a while in the rush of feelings. Elaine: "Every time that happened, I'd feel like I was back in the hurricane, going down for the third time. It took a couple of setbacks, and finding out that I lived through them, for me not to be so scared. They still come, but less often. When they do, they hurt just as much, but I know that they won't last forever."

Expect Anniversary Reactions. As we have discussed, anniversary reactions are the upsurges of memory and grief that occur on your child's birthday, the anniversary of his death, and whatever other dates carry a special significance for you. As you live with your loss, you will get a sense of the dates and anniversaries that stir up feelings.

Derek's son died on September 4. All the next year, the fourth of each month was an especially painful reminder. "I was a wreck every fourth. After a few months, I quit trying to tough it out. I'd mark it on the calendar and sometimes not go to the gallery that day. I'd spend some time at his grave and then do something to honor him: write about him, or meet a friend for coffee, someone who knew him, that I could talk about him with."

It will help your other children for you to explain the anniversary phenomenon to them. The anniversaries they feel may be different from yours. It will help all of you to let one another know when you are having a particularly bad time with missing the child.

Most religions recognize the importance of anniversaries. Jews place headstones on people's graves on the year anniversary of their death. In many Protestant denominations, special prayers are offered. Latinos honor all the dead on November 1, the Day of the Dead, a time of particular closeness to those who have died. You are wise to make use of your religious traditions, whatever they are, for marking anniversaries.

Respect the Rhythm of Your Own Grieving. Part of grief is periods of fallow: time when you do not think much, or feel much, when your grieving feels suspended. In tracing out the roots of a tree, there are times when you have worked your way out one root and do not yet see where the next one lies. These times of blankness are as much a part of grief's rhythm as the painful times. A field left fallow for a season recovers its richness. The next year its crop grows more abundantly. People also need fallow times. We push ourselves too fast at our own peril.

These are the fruits of other parents' first years without their child. They offer their wisdom generously, with an understanding of your loss and in the hope that their experiences might help ease someone else's first year.

By the anniversary of your child's death, you have learned more than you ever cared to know about pain and your own capacity to bear it. Perhaps you see some lifting of your sorrow; perhaps not. A year is a natural unit of time, a full cycle of the seasons. Yet it carries no built-in guarantee of completion. You may still feel some of the upheaval and severe disorganization of acute grief. You may still be groping for ways to stay in touch with the rest of your family, may not yet have found ways to care for yourself. The flow and timing of your grief will be your own. The passing of a year to the date of your child's death need not, should not, impose requirements on your healing. Rather, you can use the anniversary as a point from which to look back and to look forward.

The rest of your life still lies before you. In the next chapter, parents talk about how the rest of their lives changed after their child's death.

· 16 ·

The Rest of Your Life

*"Our language has no word for
a parent who has lost a child."*
—Martha

Your child has been dead a year, and your own life has been changed forever. This much you know. What you cannot know yet is the full shape and scope of the changes you will make as you build your life beyond this year. Several parents who lost a child more than five years ago agreed to talk about their lives in the time since their child's death and the changes they saw in themselves. In this final chapter, their stories illuminate the tasks all parents face as they work to fashion a life they can live beyond the loss of their child.

Although they live in different cities and lead very different lives, for the purposes of this chapter I have seated them around a table, so that we can hear the common themes that arise from their experiences.

Hank is a deputy sheriff in a rural western county. His son Colin died eight years ago, at age eight, from head injuries sustained when he fell out of a tree. Hank was divorced from Colin's mother at the time of Colin's death. Grace lost her daughter Iris to hepatitis, contracted from IV drug use, eleven years ago. She works as a bereavement counselor for a large urban hospital. Carol's daughter Maryann was killed by a

253

drunken driver; for the past eight years Carol has worked with her local Mothers Against Drunk Driving chapter, first in legal advocacy and later in community education. Dave heads the legal department of a large corporation; Naomi is a medical technologist. Their son Kyle died in a car accident, also caused by a drunken driver.

Looking back, the parents recognize that, at the first anniversary of their child's death, their healing had only begun. All of them characterize the time as a blur, full of pain and experiences whose meaning for them they could not yet sort out. Carol says, "I was working at MADD and going to court proceedings. But any little thing could trigger an avalanche of memory, and I'd be buried, out of commission for days." Hank: "Just before Colin died, I was Deputy of the Year. My job was everything to me. A year later I had to think hard to find reasons to go to work. Everything I'd thought was important felt useless. The things I used to worry about, assignments, promotions—they didn't matter to me anymore. I couldn't see anything ever mattering again."

A Deepening Realization

Sometime during the second or third year, these parents felt a shift in their awareness. They felt, to a degree that they had not experienced before, the utter finality of their loss. Nothing could ever be done to undo the death of their child and to fill the empty space it had left in their lives. It would be with them forever. This shift was not the crumbling of a pathological denial. These were psychologically healthy people, their reality-testing intact, who knew from the first that their child had died. The shift in their understanding or the deepening of it reflects the enormity of their loss. All that you lose when your child dies is simply too much to take in at one time. All the changes in your life are more than you can possibly anticipate.

"This whole thing has been like falling down a very long flight of stairs," Dave observes. "You fall a few steps and you land sprawled on your face on the landing. You rest there awhile, and then, never when you're ready, you start falling again. This time you fall farther. You know more what you've lost." Dave's metaphor rings true for other parents. They agree that their realization, in the second or third year after their child's death, that *this is final, this is the way it's always going to be* was another fall. Each of them remarks on that fall and the ways it brought her or him to a deeper level of knowing his or her loss.

This deeper knowing brought into focus for parents a new task: Without their child, how were they to make a life that still held meaning and purpose? "I thought that's what I'd been working on ever since she died," Carol observes. "In one way I was right. But some time in the second year, it sunk in harder: that part of my life, being her mother, was totally over. I realized that I had more to cope with than I'd thought. I wasn't ready to be through being a mother. Maryann's dying put me out of a job that I loved. She was my youngest, and she was nearly out of high school. That job was going to taper pretty soon. But when she was ripped away from me like that, I lost too much at once. I had to find a way to keep on being a mother, at least for a while, or my life couldn't make any sense."

Hank echoes Carol's thoughts. "I sure wasn't ready to quit being a father, not with my son eight years old. I didn't want another child just then, and I didn't want to take up with a woman just for her children. I had to find some way to keep on being a father. It forced me to think a lot about what being a father meant. Even what being a man meant." He pauses, thoughtful. "I expect I thought more about being a father after Colin died than I did all the years he was alive."

Each of these parents says that periods during the second or the third year after their child died were more painful than the first year. These were the times when the full reality of their loss came home to them, when the former structures of their lives was shattered and new ones had not yet evolved. Dave remembers the period after the driver who killed his son was sentenced as the worst time in his life. He had used his quest for revenge as a way to keep himself going. After the driver was sentenced, the bottom fell out from under him. He was faced with all the sadness and helplessness that he had not allowed himself to feel. In his words, "Three years later, I was starting from zero." He remembers that time as the most painful of all.

Grace: "I had remarried, and my husband had only known Iris when she was going downhill, so he couldn't have the feelings for her that I did. We had moved to another state a few months before she died. I felt so isolated, and I think for the first two years I lived a pretty superficial life. I didn't think that much about her. Amazing how you can do that, with someone you'd spent so many hours and days thinking about. Friday nights were always hard, because that's when she used to call. Somewhere in the third year after she died [not thinking about her] didn't work anymore. I thought about her a lot, and about her father, who'd died of cancer. I began to feel that if two of the people I loved the best had left me, there must be something very bad about me. I had a very hard time with it. I got myself into therapy and started looking at what had happened."

Rethinking Your Life, Reworking Your Self

As time unfolds after your child's death, you realize that you will never again be your old self. That self was forever changed when your child died. Who you will be now, how you will live without your child in your life, will be the work of several years of sorting out. In the sections that follow, parents describe the changes that came about as they reexamined their most basic assumptions about what mattered. As they worked to make sense of their lives in the wake of their loss, each of these parents learned that how they felt about work and relationships changed.

With those changes came some strains and, inevitably, some frictions. Rebuilding never gets done without some dust and disorder. Even if you're working from blueprints, when you're in the middle of a job you can't always see how it will come out. For the job you have—grieving—you have no blueprint. Lacking a blueprint, feeling your way through changes that you did not anticipate, toward outcomes you cannot predict, you cannot help but experience some strain.

Strains, counterpulls, and frictions occur in your relations with the people closest to you, as they watch you change. A more diffuse and widespread unease may come up with people beyond your immediate circle who do not understand what's gotten into you.

In the second and third years, most parents also saw a gradual receding of grief that left them with more energy, a restoration of their capacity for pleasure, the ability to work productively again, and a renewed investment in the relationships they valued. How they functioned in work, pleasure, and relationships were the chief markers parents used to measure their healing.

What Matters: Changes in Your Values. Nearly every parent speaks about a shift in their values in the years after their child's death. Hank: "I knew I loved Colin, but I didn't know how important he was until it was too late. My job was always such a big deal for me; it came first, and then my family. That was a terrible mistake. Now I put the people in my life first: my parents, my sister and her kids. Colin's mom and I are closer too."

Dave agrees. "All the years Kyle was growing up, I was claw-ing my way up the career ladder. Sixty-, seventy-hour work weeks. I told myself I was doing it for my family. Now I think of all the times I could have had with them, and I was at the office. I'll never have that with Kyle now. I feel blessed that I still have time with his sister and my wife. My career's probably plateaued out, because I don't put in those hours anymore. You know what? It's more important to me to get to Debbie's vol-leyball games."

Parents say that the conventional markers of success—pro-motions, a nicer house, more money and things—all mattered much less to them after their child died. Their commitments changed as well. Grace is an excellent tennis player. For years she played almost daily, and much of her social life revolved around the tennis club. "After Iris died, I'd listen to my friends fretting about their game, and I'd wonder why it mattered. When I started to do some volunteer counseling through the cancer center, it felt more important than tennis. I still play, but it matters a lot less than it used to. My tennis friends don't understand me, and I've given up trying to explain."

Internal Strains, Suicidal Thoughts. The changes that these parents describe did not come easily. Reworking what matters inevitably brings times when you feel utterly adrift. The old assumptions no longer work. New structures are not yet in place. You do not know what your life holds. All you know for certain is that your child is gone and, with him or her, the shape of your future. Each of these parents speak of periods of intense despair in the course of their rebuilding. Each of them at some point considered suicide. Their pain was so great and their way through it was so far from clear that dying seemed easier than living.

"I was pretty shocked when I realized what I was thinking," Hank says. "It didn't even come up in the first few months after he died. I felt like I'd lost all the ground I'd gained." Hank adds that his suicidal thoughts did not last long. In retrospect, he figures that they were an inevitable part of his efforts at change.

"Compassionate Friends helped me with that," Naomi remembers. "At a meeting someone said that it just hurt too much to go on. We started talking about suicide, and it turned out everyone in the room had thought about it at some point. For a lot of people it came up the most during the time when they also felt they were changing the most."

This experience, of feeling the worst in the midst of efforts to change, seems to be how human beings are built. Even as we work to change, we also fear it because change always means stepping into the unknown. We resist it, dig in our heels against it, even believe that death would be easier. Transient suicidal thoughts in the course of reworking how you will live are probably no cause for alarm. If they persist, or if you begin to think actively about methods, you should consult a mental health professional.

Changes and Stress in Your Relationship with Your Partner. No two people experience a loss, or rebuild after it, in the same way, or on the same timetable. Parents comment on the tensions they felt in relationships with partners and children whose healing inevitably took a course different from their own. Carol plunged into advocacy work for MADD; Lyle, her husband, read in his study or worked in their small orchard.

"He thought I was whipping myself into a frenzy, and I thought he was withdrawing from life. We fought about it, but mostly we went our own ways. I remember a morning when I was leaving to go to court. He was sharpening his pruning shears. I blew up and yelled, 'How can you prune apple trees when Maryann is dead?' He looked at me and said very quietly, 'Pruning is a problem I can do something about.'

"That helped me understand him better. I saw that he had to

deal with Maryann's death his way. Mine wouldn't work for him, any more than his would for me." Carol pauses, then reflects: "That's something I couldn't possibly have anticipated when she died. How much tact and respect for my partner this thing has demanded. When I talk to other parents who have lost a child, that seems to have a lot to do with whether they stay together or not—how much they were able to live with each other's way of coping."

While Dave pursued the driver who killed his son through the courts, his wife Naomi joined Compassionate Friends and thought about how she wanted Kyle to be remembered. She talked with people who had known her son, Kyle's friends and their parents, his teachers, family friends and relatives. From those conversations, she decided to endow a scholarship fund in Kyle's name at his high school, with a memorial run as a fund-raiser. The project has involved her with many of Kyle's friends, with whom she stays in touch. The fund's growth has been a source of deep satisfaction for her.

"From the day Kyle died, Dave and I reacted differently," she remembers. "When Dave looked up from his vendetta three years later, I was not the person I was when Kyle died. It was an extremely difficult time for both of us. He was depressed, and he expected me to make him feel better. By then I knew that wasn't my job. When I didn't, he blamed everything on me, even Kyle's death. That was too much. We separated. I was ready to leave him. I only came back when I saw he was serious about changing."

Rethinking what matters and reworking your self tend to be long-range projects. They are the work of months and years, not constant, but coming in and out of your thoughts. Usually they do not begin until the pain of your grieving has receded. Because much of your work and the changes that flow from it occur in the second and third year after your child dies, your relationship with your partner may continue to change in this period.

What's Gotten into You? We have seen that our culture's timetable for grieving is unrealistically short. Six months after your child dies most acquaintances and co-workers will feel that you should be over your grief, back to your old self. You may well be past acute grief and no longer at risk for coming unraveled in meetings. But your old self has been forever changed. In years two, three, and beyond, you are in the midst of building a new self, one who may not fit other people's expectations of you.

Every parent observes that the changes they made unsettled many of their friends and co-workers. People who have known you over time feel they know at least the broad outlines of who you are: which people are important in your life and where your pleasures and priorities lie. You are somewhat predictable. After your child's death, as you rethink what matters, you are likely to deal the people who know you some surprises. Hank: "I was always the go-to guy for the sheriff. He gave me the toughest assignments because he knew I wanted them, and I'd handle them right. When I told him I wanted the drug education detail, I thought he was going to fall out of his chair. I told him I needed to do something to help kids, a way to keep on being a father. He understood, but he didn't. He thinks I've gone soft in the head. I guess that's his problem."

Dave: "Usually I'm the only father at Debbie's games. The moms say nice things about my coming, but you can see it on their faces: 'It's three o'clock; he should be at the office.' "

Not all reactions are negative. Parents speak of friends who were surprised, then curious about their changes, and ultimately supportive. Grace's friends miss her at tennis, but several have told her how much they admire the work she does.

Expect that you will have to educate friends and colleagues. They will not automatically understand the changes in your priorities. Your willingness to say why you are doing x when you have always done y will be helpful. You are likely to dispel inaccurate ideas and perhaps get others thinking about what matters in their own lives. The people who care about you will try to understand; even if they can't, they are more likely to respect your need to do what you do.

How Much of Your Life
Will You Allow Your Anger to Claim?

Every parent speaks of this question and the decisions he or she made in answering it. Parents whose children died violently, in accidents, suicides, and murders, felt the question most intensely. Carol remembers talking with her husband, Lyle, a day or two after her daughter's death. "His faith never wavered. He said we needed to be guided by our Christian principles and, by our lives, set an example for others. My faith isn't always that strong, but what he said helped me get through the worst times." Two years later Carol came to another decision. She had been having dreams in which she stalked the driver who killed her daughter and then killed him. They left her shaken. "I decided that I couldn't hate him any longer. Hating him got in the way of remembering Maryann." She feels that this decision helped her refocus her life. "It's helped me spend my time remembering the good things about her. I felt like a burden had been lifted. Don't get me wrong. I'm still angry. But I had to decide what I wanted in my life."

Dave tells a similar story. "I made a three-year career out of punishing the guy who killed Kyle. It nearly cost me my marriage and my other child. I don't think you ever stop being angry for what's been taken from you. But somewhere, some time, you have to make a decision about how you're going to live. Naomi laid it out for me in pretty blunt terms. She said I could keep on blaming her and everyone else, or we could stay married, but I couldn't do both. That brought me up real short.

"That's what I worked on, one way or another, all through the counseling. I've been blaming people all my life, and I had to decide whether I could live without blaming. I guess Kyle's dying ultimately forced me to rethink how I was going to live."

Deciding How You Will Live

Your child's dying has thrust you into more pain than you thought you could bear, has torn and forever altered the tapestry of your future. Your loss is immeasurable. Yet you have miles to go before you sleep. Other people, perhaps other children, need you. You have work to do, time for pleasure, time to make a difference in other people's lives. However your child died, you must decide how you will live.

The parents in this chapter each wrestled with this decision. From their efforts, all developed a greater understanding of themselves, and a plan that would bring meaning to their lives. As different as these parents are, in the facts of their lives and in the decisions they came to, three common themes from their experiences stand out.

- All recognized that, although they had no choice about what happened to their child, they had to choose what they would make of the rest of their lives.
- All needed to continue to be parents in some fashion.
- All sought to make some memorial, public or private, to their child.

Choosing When You Have Been Robbed of Choice. Looking at the directions their lives have taken, all of the parents comment that as their lives were changing, they did not feel as if they were in charge, the ones making the choices. "I never felt I chose to work with MADD," Carol says. "It was something I had to do to survive." "When the floor you're standing on gets blown out from under you, you've got to put something in its place, just to keep yourself from falling. That sure doesn't feel like a choice," Dave adds.

There is truth in what they say. None of these parents could control what happened to his or her child. The shifts in how they live their lives were essentially reactive, initiated by the catastrophic change in their lives that they were helpless to prevent. In *When Bad Things Happen to Good People*, Rabbi Harold Kushner writes about the changes he has seen come about in himself since his son's death:

> I am a more sensitive person, a more effective pastor, a more sympathetic counselor because of Aaron's life and death than I would ever have been without it. And I would give up all of those gains in a second if I could have my son back. If I could choose, I would forgo all the spiritual growth and depth which has come my way because of our experiences, and be what I was fifteen years ago, an average rabbi, an indifferent counselor, helping some people and unable to help others, and the father of a bright happy boy. But I cannot choose.[1]

Yet Kushner and the parents in this chapter have in fact had a choice, not the one they wished for—not a choice in their child's fate. But, facing the terrible loss they have been dealt, they have had choices and have made choices about how they will live. Having lost so much, not everyone can recognize what is left to choose from. The experiences of those who have been able to recognize the choices available to them offer us models and hope.

You Are Still Your Child's Parent. Every parent speaks of the loss of being their child's parent. Even when you have other children, you have lost the possibility of being your dead child's parent. In the second and third years, as the upheavals of grief subside, parents appreciate that their child's death has cut them off from a rich and satisfying part of their lives. Each one looks for ways, direct and indirect, to continue to be a parent. Hank taught drug education in the schools. "I feel like I'm helping every kid I teach," he explains. Naomi cherishes the contacts with Kyle's friends that her fund-raising affords her.

You need not change careers or volunteer with a formal program. The ways you can be a parent are as varied as children and their needs. The place to start is with yourself. As you reflect on the parts of raising your child that you loved the most, you will discover the parts of you that now go unsatisfied. As you look to find ways to engage those parts of you, you are likely to find the avenues you need. Parents who have found their way advise other parents to have patience with themselves. It may take a while to sort out what will fit, what will work. Martha, who helped organize a gardening program, recalls that it was seven years before she knew what she wanted to do. "I couldn't have moved any faster," she says.

Making Memorials. Parents say they want their child to be remembered. Many voice the fear that their child, who was so central in their lives, will be forgotten. Discussing memorials, Wanda Henry-Jenkins advises that you allow yourself time to work through the worst of your grief and anger. A memorial should not be an expression of your grief but should be a celebration of your child's life.

Dave: "When you name a Jewish child, there's a line in the ceremony, 'May this be a name honored in the house of Israel.' That phrase came back to me after I started to grieve for Kyle. I knew I wanted Kyle's name to be honored in every house and every heart that ever knew him. Naomi understood that a long time before I did. That's what the scholarship fund is about. I guess that's our public memorial.

"I also have more private ways to honor him. Every time I leave the office at six so I can get home for dinner with Naomi and Debbie, I feel like I'm honoring my son. He used to tease me about the spare tire I was developing. Every year I run in the scholarship run, but this year I've kept it up. That tire's down from a truck tire to a bicycle size. When I'm running I talk to [Kyle], so he'll know I'm getting it down."

Grace works as a bereavement counselor with families who have lost a parent or a child to cancer. "You could call the work I do my private memorial to Iris," she says. "I think I've been very, very fortunate. This work has given me a center to my life and a chance to help. That's what was so horribly painful with Iris, that I wanted to help and I couldn't ever make it work for her. Now when I can help someone, I just feel I've been fortunate."

Sometimes a memorial for your child is clear in your mind from the start. For other parents, it may take a time of grieving and rebuilding before it becomes clear how you want to mark your child's life. Your tribute may be as private as a prayer you utter to yourself or as public as a memorial basketball tournament. It may lie in new work that you take up or in the transformed spirit with which you approach what you have always done. You may plant a tree in his honor, or a forest, or you may work toward a cure for the disease that claimed him. As your memorial takes shape, first in your own mind, then in the hearts and imaginations of others who knew your child, you are likely to feel some easing of your ache.

Sarah's Picnic. An easing of their ache was what Sarah's family sought when they planned her picnic. "We wanted to remember Sarah's joy and all the joy she brought us," her parents explain.

Sarah's family moved into the house that faced the park when she was six months old. Every warm day her mother rolled her along its paths in her stroller. As a toddler Sarah explored the sandbox and swings of the park's playground. By the time she was four, she greeted the old women who sat on the benches, the homeless people asleep under the trees, and the big boys and girls who rode their bicycles down the park's hills. Her family joked that Sarah thought the park was part of her yard, and she its official hostess. In the summer she fed the ducks at the lake, and in winter she hung a feeder for the cardinals who spent the season there. When she got her first two-wheeler, she learned to ride it in the park. Sarah and her brothers rode their bikes on its leafy paths every day after school.

In Sarah's eight years, the neighborhood around the park got better, but somehow the park got worse. More and more strangers slept in its woods, sold drugs from its benches. Sarah's parents told their children they could not ride there unless an adult was with them.

Sarah hated the new rule. On a sunny October afternoon she sneaked her bike out of the garage and pedaled into the park. Searchers found her bike under the sumac bushes near the ball fields, and three days later her body floated to the surface of the lake.

From the shock and outrage about her death a new resolve arose in the neighborhoods around the park. Residents started a volunteer patrol. They walked the park in twos, watched for children, called the police to report drug dealing. The park got cleaner and safer. "For a long time I couldn't even look out my window at the park," Sam, Sarah's father, says. "When I finally took a walk there, it was spring, and the lilacs were blooming. I remembered why Sarah loved it. I told Liza, my wife, that when we felt up to it, we needed to have a picnic for Sarah."

The picnic happened that summer. Sam and Liza and Sarah's brothers invited everyone who had known Sarah, and all the volunteer patrol. "Everybody brought food, we had enough to feed an army. There was a softball game, and at the end, we made a huge circle, and Liza and I and the boys talked about Sarah. How she loved the park, and how we wanted to remember all the joy she brought us.

"The next year I said, 'Let's do this again.' We invited our Compassionate Friends group. It's been going seven years now, and it's turned into a picnic for all families who have lost a child. New people come each year, and every year some things change. Last year we got a country band that played all afternoon. Sometimes we play softball, sometimes not."

The part of Sarah's picnic that does not change is the ending. As the light is fading, parents gather their children and form a large circle at the edge of the woods. Sam invites everyone—parents, brothers, sisters—to speak about the child they have lost. Each speaker says how old the child would be now and tells something he remembers about him.

The sky darkens to deep violet, and cooler air from the woods moves across the field. As people hear one another's recollections, the circle fills with the presence of all the lost children, restored to their families by love and memory. Sam speaks last, about Sarah. There is silence for a while, and then, one by one, each family releases a balloon. They watch them float up until they disappear in the night sky.

The Rest of Your Life

As they look back at the years since their child died, and forward toward the rest of their lives, the parents I spoke with think about what they would want other parents to know. You never get over a loss like this, they say, any more than you would get over the loss of a leg. Instead, you find ways to live your life despite it. You continue to hold your child in your mind. You find people you can talk to about your child. You work at keeping the lines of communication open with your partner and your other children. You put your energy into what's important, and you let the rest go. You make a decision that you will let yourself feel whatever you feel and deal with it as it comes. You get through the bad days because you've learned that they do end. The pain overwhelms you, but then it recedes. You are stronger than you ever thought, stronger than you ever wanted to be.

You never forget what you lost. You learn to value what you have.

Appendix

The following national organizations may be of use to you. The list is by no means exhaustive; consider it a starting point. Many cities have local organizations that will also address your needs. Keep searching until you find the group that fits your need.

AIDS

Call a Mom Hotline
Mothers Initiative of the
   People with AIDS Coalition
50 W. 17th Street
New York, NY 10011
(800) 828-3280

Federation of Parents &
   Friends of Lesbians &
   Gays
PO Box 24565
Los Angeles, CA 90024
(213) 472-8952

National Association of
   People with AIDS
1413 K Street NW
Washington, DC 20005
(202) 898-0414

Cancer

American Cancer Society
90 Park Avenue
New York, NY 10016
(212) 586-8700

The Candlelighters
   Childhood Cancer
   Foundation
7910 Woodmont Avenue, Suite
   240
Bethesda, MD 20814
(301) 657-8401

Children's Hospice
   International
901 North Washington Street,
   No. 700
Alexandria, VA 22314
(800) 2-4-CHILD (242-4453)

Death of a Child

Compassionate Friends
PO Box 3696
Oak Brook, IL 60522-3696
(708) 990-0010

SHARE, St. John's Hospital
800 East Carpenter Street
Springfield, IL 62769
(217) 544-6464

Death of a Child by Drunk Driving

Mothers Against
  Drunk Driving (MADD)
PO Box 541688
Dallas, TX 753554-1688
(800) GET-MADD (438-6233)

Murder

Parents of Murdered Children
100 East 8th Street, Room B41
Cincinnati, OH 45202
(513) 721-5683
Fax (513) 345-4489

Sudden Infant Death Syndrome

Counseling &
  Research Center for SIDS
PO Box 1997
Milwaukee, WI 53201
(218) 739-5252

SIDS Alliance
10500 Little Patuxent Parkway,
  Suite 420
Columbia, MD 21044
(800) 638-7437

Suicide

American Association
  of Suicidology
2459 South Ash Street
Denver, CO 80222
(303) 692-0985

Sharing and Healing Newsletter
3586 Trenton Avenue
San Diego, CA 92117

Notes

1. A Loss Like No Other

1. Linda Edelstein, *Maternal Bereavement: Coping with the Unexpected Death of a Child* (New York: Praeger Scientific, 1984), p. 49.
2. Beverly Raphael, *The Anatomy of Bereavement* (New York: Basic Books, 1983), p. 233.

2. The Family Undone

1. Stephen Bank and Michael Kahn, *The Sibling Bond* (New York: Basic Books, 1982), p. 59.
2. Ibid., p. 282.
3. Monica McGoldrick, "Loss and the Family: A Systemic Perspective," in *Living Beyond Loss: Death in the Family,* ed. Froma Walsh and Monica McGoldrick, (New York: Norton and Co., 1992), p. 26.

3. How Could It Happen?

1. Diary of Mary White, unpublished manuscript, The Huntington Library, cited in Paul Rosenblatt, *Bitter, Bitter Tears* (Minneapolis: University of Minnesota Press, 1983), p. 18.

2. Lewis Thomas, *The Youngest Science: Notes of a Medicine Watcher* (New York: Viking Press, 1983), p. 35.

4. Why Must We Grieve?

1. Sigmund Freud, "Mourning and Melancholia." In *The Standard Edition of the Complete Psychological Works of Sigmund Freud*, vol. 14, ed. J. Strachey (London: Hogarth Press, 1963), p. 246.

6. The Long Haul

1. Edelstein, *Maternal Bereavement*, p. 73.
2. "When a Child Dies," pamphlet, The Compassionate Friends, Oakbrook, Ill., 1987.

8. How Children Grieve

1. Janice Harris Lord, *Beyond Sympathy* (Ventura, Calif.: Pathfinder Publishing, 1988), p. 121.
2. Susan Scrimshaw and Daniel March, "I Had a Baby Sister but She Only Lasted One Day," *Journal of the American Medical Association* 251, no. 6 (February 1984): 732–33.

9. Suspended in Pain

1. J. M. Barrie, *Margaret Ogilvy* (New York: Charles Scribner's Sons, 1913), pp. 231–32.

10. The Loss of Possibility

1. Scrimshaw and March, "I Had a Baby Sister," 733.
2. Erna P. Furman, "The Death of a Newborn: Care of the Parents," *Birth and the Family Journal* 5, no. 4 (1978): 214.

3. Judith Lewis Herman, *Trauma and Recovery* (New York: Basic Books, 1992), p. 70.

4. Irving G. Leon, "The Invisible Loss: The Impact of Perinatal Death on Siblings," *Journal of Psychosomatic Obstetrics and Gynecology* 5, no. 1 (1986): 9.

13. Murders

1. From a speech before the First World Congress of Victimology, Washington, D.C., August 1981. Quoted in Ronald Knapp, *Beyond Endurance* (New York: Schocken Books, 1986), p. 90.
2. Wanda Henry-Jenkins, *Just Us* (Omaha: Centering Corporation, 1992), p. 39.
3. Knapp, *Beyond Endurance*, p. 101.
4. Henry-Jenkins, *Just Us*, p. 48.

14. Suicides

1. Iris Bolton, "Death of a Child by Suicide," *Parental Loss of a Child*, ed. Therese Rando (Champaign, Ill.: Research Press, 1986), p. 206.
2. Edwin Schneidman, "Postvention: The Care of the Bereaved," *Suicide and Life-Threatening Behaviors* 2, no. 4 (1981): 358.
3. Mary Giffin and Carol Felsenthal, *A Cry for Help* (New York: Doubleday, 1983), p. 289.
4. Furman, "The Death of a Newborn," 214.

15. Getting Through It

1. Mary Spratt and Douglas Denney, "Immune Variables, Depression, and Plasma Cortisol over Time in Suddenly Bereaved Par-

ents," *Journal of Neuropsychiatry and Clinical Neurosciences* 3 (1991): 299–306.

16. The Rest of Your Life

1. Harold S. Kushner, *When Bad Things Happen to Good People* (New York: Avon, 1984), p. 133.

Bibliography

Arnold, Joan, and Penelope Gemma. *A Child Dies: A Portrait of Family Grief.* Rockville, Md.: Aspen Systems Corp., 1983.

Bank, Stephen P., and Michael D. Kahn. *The Sibling Bond.* New York: Basic Books, 1982.

Barrie, J. M. *Margaret Ogilvy.* New York: Charles Scribner's Sons, 1913.

Birenbaum, Linda K. et al., "The Response of Children to the Dying and Death of a Sibling." *Omega* 20, no. 3 (1989–90): 213–28.

Bohannon, Judy. "Grief Responses of Spouses Following the Death of a Child: A Longitudinal Study." *Omega* 22, no. 2 (1990–91): 109–21.

Burton, Iris. "Death of a Child by Suicide." In *Parental Loss of a Child,* ed. Therese Rando. Champaign, Ill.: Research Press, 1986, pp. 201–12.

Centering Corporation. *Dear Parents.* Omaha: Centering Corporation Press, 1989.

Davies, B. "Family Responses to the Death of a Child: The Meaning of Memories." *Journal of Palliative Care* 3 (1987): 9–15.

Donnelly, Katherine. *Recovering from the Loss of a Child.* New York: Macmillan, 1982.

Edelstein, Linda. *Maternal Bereavement: Coping with the Unexpected Death of a Child.* New York: Praeger Scientific, 1984.

Florian, Victor. "Meaning and Purpose in Life of Bereaved Parents Whose Son Fell During Active Military Service." *Omega* 20, no. 2 (1989–90): 91–102.

277

Franciosi, R., and G. Friedman. "Sudden Infant Death Syndrome: A Medical and Psychological Crisis." In *Acute Grief,* ed. Margolis et al. New York: Columbia University Press, 1981, pp. 120–25.

Freud, Sigmund. "Mourning and Melancholia." In *The Standard Edition of the Complete Psychological Works of Sigmund Freud,* vol. 14, ed. James Strachey. London: Hogarth Press, 1963. Originally published 1917.

Furman, Erna P. "The Death of a Newborn: Care of the Parents." *Birth and the Family Journal* 5, no. 4 (1978): 214–18.

Giffin, Mary, and Carol Felsenthal. *A Cry for Help.* New York: Doubleday, 1983.

Grollman, Earl. *Living When a Loved One Has Died.* Boston: Beacon Press, 1977.

———. *Explaining Death to Children.* Boston: Beacon Press, 1967.

Harrison, S., C. Davenport, and J. McDermott. "Children's Reactions to Bereavement." *Archives of General Psychiatry* 17 (November 1967): 593–97.

Henry-Jenkins, Wanda. *Just Us.* Omaha: Centering Corporation, 1992.

Herman, Judith Lewis. *Trauma and Recovery.* New York: Basic Books, 1992.

Klass, Dennis. "John Bowlby's Model of Grief and the Problem of Identification." *Omega* 18, no. 1 (1987–88): 13–32.

———. *Parental Grief: Solace and Resolution.* New York: Springer Publishing Company, 1988.

Klass, D., and S. Marwit. "Toward a Model of Parental Grief." *Omega* 19, no. 1 (1988–89): 31–50.

Knapp, Ronald. *Beyond Endurance.* New York: Schocken Books, 1986.

Kübler-Ross, Elisabeth. *Living with Death and Dying.* New York: Macmillan, 1982.

———. *On Children and Death.* New York: Macmillan, 1985.

———. *AIDS.* New York: Macmillan, 1989.

Kushner, Harold S. *When Bad Things Happen to Good People.* New York: Avon, 1984.

Legg, Cecily, and Ivan Sherrick. "The Replacement Child—A Developmental Tragedy." *Child Psychiatry and Human Development* 7, no. 2 (1976): 113–26.

Leon, Irving G. "The Invisible Loss: The Impact of Perinatal Death on Siblings." *Journal of Psychosomatic Obstetrics and Gynecology* 5, no. 1 (1986): 1–14.

Limbo, Rana, and Sara Wheeler. *When a Baby Dies.* LaCrosse, Wisc.: RTS Bereavement Services, 1986.

Lindemann, Eric. "Symptomatology and Management of Acute Grief." *American Journal of Psychiatry* 101 (1944): 141–48.

Lord, Janice Harris. *Beyond Sympathy.* Ventura, Calif.: Pathfinder Publishing, 1988.

Margolis, Otto et al. *Acute Grief: Counseling the Bereaved.* New York: Columbia University Press, 1981.

Miles, Margaret. *The Grief of Parents When a Child Dies.* Oak Brook, Ill.: Compassionate Friends, 1980.

Moriarty, D. M., ed. *The Loss of Loved Ones: The Effects of a Death in the Family on Personality Development.* Springfield, Ill.: Charles C. Thomas, 1967.

Moriarty, Irene. "Mourning the Death of an Infant: The Siblings' Story." *Journal of Pastoral Care* 32, no. 1 (1978): 22–33.

Osterweis, M., F. Solomon, and M. Green, eds. *Bereavement: Reactions, Consequences, and Care.* Washington, D.C.: National Academy Press, 1984.

Panuthos, Claudia, and Catherine Remeo. *Ended Beginnings.* South Hadley, Mass.: Bergin and Garvey, 1984.

Parkes, Colin Murray. *Bereavement,* 2d ed. London: Tavistock Publications, 1986.

Pollock, George. "On Siblings, Childhood Sibling Loss, and Creativity." *Annual of Psychoanalysis,* vol. 6. New York: International Universities Press, 1978, pp. 443–81.

Rando, Therese, ed. *Parental Loss of a Child.* Champaign, Ill.: Research Press, 1986.

Raphael, Beverly. *The Anatomy of Bereavement.* New York: Basic Books, 1983.

Rosen, Elliot J. "Family Therapy in Cases of Interminable Grief for the Loss of a Child." *Omega* 19, no. 3 (1988–89): 187–202.

Rosenblatt, Paul. *Bitter, Bitter Tears.* Minneapolis: University of Minnesota Press, 1983.

Rubin, Simon S. "Death of the Future? An Outcome Study of Bereaved Parents in Israel." *Omega* 20, no. 4 (1989–90): 323–39.

Sahler, Olle Jane Z., ed. *The Child and Death.* St. Louis, Mo.: C. V. Mosby, 1979.

Savage, Judith A. *Mourning Unlived Lives.* Willmette, Ill.: Chiron Press, 1989.

Schiff, Harriet Sarnoff. *The Bereaved Parent.* New York: Crown Publishers, 1977.

Scrimshaw, Susan, and Daniel March. "I Had a Baby Sister but She Only Lasted One Day." *Journal of the American Medical Association* 251, no. 6 (February 1984): 732–33.

Shorter, Edward. *The Health Century.* New York: Doubleday, 1987.

Solnit, Albert, and Morris Green. "Psychologic Considerations in the Management of Deaths on Pediatric Hospital Services." *Pediatrics* 24 (1959): 106–12.

Spratt, Mary, and Douglas Denney. "Immune Variables, Depression, and Plasma Cortisol over Time in Suddenly Bereaved Parents." *Journal of Neuropsychiatry and Clinical Neurosciences* 3 (1991): 299–306.

Statistical Abstract of the United States. Washington, D.C.: U.S. Department of Commerce, Bureau of the Census, 1992.

Sugar, Max. "Normal Adolescent Mourning." *American Journal of Psychotherapy* 22 (1968): 258–69.

Thomas, Lewis. *The Youngest Science: Notes of a Medicine Watcher.* New York: Viking Press, 1983.

Walsh, Froma, and Monica McGoldrick, eds. *Living Beyond Loss: Death in the Family.* New York: Norton and Co., 1992.

Index

281

Family (*cont.*)
  and memorials, 266–68
  reconnecting with, 148
  sharing grief, 38–39
  sibling's knowledge of life in,
    24–25
  and suicide, 229–30
  talking about child with,
    87–88
  and terminal illness, 176–85
Family, friends, and community
    (other people)
  and AIDS, 181–82
  as barrier to grieving, 137, 139
  connecting with, during first
    year, 240–41
  and death of infant, 158–62,
    167–68
  educating, 241, 262
  after first year, 261–62
  and grieving, 98–99
  and murder, 214–15
  and suicide, 227–28, 233, 235
  and terminal illness, 186–87
Fantasies, 52, 53
Fathers, 5, 12, 93, 176. *See also*
    Men
Fatigue, 68
Fears, 5, 45, 210–11, 212
Feelings
  allowing, to emerge, 243–44
  naming, 124
Fifteen and older adolescents,
    and understanding of death,
    119–20
Fighting, by siblings, 125
Five to seven year olds, and un-
    derstanding of death, 114–
    15, 120
Food, 68
Foster child, 16–17
Freud, Sigmund, 47, 53

Funeral, 70–71, 72–73, 128–29
  and stillbirth, 159
  and unresolved grief, 145
Furman, Erna, 164, 216, 234
Future, 18–19, 177, 211

Giffin, Dr. Mary, 229
Gorbach, Nina, 125–26
Grade school–age siblings, 37
Grief and grieving, 5, 47–151
  allowing other children to see,
    36–37, 129–30
  and circumstances of death,
    44–45
  concealed by children, 38, 127
  and creating climate for chil-
    dren to grieve, 37–39, 110–
    11, 117, 120, 124, 127–30
  culture's timetable for, 261
  and different styles of partners,
    93–100
  factors interfering with, 136–41
  after first year, 257
  four principles of, 108
  as journey, 47–48
  reason we must grieve, 49–60
  and respecting rhythm of,
    251–52
  styles of children, 107–30
  styles of men vs. women, 59,
    95–97
  taking breaks from, 38, 52,
    123, 125–26
  tasks of, for parents, 51–60
Groups
  bereavement, 34–35, 88, 168
  for children, 34–35, 108
  and first year, 240–41
  and holding child in your
    mind, 88–89
  and homicide survivors, 212,
    218–20